Digital Sub-Editing And Design

Rajesh K. Singh

MANGLAM

MANGLAM PUBLICATIONS

DELHI-110053 (INDIA)

Published by :

MANGLAM PUBLICATIONS

L-21/1, Street No. 5, Shivaji Marg, Near Kali Mandir,
J.P. Nagar, Kartar Nagar, West Ghonda, Delhi-110053
Phone : 011-22945677, (M.) 9968367559, 9868572512
E-mail: manglam.books2007@rediffmail.com,
manglam.publications2007@rediffmail.com

Digital Sub-Editing And Design

First Edition 2010

ISBN 978-93-80013-30-5

PRINTED IN INDIA

Published by Ravindra Kumar Yadav for Manglam Publications, Delhi-110053 Laser Typesetting at M. K. Graphics, Delhi- 53, Printed at Sachin Printers, Moujpur Delhi- 53

PREFACE

In the beginning of the nineteenth century the information flow via specialised journals, in particular journals published by specialised learned societies, was increasing. The information flow, however, was far from smooth: there was an unacceptable publication delay. One of the causes for the delay was the habit of reading submitted papers in the annual society meeting before they could be published in the journal. Further delay was caused, in particular in smaller learned societies, by the fact that it took a long time to collect sufficient articles to warrant the publication of a journal issue. Distribution was hampered by the high costs of postage and it was so limited that a large part of the potential readership could not be reached. The situation improved when the publishing efforts of the learned societies became as professional as the scientific effort of the members. This professionalisation of the publishing effort was boosted after the Second World War by the sudden growth of the number of journals published by commercial publishers.

In response to the growth of the number of journals, secondary literature was established at an early stage: 'abstract journals' assisting the scientist in managing the primary literature. At first, abstracts were only published separately in abstract journals, but later abstracts were also included in the article itself. A present-day example of secondary literature is Current Contents, published by the Institute for Scientific Information (ISI), which contains bibliographic information about primary journals in a particular domain. With the professionalisation of science, the nature of the scientific experiments changed. The content and format of scientific articles changed accordingly.

— *Author*

CONTENTS

1

INTRODUCTION

Sir Isaac Newton wrote: "If I have seen farther than others, it is because I have stood on the shoulders of giants" And if Newton stood on the shoulders of giants, it is because he had located helpful giants and found the means to climb on their shoulders. Without communication, he wouldn't even have been aware of their existence. In the words of Francis Crick, who won a Nobel prize for the discovery of the molecular structure of DNA: "Communication is the essence of science". The problem is that this communication is not always as effective and efficient as it could be. These days, two major trends can be identified: firstly, scientists are increasingly dissatisfied with the communication process; secondly, new, electronic communication channels are emerging.

These two trends invite the question of how the new technology can contribute to a substantial improvement of scientific communication. Only part of the answer to this question can be found in further technical developments for it. It is also important to examine the organisation of the communication process, as well as the organisation of the scientific information that is communicated.

THE EXPLOSION OF SCIENTIFIC JOURNALS

In general, two types of communication channels can be distinguished: informal channels such as discussions between colleagues, and formal or archival channels. To communicate science to a larger audience systematically, across both distance and time, formal channels are indispensable. The predominant formal means of communication in science is the scientific journal article. In our research we focus on communication via this channel. The emergence and evolution of the scientific journal, and of the process of scientific communication by means of journals, have been prompted by the needs of scientists and by the possibilities offered by the publication media.

A significant factor in the shaping of scientific journals is the continuing endeavour to protect the scientists from being 'inundated' by the information flow. The amount of information communicated via journals has been growing considerably since the emergence of the scientific journal. Roughly speaking, the number of titles doubles every 10-15 years and, at the same time, more articles are published in each journal and the articles get longer. Scientists have long been struggling to manage this increasing information flow and to find the relevant drops of information without drowning. Nowadays, scientists believe they are only reading 40% of the relevant literature. Faraday reported the same problem already in 1826:

It is certainly impossible for any person who wishes to devote a portion of his time to chemical experiment, to read all the books and papers that are published in connection with his pursuit; their number is immense, and the labour of winnowing out the few experimental and theoretical truths which in many of them are embarrassed by a very large proportion of uninteresting matter, of imagination, and error, is such, that most persons who try the experiment are quickly induced to make their selection in their reading, and thus inadvertently, at times, pass by what is really good. To manage the information flow, the scientific community has for centuries been adjusting their communication channels.

The first scientific journals were established in the second half of the seventeenth century. Until then small groups of scholars communicated with each other via private correspondence. Taking Great Britain as an example, we see that the subsiding of social unrest allowed for a more systematic organisation of the scientific effort. As a result the Royal Society was formed in 1662. In the beginning, Henry Oldenburg, the secretary of the society who corresponded extensively, read relevant letters aloud at the meetings of the society. However, the correspondence soon started to overburden him. He tackled this problem by printing and distributing the most important letters; thus, the journal Philosophical Transactions: Giving Some Accompt of the Present Undertakings, Studies and Labours of the Ingenious in Many Considerable Parts of the World was established. This development was possible because of the `inventio sine qua non' of the printing press.

By 1789, the Neues medicinisches Wochenblatt für Aerzte complained: ``This is truly the decade of the journal, and one should seek to limit their number rather than to increase them, since there can also be too many periodicals". At that time, the sciences started to differentiate and, in fact, the problem was that there were too many general science journals but not enough specialised journals to allow the reader to filter the information flow. Thus, in response to this problem, many specialised journals were founded in the nineteenth century. The trend of specialisation, and the related trend of professionalisation, have restricted the number of journals that a scientist must consult in order to stay informed of the developments in his domain. These trends also have restricted the readership of specialist journals: nowadays only scientists in a very specific branch of a domain can understand the articles published in such journals.

In the beginning of the nineteenth century the information flow via specialised journals, in particular journals published by specialised learned societies, was increasing. The information flow, however, was far from smooth: there was an unacceptable publication delay. One of the causes for the delay was the habit of reading submitted papers in the annual society meeting before they could be published in the journal. Further delay was caused, in particular in smaller learned societies, by the fact that it took a long time to collect sufficient articles to warrant the publication of a journal issue. Distribution was hampered by the high costs of postage and it was so limited that a large part of the potential readership could not be reached. The situation improved when the publishing efforts of the learned societies became as professional as the scientific effort of the members. This professionalisation of the publishing effort was boosted after the Second World War by the sudden growth of the number of journals published by commercial publishers.

In response to the growth of the number of journals, secondary literature was established at an early stage: 'abstract journals' assisting the scientist in managing the primary literature. At first, abstracts were only published separately in abstract journals, but later abstracts were also included in the article itself. A present-day example of secondary literature is Current Contents, published by the Institute for Scientific Information (ISI), which contains bibliographic information about primary journals in a particular domain. With the professionalisation of science, the nature of the scientific experiments changed. The content and format of scientific articles changed accordingly. In [Bazerman, 1988, p.66,68], experimental reports published in the Philosophical transaction between 1665 and 1800 are compared:

Thus, the article had started to play a role in the scientific debate. Consequently, methodological issues gained in importance, and the results of the experiments were reported with increasing attention to precise and quantitative detail. At the same time this professionalisation was reflected in the formalisation of the discourse in the article. This led to the prototypical sections in scientific articles: Introduction, Methods, Results, Discussion and Conclusions.

These changes not only involved the content of the scientific discourse of the article, but also the bibliographic aspects of the article. Since the first scientific articles simply reported loosely connected experiments, they contained few references if any. In the second half of the nineteenth century, however, most articles do refer to previous work, which may be a sign of the increasing integration of scientific effort. However, many readers had difficulties in locating the cited work using the incomplete references that were given at that time. The situation improved with the standardisation of the references in particular and of the bibliographic information in general. Since the Second World

War, the problem of the information overload has become acute. The information flow has increased so dramatically that it is sometimes referred to as an `information explosion'. For the individual scientist it has become difficult to keep up even with the secondary literature, let alone the primary literature. The scientist not only has to cope with the current journals, but also with the accumulated archives. As an indication of the scale, the Institution of Electrical Engineers scans over 4000 scientific and technical journals and some 2000 conference publications for the bibliographic INSPEC database. At the end of 1997, the Database contained nearly 6 million bibliographic records and is growing at the rate of 330,000 records a year [IEE, 1999].

The main cause of the information explosion is the rapid growth in the number of scientists since the Second World War. Another factor is the mechanism of funding research on the basis of the number of publications [Coles, 1993, p.12]:

The case study interviewees agreed that, although publications are necessary to establish the worth of a scientist, the importance placed on publications by assessment régimes fuels the volume of published science. The pressure to publish was seen to lead to 'salami slicing', multi-authored papers, repetitious publishing and the continuance of some journals of dubious quality.

The communication system has not been able to keep up with this information explosion. Consequently, ``in some disciplines it is occasionally easier to repeat an experiment than it is to determine that the experiment has already been done." [Garvey, 1979, p.8].

Thus, although a massive amount of information is available, it does not flow to the scientists who need the information. The emergence of electronic media can help to tackle this problem, as the new technology can greatly facilitate the storage, retrieval, and dissemination of scientific information. However, simply increasing the amount of available information using this technology will only aggravate the information overload. It follows therefore, that the communication system and the information that is to be communicated must be well-organised, taking into account the possibilities offered by the technology.

THE EMERGENCE OF THE ELECTRONIC MEDIA

Nowadays, the computer has become pervasive in scientific communication. It has played an important supportive part in the communication process since scientific texts have been written using word processors, rather than typewriters, so that they are immediately available in digital form. In that form, they can be stored electronically and either consulted on the screen or printed on paper. With the advent of networking technology, the electronic media have started to play a leading part in communication processes: the electronic transmission of messages.

Although electronic communication channels also include carriers like CD-ROMs, the most popular channel is the Internet and its various services. The Internet is a network of electronically linked computer networks. Its development started with the ARPAnet: a network established in 1969 by the US Department of Defence to connect the military with their contractors and with the universities doing military-related research. Using this network, files could be transferred and computers could be accessed remotely. Electronic mail quickly became the most popular application. Other networks were added. TCP/IP software (developed in the seventies and adopted in the early eighties) provided computers in different networks with a common language, so the loose collection of dozens of networks was welded into a real `internet'.

The World Wide Web (WWW) was initiated in 1990 at the Centre Européen de Recherches Nucléaires (CERN), as a new service on the emerging Internet. Tim Berners-Lee, the `inventor' of the WWW, describes it as a ``distributed heterogeneous collaborative multimedia information system" [Berners-Lee, 1991]: all information, from any source, can be accessed in a consistent and simple way. The main feature of the Web is that it is a hypertext system. It was after the introduction of the graphical interface Mosaic in 1993, that the

Internet became a `household appliance'. To give an indication of the scale of the Internet, the online population in June 1999 is estimated to be about 200 million people and the number of hosts more than 43 million.

The Internet can assist scientists in the communication process at different levels. Electronic mail is used for informal discussions, instead of the telephone. Electronic mail services also take the place of traditional mail for a rapid exchange of data and manuscripts, for example between authors, between authors and editors and between editors and referees. The computer files can be distributed via the Internet and stored in on-line electronic databases, from which they can be retrieved again via the Internet. In this way, both scientific articles and practical messages can be made public. For example, The Internet Pilot To Physics [TIPTOP, 1999] is a unified physics resource, which includes an index of physics resources around the world, bulletin boards and notification services concerning practical issues, such as conference deadlines and job openings, and a forum for informal communication.

In the recent years, we have seen an explosive growth of the use of the Internet for the publication of electronic scientific articles. In [Hitchcock, 1995], which is titled `A survey of STM on-line electronic journals 1990-1995: the calm before the storm', 83 online journals in the domain of science, technology and medicine (STM) were examined. Since then, the storm has broken: the major science publishers have created electronic versions of all, or most of, their journals and made these available on the World Wide Web. According to [Butler, 1999, p.195] ``A journal without a web version is now rare, and probably endangered." To give an indication of the scale of the electronic endeavour, the distributor and agent Swets & Zeitlinger provided in June 1999 access to 9624 electronic journals in the domain of science technology and medicine.

The first electronic journals were close copies of their printed ancestors. Printed articles were scanned and made available as bitmap files after the publication of the original articles. In this approach to electronic publishing, the new technology was merely used for `long-distance photocopying'. Many publishers of electronic journals even stated explicitly that their electronic journal had to look as closely as possible like a printed journal. This seems characteristic of the application of a new technology: in a similar way, the first automobiles mimicked coaches to be horse-drawn. But the coach-like appearance of automobiles was gradually replaced by a form more appropriate to the new technology, when the advantages of an aerodynamic design were taken into account. So, the question now is: how to `streamline' electronic journals to make them more suitable vehicles for the `information highway'?

Since the beginning of the nineties, various electronic publishing initiatives have been taken. Different possibilities offered by the new technology were used to improve particular aspects of scientific communication, such as the distribution of articles, the presentation of information in the articles, and the organisation of feedback.

One of the first important initiatives for electronic publishing in physics was concerned with `preprints' (or `e-prints', as the electronic versions are called) rather than regular articles. Preprints are part of the `grey literature', i.e. in the grey area between informal and formal communication. The Los Alamos e-print archives provide a fully automated electronic archiving and distribution of preprints. For current awareness, the reader can browse a daily list of e-prints submitted in his area of interest (on the World Wide Web or sent by e-mail). In practice, the reader prints an e-print on paper in order to read it. Thus, the Internet is used for the dissemination of the same document that used to be disseminated via traditional preprint mailing lists.

This e-print service has proven so efficient that in certain domains it has supplanted traditional scientific journals as a channel for communication between scientists. Thus, this communication channel for grey literature is becoming more formal. The main difference is that the e-prints have not been certified by means of peer review. To fill that gap, a peer reviewed electronic journal has been established in collaboration with the e-print archives: the Journal of High Energy Physics [JHEP, 1999]. In the publication of this journal, as much as possible of the administrative work involved in the refereeing and editing process, in addition to the archiving and distribution, is automated or mediated by software robots.

Another initiative that bridges the gap between informal and formal literature using the Internet has been taken by Steven Harnad [Harnad, 1991]: Psycoloquy is a refereed electronic journal, in the domain of psychology and some related disciplines, established in 1989 on the basis of an electronic bulletin board [Psycoloquy, 1999].

In this journal, articles are published along with peer commentary, all contributions being refereed by an editor. The purpose of this journal is to provide scholars with an international forum of colleagues, to whom ideas in the formative stage of their research may be submitted and from whom rapid feedback obtained. Once the research has been completed the outcome can be published elsewhere.

With respect to purely formal communication, most electronic journals currently available on the World Wide Web were launched as electronic versions of existing printed journals. The electronic versions of articles published in such journals have some additional features, although often these are limited to the implementation of references in hyperlinks, at least within the article and preferably also to the publications cited in the article. However, in some electronic journals it is possible to include items that cannot be printed. For example, the publisher of the electronic journal (with an additional paper version) New Astronomy [New Astronomy, 1999] emphasises the possibility of including large data sets and multimedia files (e.g. animations). An important feature of this journal, and of other journals in the domains of astronomy and astrophysics, is its link with major scientific data centres (the cited data being too extensive for efficient publication in print).

In some electronic journals, particular aspects of electronic publishing technology are used to add features to the communication process, rather than just to the article itself. For example, it is possible to search the full text of all issues of the electronic version of The Astrophysical Journal [APJ, 1999]. The Institute of Physics offers personalised services, such as alerting services, to assist the reader in managing the information flow in its journals [IOP, 1999].

In short, some aspects of the communication process are facilitated by the new media. In addition, compared with print articles, electronic articles have some additional features. However, the organisation of the information in present-day electronic journals does not differ fundamentally from the way the information is organised in the print version.

THE PROJECT 'COMMUNICATION IN PHYSICS'

In the physics community, different programmes have been initiated to deal with the issue of scientific communication in the context of the emerging technology.

In 1989, the American Physical Society (APS) formed a `Task Force on Electronic Information Systems' to review the state of affairs and develop a plan for the physics information system, because: [it] is clear that the world of physics is on the verge of a revolution, a revolution that is driven by technology, but whose true nature will be determined by the response of the world scientific community. The revolution will change what and how physicists read, how they become aware of what they read, and even what `read' means. [APS, 1991]

The task force has defined a long term goal: a world scientific information system. In this system, the world's formal and less formal literature would be available on-line in an interactive environment. Individual documents, rather than entire journals, would be the fundamental entities.

In 1993, the International Union of Pure and Applied Physics (IUPAP) also formed a task force to ``investigate how the means presently available, and new means expected to become available soon, can be integrated into a first version of a system of communications, to provide fully electronic submission, publishing, large scale storage, fast retrieval and selection." [IUPAP, 1993].

Here in The Netherlands, the research programme `Communication in Physics' was launched in 1994 by the Foundation Physica, an organisation promoting the advancement of physics in The Netherlands. The foundation was moved to initiate this programme as a result of a meeting at which both the increasing dissatisfaction with the flow of scientific information was voiced and the emergence of the new technologies of computer networks and electronic publishing were signalled [De Waard, 1993]. This thesis reports on research performed in the context of this programme.

The starting point of the programme is the following: rather than being dragged along by the technological developments, the physics community should determine how it prefers the scientific communication process to function. Subsequently, the specific technology can be developed to implement this vision. Therefore, the first goal of the research programme is to gain insight into the nature of scientific information itself and of the management of this information. The second goal is to develop new models for the representation of scientific information and for scientific communication that can be implemented using the particular features of the new technology.

In order to increase our understanding of scientific information and the communication system, different aspects have to be considered: technical, social and financial aspects, as well as more `conceptual' aspects. With respect to the technical aspects, for example, presentation, storage and automatic indexing techniques have to be developed.

With respect to the social and financial aspects, issues like intellectual property and research policy and motives of scientists must be addressed. Many of these issues are the subject of current research and reported in journals like the Journal of Electronic Publishing, the Journal of Documentation and the Journal of the American Society for Information Science.

In the literature, however, the organisation of the scientific article itself is not considered systematically. Usually the authors aim to solve communication problems by developing sophisticated new techniques to deal with the article as it is. For instance, we agree with Liddy that there is a problem with the retrieval of information [Liddy, 1991, p.78]:

> *Current retrieval systems allow users to require only that the concepts they are interested in occur somewhere within the free-text representation. It is not possible for the user to specify what roles the concepts of interest should play in the retrieved documents or to specify the relationships that should hold between the concepts.*

However, we approach this problem from a different angle. Liddy proposes. [a] system that can detect the structure of abstracts and is capable of providing this type of detailed representation [that] could improve the retrieval process by allowing the user to specify in advance the particular role they require each searched concept to play.

Contrary to Liddy, who aims to improve information retrieval by improving the retrieval system, we propose a fundamental restructuring of the article itself, so that the same retrieval system can work more effectively and efficiently. Thus, we take a step back and focus on a fundamental question concerning the scientific article: what is the basic `streamlined' shape that allows for substantial improvement of scientific communication in the context of the new technology of electronic information transfer? Our basic idea is that, in an electronic environment, scientific information may be communicated more effectively and efficiently if it is presented as a network of articles with a modular structure, rather than as a set of linear, essay-type articles. An article with a modular structure consist of a coherent collection of explicitly linked modules, representing a coherent network of related conceptual information units within the larger network of published information. This structure allows the user to take into account the role that concepts of interest should play within a document, as well as the relations between specified concepts.

OUTLINE

Here we will discuss about the general problem of how to structure the presentation of scientific information in electronic articles. Given the idea of modularity, we focus on the following questions: (1) Is it possible to develop a systematic model for a modular structure for electronic scientific articles? (2) Does the modular structure indeed allow for more effective and efficient scientific communication?

The adequacy of the structure of such a presentation depends on the needs of the scientists involved in this type of communication. Therefore, we first analyse in chapter 2 the characteristics of scientific communication via articles in order to formulate an `interactants profile'. This profile summarises the characteristics and the needs of the prototypical readers and authors of scientific articles, and it yields communication criteria for the presentation of scientific information.

The definitions pertaining to the idea of a modular structure are given in chapter 3. In chapter 4, the idea of a modular structure is realised in a modular model for articles on experimental sciences: a model for the creation and evaluation of modular articles. In the modular model, the basic notions are complemented with a typology for the different types of modules and one for the different types of structured links that can be created using the model.

In order to make the modular model applicable to the creation and evaluation of concrete modular articles, the typologies have to be specified for the scientific domain at hand. In addition, specific rules for the composition are necessary, in order to determine which modules and links are required, and which are allowed, in a particular modular article in this domain. In appendix A, we provide such a specification in terms of guidelines for authors of modular articles in the field of experimental molecular dynamics.

The general modular model for experimental science and its specification for experimental molecular dynamics are developed in conjunction with an empirical analysis of a corpus of published, linear articles. The bibliography of this corpus is given in appendix B. This analysis involved modularising articles from the corpus, i.e. reconstructing linear articles in modular form, rather than writing new modular articles, in order to ground our work in the existing scientific practice. We firstly aimed to determine whether it is indeed possible to write articles with a modular structure that satisfies both the abstract definitions and the concrete guidelines. Secondly, we compared the modularised versions with the original articles in the light of the communication criteria, to see if the modular structure can indeed meet the requirements specified in the interactants profile, better than the structure of the original articles. Thus, we tested if the model allows for more effective and efficient scientific communication via electronic articles.

A MODEL OF THE PROCESS OF COMMUNICATION VIA SCIENTIFIC ARTICLES

In this thesis, we concentrate on the structure of scientific articles. For that purpose, we have to distinguish in our analysis between the organisation of the information and the actual phrasing used to present the information in the article. In addition, we have to separate the organisation of the article from the organisation of the communication process, which for instance involves the question of how peer review is organised. In this endeavour, we also have to separate between, on the one hand, conceptual issues pertaining to the organisation of the information and the communication process, and, on the other hand, the technical issues of the implementation of the article and the communication system. These different aspects are taken into account in the model of the process of scientific communication via articles that we give in this section.

Here, we first clarify how we use the terms `information' and `communication' in this thesis, because in the literature these terms are used in different ways. By communication we mean the transfer of information from a human sender to a human receiver, for the purpose of increasing the receiver's knowledge, enabling him to carry out tasks, or influencing his attitudes and behaviour. If the receiver also acts as a sender, the one-way transfer of information becomes a two-way exchange of information between human interactants. Depending on the type of communication, the senders and receivers are the speaker and listener in oral communication, or the writer and reader in the case of written communication.

By information we mean a conceptual representation of aspects of a `universe' for the purpose of communication. Because information is a conceptual representation, it cannot be directly communicated to others: it first has to be represented in a message that can be encoded and transmitted. Thus, communication entails at least three `representation levels':

1. *Conceptual Level*: *Information*: Information is a conceptual representation of particular aspects of the universe.
2. *Symbolic Level*: *Message*: The message is a symbolic representation of the conceptual representation of an aspect of the universe. It can be formulated textually, in mathematical or chemical formulae, in pictures, or in any other `language'.
3. *Technical Level*: *Signal*: The message is encoded (in different stages) in a physical or electronic signal that can be transmitted.

In a universe, separate entities can be distinguished, as well as relations between these entities. The same 'granularity' can be seen at the conceptual level: the information about these entities forms related information units. For example, information about the results of a particular type of measurement on different specimens can be divided into different information units. The complete set of rules for the performance of a particular task also form an information unit. We need such a notion of a `quantity of information' to be able to develop an adequate structure for the representation of scientific information. If information can be considered as a network of units, we should structure a scientific article (in which the scientific information is represented) as a network of modules, each representing a unit. The question as to what can constitute an information unit, however, can only be answered in the context that determines what is similar information about similar subjects. The notion of information we use allows us to follow an information unit through the communication process, from the sender to different types of receivers. In this process, the amount and the nature of information conveyed is considered fixed, regardless of the question as to whether a particular receiver already is aware of the information or whether the signal is intact when it reaches him.

Our notion of communication is based on sending and receiving. In this respect, it fits with most models for communication, according to the International Encyclopaedia of Communications [Barnouw et al., 1989]: Most communication models employ a small number of basic concepts: a sender; a process of encoding into signals or symbols; a message; a channel; a receiver; a relationship; a process of decoding; a range of things to which the messages refer (`referents'); and an actual or probable effect, intended or not. Some models incorporate a feedback link from receiver to sender.

The communication models of this type are based on the mathematical theory of communication developed in [Shannon and Weaver, 1949]: a sender encodes a message in a signal that is transmitted through a channel and then decoded by a receiver. Shannon and Weaver developed their model to describe telephone conversation from an engineer's point of view. They were not concerned with either the meaning of the message or the reason for its transmission. Unlike Shannon and Weaver, we do take these aspects into account. For that purpose, we add steps to their model of the communication process. We describe the meaning of the message as the information represented in it. The reason for transmission is then taken into account in the goals of the sender and the receiver and thereby in their criteria for the adequacy of the communication.

We visualise communication between senders (authors in particular) and receivers (readers) as follows: packages containing information are transmitted to a receiver via a communication conduit (e.g. a telephone line, or a regular mail service). The communication, however, involves more than the transmission of packages through the conduit. Analytically, we distinguish four main stages. In the first stage, the sender creates the information package.

Then, a connection has to be established with the receiver and the package has to be transmitted. This involves two stages: in the second stage, the dissemination, the package is made available to the receiver, and in the third main stage the receiver acquires it.

The fourth stage is the assimilation, in which the receiver unwraps the package, consumes the information. For the process of communication via scientific publications, these four main stages can be further refined into an idealised sequence of seventeen different activities. We emphasise that this is an analytical model of the communication process; in practice, the activities may be performed in a different order or simultaneously, or they may be repeated, guided by feedback, until the result is satisfactory. In the following, we examine the model in more detail.

Stage I: Creating

(1) We start with the scientist generating and gathering raw scientific information in some research activity, by forming a conceptual representation of some aspects of the universe at issue.

(2) This information is organised and characterised at the conceptual level, based on an evaluation of the raw material in the context of the research programme. In this step, the `raw output' is both moulded and filtered. Some information is discarded as uncertain, irrelevant, superfluous or unimportant.

(3) Then, the author actually writes the article, i.e. he creates a symbolic representation of the information. The author decides which `language' or symbolic means he will use to communicate the different types of information: natural language (and which one), mathematical or chemical formulae, pictures, tables, animations, et cetera. Then, he chooses the structure of

the document, the exact wording, the appearance of the non-verbal presentation, and the precise terms (e.g. key words) by which the information is characterised.

(4) In order to allow for transmission, the document is encoded in an analog signal (e.g. by printing it on paper) or a digital signal (a computer file) that can be transmitted.

Stage II: Disseminating

(5) The first activity in this stage is the collection of encoded documents for publication. The editor of a particular journal can actively solicit them, or the author can submit them directly. The encoded document can be made public and archived immediately, in a `preprint' archive [Ginsparg, 1996]. In communication via articles published in a journal, however, more value is added first.

(6) For scientific quality control, the correctness of the information and the clarity of the presentation are judged in some form of peer review. In principle, quality control does not have to take place before publication. Comments and `quality labels' could be added to the article after publication. Different forms of peer review are proposed, for example, in [Harnad, 1991]. If this control takes place before publication, feedback can lead to an improvement of the article to be the published article. The editor of the journal may further enhance the quality.

(7) Indexing also adds value to the document. The document can be characterised using controlled index terms chosen from a thesaurus, for example, or using free terms. The next activities are not concerned with the scientific content of the article but with other added value. Usually, these mainly technical, administrative and financial tasks are performed by publishers and librarians.

(8) Value can be added to the technical aspects of the presentation of the document and its encoding in a

signal. The presentation can be professionalised and the document can be encoded (in different steps) in several types of signals. The technical aspects of editing and presentation involve, for example, visual design, typesetting, printing and format conversion.

(9) The publication, in the literal sense of making the information public, then allows the audience to become aware of the existence of the information. At this stage, the (encoded) article can be distributed directly to the intended readership. However, it is usually transmitted to a (physical or digital) library, from which the receiver can retrieve it immediately after publication or later.

(10) Thus, value is added by archiving the article for future reference.

Stage III: Acquiring

Supposing that the article created and disseminated in the previous stages contains information that is of interest to a prospective receiver, that receiver first has to acquire the signal in which the entire article, or the relevant part of it, is encoded.

(11) In this stage, the first activity involves locating relevant information, which implies a selection process. Relevant information can be found in two ways: by scanning or browsing, and by searching. When browsing, the receiver navigates through (selected) sources, trying to encounter interesting information he was previously unaware of. Using this method, the browsing scientist locates information by recognising it as relevant. The searcher specifies in advance the characteristics of (potentially) relevant information. For both searching and browsing, both the contents of articles and the `meta-information', i.e. the information about the articles, can be used.

(12) After locating the relevant information, the prospective receiver has to retrieve the `signal' (e.g. the computer file).

Stage IV: Assimilating

(13) Once the receiver has retrieved the signal, he first decodes it, to obtain the document (i.e. the article, or the relevant part of an article) it contains.

(14) Then he reads the document, reconstructing the information underlying it. Comprehensive reading involves following the discourse linearly from the beginning to the end. In their field of interest, however, scientists often read selectively: they usually neither study the article as a whole, nor in the prescribed order [Dillon et al., 1989].

(15) The receiver `absorbs' the information (by fitting it into his own conceptual representation of the universe), and

(16) evaluates it.

(17) If it is satisfactory, he incorporates the information in his own research. This can involve increasing his personal knowledge, as well as a concrete utilisation of specific information. Generating new scientific information, the scientist now exchanges his role of receiver for that of sender, which brings us back to (1).

Scientific Articles

In this section, we specify the means of communication: published documents, in particular scientific articles. By a document we mean a symbolic representation of a quantity of information that can be stored and retrieved separately (when it has been encoded in some medium). Communication via published documents has two distinguishing features that may compromise its effectiveness and efficiency: it is strongly indirect and heterogeneous. In strongly indirect communication, there is no immediate feedback. In addition, the interactants are not connected to each other by a direct communication channel. This means that the transmission of a message from the sender to a receiver is nontrivial. The message is put into some `information pool', from which the receiver has to retrieve it, and the sender cannot be sure that the prospective receivers have indeed done so.

Communication by means of published documents is not only strongly indirect, but also heterogeneous: the audience consists of (potential) receivers with different needs. The needs of a receiver depend on the goals that he pursues at that particular moment and on his background, which determines what the receiver understands, accepts and finds interesting.

Narrowing down the type of documents, we concentrate on scientific articles. In a broad sense of the word, a scientific article is any document in which information on a particular subject obtained from scientific research is presented. We focus on scientific articles in a more narrow sense of the word: by a scientific article we mean a refereed full, original account of a research activity published in a scientific journal, that constitutes a coherent unit for the purpose of communication to peers. In other words, the article forms a self-contained publication unit, in the sense that it provides what the target audience is supposed to consider a full account of a finished `piece of research'.

By a scientific journal we mean a documentbase in which certified documents of a particular type, on a specified subject in science, aimed at a specific target audience are published, and in which some form of peer review is implemented. A documentbase is a structured collection of documents of a particular genre, which can be accessed by more than one person and/or used for more than one purpose. Thus, a journal is defined by its functions of certification and registration of articles, of (allowing for) archiving and of making the audience aware of it. In our broad definition of the word `journal', we do not specify the medium. The journal may be published by any suitable means. The most obvious media in this context are the electronic medium and the paper medium. We do not specify the journal's schedule either. A journal traditionally is a periodical, but `continuous journals' can also be envisaged: articles can be published as a continuous stream instead of being gathered into periodically appearing issues.

The kinds of documents that can be published in a journal include scientific articles according to our narrow definition, rapid communications, comments and reviews. The requirements or guidelines for articles that are to be published in some particular journal are usually specified by the editorial board. The aims and scope of a journal are often explicitly stated. The subject may for example be chemical physics and the intended audience chemical physicists or all broadly interested physicists. The target audience of the journal, and more particularly of the article, is restricted to a specified range of fellow experts or at least fellow scientists. Nevertheless, it is still rather heterogeneous, as not every member of the target audience has exactly the same needs.

Requirements for Scientific Articles

In this section, we consider the specific requirements that the information, the representation of the information in scientific articles, and the `information system' for the transmission of those articles have to meet in order to allow for effective and efficient communication.

Rational Communication

Rational communication is a goal-oriented interactional activity, which has three aspects. Firstly, the messages of the interactants are means to achieve some end and responsive to the requirements of the situation. Secondly, rational interactants take into account the goals and plans of the other interactants. And thirdly, rational interactants actually take up the other's purposes working towards an accepted common goal, so that their interaction truly is a joint activity [Van Eemeren et al., 1993, p.6]. Scientific communication, in particular, is rational communication in which the interactants are scientists and the primary common goal of the interaction is the advancement of science.

An influential theory that articulates standards of rationality for the usage of ordinary language is `speech act theory'. According to [Searle, 1969], speech acts are performed successfully if they satisfy specific `felicity conditions' for rational communication. The felicity conditions imply an abstract model of presumptions and expectations, shared by all language users, of what rational communication involves. The best known example of such a model is Grice's Co-operative Principle, to which the participants of a conversation are assumed to adhere [Grice, 1975, p.45]:

Make your conversational contribution such as is required, at the stage at which it occurs, by the accepted purpose or direction of the talk exchange in which you are engaged.

Although the Co-operative Principle is formulated for conversation, Grice explicitly states that this principle also applies to other types of rational interaction. The maxims that Grice derived from this Co-operative Principle have been reformulated by Van Eemeren and Grootendorst, in terms of five rules of communication based on Searle's felicity conditions. These rules read as follows [Van Eemeren and Grootendorst, 1988, p.501]:

1. Perform no incomprehensible speech acts.
2. Perform no insincere speech acts.
3. Perform no unnecessary speech acts.
4. Perform no pointless speech acts.
5. Perform no new speech acts that are not an appropriate sequel or reaction to preceding speech acts.

Grice's Co-operative Principle and the ensuing maxims and rules represent the basic expectations of participants in a conversation: speakers generally act according to them and listeners may base their interpretation of an utterance on the fact that they expect the speaker to adhere to them. In discourse analysis, adherence to the maxims is often taken as a starting point and the Co-operative Principle is used as a tool for the reconstruction of discourse.

The maxims, and the rules for communication derived from them, can also be interpreted as norms for a rational, effective exchange of information. As such, they can be made explicit into the following-intenrtwined-basic requirements for rational communication and then used to provide senders with guidelines: quantity, clarity, quality and relevance.

In order to determine if a particular message satisfies these requirements, the requirements have to be further specified, by determining the goals of the sender and receivers, and thereby the `communicative purpose' of the message. Therefore, the `genre' and domain of the message have to be specified. A (rather general) working definition of the concept `genre' is given in [Swales, 1990, p.58]: A genre comprises a class of communicative events, the members of which share some set of communicative purposes. These purposes are recognised by the expert members of the parent discourse community, and thereby constitute the rationale for the genre. This rationale shapes the schematic structure of the discourse and influences and constrains choice of content and style. Communicative purpose is both a privileged criterion and one that operates to keep the score of a genre as here conceived narrowly focused on comparable rhetorical action. In addition to purpose, exemplars of a genre exhibit various patterns of similarity in terms of structure, style content and intended audience.

In this thesis, we focus on the genre of experimental scientific articles, and we concentrate on the domain of experimental molecular dynamics in particular. As communication via articles is strongly indirect, the author has to pay particular attention in advance to the fulfilment of the receiver's potential requirements. These requirements are particularly important in scientific communication, because scientific research is a co-operative effort. Incorporating existing scientific information into new work is constructive only if the information has a high quality and if it is relevant to the new situation. It is feasible only if it is presented sufficiently clearly to allow the scientist to understand and evaluate it, and it is practical only if the information is presented in an appropriate quantity.

Quantity: The message is required to represent all information that is necessary for the achievement of the sender's and the receiver's goals, and no unnecessary or pointless information. In other words, the sender has to provide precisely the appropriate amount of information. This requirement is derived from the communication rules to perform no unnecessary and no pointless speech acts.

The existence of a research programme (an accepted model or pattern) in science has a direct impact on the quantity requirement of scientific communication. The sender is required to provide the receiver with all necessary information. This implies that he not only has to give a full account of his latest findings, but that he also has to make all relevant background information available. In the context of a shared programme, that background has already been established. Once the background has been properly presented, it does not have to be repeated in each publication.

The consequence of the heterogeneity of communication via articles is that it is difficult to fulfil the quantity requirement for all potential receivers.

Clarity: The message has to be clear, orderly and brief, avoiding obscurity and ambiguity, so that the receiver can understand and critically test it. This requirement is based on the communication rule to perform no incomprehensible speech acts. This implies that the restrictions of the information and all relevant dependency relations between information units must be made explicit. It also implies that the problem-solution pattern of the research has to be taken into account in the presentation.

As all scientists are in principle supposed to study the same `real universe' systematically, regardless of place and time, they must be able to communicate with each other, regardless of place and time. Furthermore, In experimental science, relevant information is related to the `real world', so that scientists require the possibility to claim their priority: [Scientists believe] that there is just one real world waiting to be explored. Since several scientists may be working along similar lines at the same time, this means that the first to give public notification of a discovery pre-empts the work of the others. Consequently, the communication system must be able to establish clearly who has priority for each step forward. [Meadows, 1998, p.49]

Therefore, the organisation, presentation and implementation of scientific information has to be compatible with the practices of scientists in other places and times. Consequently, there are handbooks about writing scientific publications (such as [Day, 1979]), and there is a prototypical format of (some types of) scientific publications.

Quality: The message is required to be correct or to have adequate grounds for belief. The sender is supposed to be honest and to be reasoned, and he can be held accountable for the message. This requirement is based on the communication rule against insincere speech acts.

Absolute correctness can be guaranteed only in cases where rigorous proofs are possible. Therefore, the requirement of quality is specified to the requirement that the information has to be correct given the current state of affairs in science, i.e. that it has to be based on adequate grounds for belief. This implies that the information has to be controllable.

Consequently, scientific communication has to meet particular clarity and completeness requirements. To control a scientific claim, the receiver requires a full and clear description of the procedures and methods that have been used. In particular, the receiver has to be made aware of the restrictions of these methods, and the consequent restrictions of the validity of the findings.

Furthermore, if information depends on other information, that dependency relation has to be explicit. In particular, it is necessary to specify the sources of previous results used in this work.

When the dependency relations are made explicit, it is possible to trace the consequences of adjustments or refutations of particular information to the validity of other information. If, for example, an assumption used in a method turns out to be unwarranted, all findings based on that method are suspect.

Relevance: The message has to be relevant given the goals of the interactants at each stage of the interaction. In other words, the sender has to provide the appropriate type of information. The requirement for relevance follows from the rule to perform no speech act that is not appropriate at that point in the sequence of speech acts.

A PROFILE OF THE INTERACTANTS IN SCIENTIFIC COMMUNICATION VIA ARTICLES

Scientific information via articles is a particular type of goal-oriented communication. Therefore, we have to specify who are the interactants, what are the goals that the interactants try to achieve, and what requirements the communication system and the article must fulfil in order to allow the interactants to achieve these goals.

The interactants are scientists who play various roles, as senders and receivers, in the communication process. In this discussion, the emphasis lies on the receiver's requirements, because the authors also concentrate on the prospective receivers (they must tailor their article to the receivers' needs) and the requirements of the senders concerned with the added value coincide with receiver requirements.

Senders

In pure science, researchers both publish and read articles, alternating the roles of sender and receiver. Authors are scientists who create scientific information and represent it in scientific articles, in the first main stage of the communication process. We assume that these scientists not only have research skills, but also have sufficient presentation skills, such as writing skills. They may be assisted by referees and editors.

We concentrate on what we assume to be the author's primary goal: the advancement of science. This goal has two aspects: firstly, the author aims to add to the body of scientific knowledge, offering present and future colleagues information that they can use in their own research. Secondly, the author wants to advance his own research by soliciting feedback from colleagues.

In order to achieve this primary goal, the author has to achieve three interactional goals in the article: he has to

(1) inform the receiver of his work, (2) convince him of its reliability, and (3) convince him of its relevance

Now, let us consider the requirements that must be fulfilled to allow the author to achieve his goals. The author's primary goal can be achieved only if the receiver's requirements for effective and efficient communication are met. Therefore, the author has to present the information in a clear and acceptable way when creating the document in the first stage. For that purpose, the standard format for articles has to be clear, so that the author understands how and where he has to represent the information.

Furthermore, he needs appropriate tools and guidelines allowing him to present and encode, in a convenient way, all the information he considers relevant. This implies that the author should not be limited to textual or `printable' representations, or limited by restrictions with regard to the amount of information. It also implies that the author should not be obliged to do unnecessary work: if part of the information that the author wants to convey has already been presented, he has to be able to re-use that previous presentation. Since the representation of scientific information requires a profound understanding of the information itself, it is more efficient for the scientist to write the article himself then to explain everything to a non-scientist professional writer and delegate the representation of the information.

SENDERS DISSEMINATING DOCUMENTS: EDITORS, REFEREES AND INDEXERS

In the second main stage of communication (disseminating the message), scientists can play the role of journal editor, referee and indexer. Editors who actively solicit articles for publication aim to elicit all relevant information available, steering the flow of the information. For that purpose, they have to be aware of existing knowledge and interesting developments in the field.

The referees responsible for the scientific quality control must be experts on the subject of the article. The goal of the referee is to ensure the scientific quality of the article, by either eliminating or ameliorating incorrect, incomplete or unclear articles.

The goal of indexing is to provide index terms that characterise the information represented in the document in such a way that the receivers are enabled to locate the document if it is relevant to their information needs. These index terms can be provided by the author, by a professional indexer, or by an automatic indexing computer programme. If the author is responsible for the characterisation of the article, it can be seen as part of the creation of the article. If a professional indexer has to find adequate index terms, he has to read and understand the article. Thus, the requirements of the scientists adding value to an article that they have not written themselves correspond to requirements of the receivers. Therefore, we shall consider the requirements of these types of senders in conjunction with the requirements of the receivers.

Receivers

The intended receivers (or `target audience') of scientific articles are peers, i.e. scientists who have approximately the same background as the author. Nevertheless, as we already stated in section 2.1.3, scientific communication via articles is heterogeneous: not all members of the target audience are equally familiar with the subject. The receivers' `degree of familiarity' ranges from the least-informed to the most-informed receiver. The most informed receiver is the expert. The question as to who is the least informed receiver, i.e. what is the minimum of knowledge on a specified subject that the receivers are presumed to have, depends on the domain and the level of specialism of the article. The `degree of familiarity' with the subject affects the receivers' goals and their requirements for effective and efficient communication.

Receivers Acquiring Documents: Searchers and Browsers

The receiver can have different specific goals in the stage of information acquisition: (1) to find specific information, (2) to look for new ideas, and (3) to keep informed. To achieve these goals, the scientist engages in different activities. To locate the desired type of information in activity (11), the receiver needs the means to differentiate between information sources, with respect to their nature and quality. Therefore, articles are required to be certified, as an outcome of the quality control (6).

Browsing: To see what is available, the scientist browses. In other words, he performs a semi-directed or an undirected search, skimming articles or tables of contents of journals, or wandering through larger repositories of information (e.g. the shelves in the library or an electronic documentbase). The browser's goal is to encounter interesting information. Informed browsers mostly monitor the information system to keep informed [Ellis et al., 1993]. Scientists who are less familiar with the subject rather look for new ideas, in what is called in [Chang, 1993] `serendipity browsing'.

Especially for the less-informed browser, both the article itself and the larger depository of documents (e.g. the library) are required to be structured clearly and relevantly. This implies that the structure needs to be compatible with what the receiver expect and that it has to be made explicit. Therefore, both the documents and the connections between them must be characterised properly, so that the browser can decide quickly whether a particular document is worth inspecting or not. Making the structure explicit in a `road map' would greatly assist the browser.

In order to obtain a clear structure, it has to be properly conceived on the conceptual level in (2) and properly realised in the writing activity (3). The archives have to be clearly structured in (10). The informed browser mainly tries to keep abreast of the latest developments in his field. Therefore, he wants to be alerted when potentially relevant information is published (9). The time delay in the publication process has to be minimised, in order to ensure the actuality of the information. For the sake of efficiency, the informed browser wants to see immediately what is the novel information (as opposed to the background information) that warranted the publication of the article.

Searching: In order to find specific information, the scientist performs a directed search. For example, he can search for a number or a definition, for advice to help him solve a problem, for a review on a specific subject, or for the precise address of an author. The more informed the searcher is about the subject, the better he is able to perform such a search, either with or without the support of an information specialist assisting in the technical aspects of the manipulation of the information system.

The basic requirements for searching information are completeness and findability: if the particular information unit the receiver needs exists, (1) it has to be available, and (2) the receiver has to be able to locate it. For completeness, all potentially relevant information has to be taken into account in the author's organisation of the information at the conceptual level (2). A fundamental problem concerning the completeness is that the author does not know what information could be relevant in other contexts, even if he strives for the completeness of what he thinks essential. Then, all potentially relevant information is required to be expressed in the article in (3) (the actual writing of the article) and subsequently encoded in (4). Relevant information can be lost for technical reasons in these activities.

Completeness also implies that all articles containing relevant information must be made available. They risk being lost altogether, when they are not included in some appropriate collection (in activity (5)). In the quality control (6), relevant information can get lost, if it is rejected along with incorrect information. Furthermore, the information should not stay in the `publication pipeline' too long, but it has to be published (9) quickly. Once articles have been made available, the searcher requires that they remain available, i.e. that the articles are properly archived (10). Access to the archives and the security of the articles have to be guaranteed permanently.

Supposing that relevant information is available, the next step is to find it. For that purpose, a correct characterisation is indispensable. The information has to be adequately characterised, and that characterisation has to be represented at the symbolic level in a set of index terms, which then must be associated to the signal encoding the document.

The characterisation must be correct (i.e. the index terms must correspond to the information they describe), clear and relevant (i.e. they should describe the information in a way that fits the receivers' expectations and needs). It is also required to be complete (i.e. all information must be characterised), to reduce the risk of the receiver missing the target altogether.

In terms of Information Retrieval, this point is mostly concerned with the `recall' of the search result. For the enhancement of the `precision' of the search result, the characterisation must also be sufficiently precise: it should be narrow (i.e. the combined index terms should not be more general, for example, than the information) and fine-grained, in the sense that the representation of each different type of information that the receiver may be looking for should carry its own index terms.

The information that the searcher is trying to locate is not necessarily what is represented in an entire article. Therefore, the precision of the search not only implies that no irrelevant documents should be retrieved, but also that the retrieved documents that contain relevant information do not contain any irrelevant information, or that the representation of the relevant information is highlighted within the document.

Therefore, smaller publication units than the article have to be explicitly labelled in the case that an article is composed of parts representing different types of information. In the next chapter, we shall see that in a modular article, each module carries a unique characterisation.

Retrieving: Then, the receiver wants to retrieve the article quickly, easily and cheaply in activity (12). Therefore, there should not be insurmountable technical or financial barriers blocking the archives. Receivers assimilating the information contained in documents: comprehensive and selective readers, and users

Decoding: For the transmission (and in particular storage) of the document, the symbolic representation of the information may have been translated into some computer language. In that case, the receiver has to decode the signal (13) in order to obtain the article itself. For example, if information represented in terms of a picture has been transmitted as a computer file in a picture format, it has to be translated back to the pictorial language that the (human) receiver can interpret. For this purpose, the receiver requires appropriate `tools'. In cases of exotic or obsolete encoding formats such tools may be unavailable.

Reading: The receiver aims to learn from the article and to use the information represented in it in his own research. When consulting a scientific article, he therefore has the following specific goals, which reflect the author's interactional goals: 1) to get informed, 2) to evaluate the reliability of the information, and 3) to evaluate the relevance of the information in the light of his own needs. For this purpose, the receiver can read the article comprehensively or selectively in activity (14) of the communication process.

In the case of comprehensive reading, the receiver consults the article as a whole, following the discourse linearly from the beginning to the end. Traditionally, articles are written to be read in this way.

According to [Bazerman, 1985], most comprehensive reading is for self-instruction in areas beyond the intimate knowledge of the receiver. Thus, the receiver studies the article as a tutorial [Dillon et al., 1989]. He has to be sufficiently informed to be able to read an article written for peers comprehensively without additional background information. The most informed receivers may read an article comprehensively, in order to judge its quality. However, they are not always interested in reading the entire article, being already familiar with most of its contents.

In the case of selective reading, the scientists do not consult the article as a whole. Instead, they extract only the specific parts they need. Bazerman has interviewed informed physicists, to analyse their reading strategies. He found that the majority of the interviewees read the larger part of the articles selectively [Bazerman, 1985, p.11].

Receivers do not consult the article sequentially either. Instead, they start with the interesting part and then jump to additional information. Rather than studying the article like a tutorial, the `selective receiver' consults the article more like a reference book. A special type of `selective reader' consults the meta-information of an article, rather than its scientific content. This role is played by non-scientists for administrative purposes, but also by scientists who want, for instance, to contact an author or to find a specific reference.

To allow the receiver to assimilate the information represented in an article, it has to be structured and expressed in a clear and readable way, so that the receiver can absorb (15) and evaluate (16) the information easily.

In particular, the coherence of the information has to be expressed. In this context, the problem of incompleteness, already mentioned for the acquisition of information, also affects the receiver: explanations, extensive calculations and interesting proofs cannot be replaced by a statement like ``you can easily show that".

We assume that, for the sake of clarity, the distinction between old and new work has to be made explicit. We also assume that the receiver wants the main claim of the article to be highlighted and that the receiver wants to be able to asses the contents of the article and evaluate its potential interest quickly. Therefore, it also has to be clear how the article fits in its context.

For comprehensive reading, readability implies that the receiver is guided smoothly from the beginning of the article to the end, while in the structure the main issues are separated from side-issues. For the purpose of selective reading, the article has to be organised in small coherent units, so that the relevant specific information is not encumbered by the rest. For the selective consultation of the meta-information, these data in particular are required to be grouped and clearly structured. Thus, comprehensive readers and selective readers have conflicting requirements. If receivers must be able to read same article in two different ways, the article will have to be structured in a particularly clear and flexible way.

Furthermore, the article has to be produced (8), published (9) and stored (10) in such a way that its (physical or electronic) `technical presentation' is either directly user-friendly, or easily re-formatted as such. The reader has to be able to transport and store the article for (re)use at a later time, to compare information and annotate the article.

Incorporating: If the receiver judges the information to be sufficiently reliable and relevant, he can incorporate it in his own work. For instance, he can utilise it directly as input in a calculation, as a guideline for the fine-tuning of his own experimental set-up, or for comparison with his own results. This implies, from a technical point of view, that the information has to be presented and stored in a manipulable form.

The information can only be used wisely if it is complete, in particular with respect to its restrictions. The more familiar the scientist is with the subject, the more natural it is for him to use information from the article, without first reading the whole story. If the receiver does not accept the information, he can contribute to science by explicitly refuting that information.

In the context of scientific articles, this implies that the information has to be controllable. Therefore, the source of cited information must be made explicit and the acquisition of the cited material has to be easy, so that the information can easily be checked. Furthermore, the receiver requires assistance in judging the article, in particular if he is not sufficiently well-informed to recognise unreliable information as such, or if he wants to use the information directly. Therefore, certification plays a crucial role in this stage, informing the receiver about the reliability of the information.

Related to the requirement of scientific quality is that of the integrity of the information. In the archives, the article has to remain `intact'. However, the archives must be flexible enough to allow for the addition of new versions, comments and explicit corrections, to keep the information up to date and ensure that obsolete information can be recognised as such. The original version of a published article must not be changed.

Summarising, we have discussed the following requirements of the interactants in the process of scientific communication.

As a prerequisite, the communication system in general has to fulfil the following requirements, including dissemination requirements. It should:

- prov' le practical tools and guidelines that facilitate authoring;
- register publications, establishing their existence and securing the authors' intellectual ownership and priority;
- disseminate rapidly;
- durably store publications in such a way that receivers can easily locate and retrieve them;
- guarantee that the authenticity and integrity of publications are preserved;
- enable receivers to obtain publications in a (physical, digital) form that allows them to easily consult, annotate, transport and store the publications, and to manipulate their contents;
- provide practical tools and guidelines for navigation, and for searching, retrieving and consulting publications.

  Concerning the article, the author has the following requirements

- `Creation requirements': The prescribed format of the article has to
  - * spare the author unnecessary work;
  - * be clear.

The scientific article itself has to meet the following criteria to satisfy the receiver:

- `Acquisition requirements': The representation of the information has to be characterised completely, sufficiently precisely, correctly, clearly and relevantly
- `Assimilation requirements': The represented information has to be:
    * the appropriate quantity, i.e. sufficient and not excessive;
    * clear, i.e. clearly structured and clearly formulated (or, generally speaking, clearly expressed in any language, e.g. natural language, formulae, graphics);
    * high-quality, i.e. based on adequate grounds for belief, and therefore it has to be controllable and certified;
    * relevant to the central problem of the article.

2

ELECTRONIC PUBLISHING

In the previous section, we have specified the requirements for efficient and effective scientific communication independently of the publication medium. In this section, we discuss the intrinsic characteristics of the electronic publishing technology (compared with the paper based technology) in terms of the impact they may have on the fulfilment of the requirements on scientific communication.

DISTRIBUTION

The electronic distribution of scientific articles is more efficient than the distribution of printed articles by the traditional distribution channels, as it is distributed more quickly and more directly. Information can be made available more quickly, when it is published on-line. Firstly, the distribution itself causes no delays. Secondly, articles or other publication units can be published as soon as they are ready, without waiting for the next issue of the journal. Thus, an electronic journal can lose its periodical character and the flow of information can become continuous. The issue of speed and ease with which an article can be obtained has two sides. On the one hand, navigating within an on-line article, once it has been found, may be relatively slow due to network congestion. On the other hand, on-line publications from different sources are accessible directly from the scientists desktop, whereas a paper or off-line publication in most cases has to be separately consulted in or fetched from the library or some other central service. Thus, electronic publications can be obtained quickly and easily, provided that the infrastructure is sufficient and the user interface is adequate.

The author's requirement for high visibility is not fulfilled by most of the present day electronic journals. At this moment, paper journals have a more serious image, a much higher status and a far larger audience then electronic journals. This is not an intrinsic characteristic of the medium, but a description of the status quo. We assume that the prestige of the new media will increase when enough important scientists have published articles in scientifically adequate electronic journals.

STORAGE

As a storage medium, an electronic memory is much more efficient than paper. Therefore, it is possible to present in an electronic article large amounts of information that cannot reasonably be published in a printed article. In an electronic environment, it is also possible to store and present messages that cannot be printed at all. For example, in an electronic article, the symbolic representation of the information can be a sound or a movie, instead of a text or a picture. The choice of the medium does not have an impact on the requirements with respect to the writing itself, but the electronic media can enhance the clarity of the article, because the most appropriate type of representation can be chosen. The impact of electronic storage on the requirement of completeness is mixed. On the one hand, an electronic article can present material that cannot be printed, including intrinsically unprintable animations and amounts of data that are too large to be printed in practice. On the other hand, information may be lost, because the electronic media are not as secure as the print medium (yet).

COMPLEX SEARCH OPERATIONS

An important advantage of electronic storage is that it allows for complex search operations, within a document as well as within an entire archive. The receiver can locate relevant articles by searching in bibliographic databases with abstracts (e.g. INSPEC), as well as in full text `document bases'. In order to allow the receiver to take advantage of this possibility, the representation of the information has to be characterised clearly and correctly.

Separating the Storage from the Presentation Format

Another advantage of electronic storage is that information can be stored independently of the presentation. Upon each retrieval of the information, it can be decided how it is to be presented-on screen or on paper, and which font, format and appearance are most suitable for a particular task. This feature is explicitly used in descriptive languages as Standard Generalized Markup Language (SGML) or Extensible Markup Language (XML), where the structure of the presentation is marked up in a functional way (labelling headers and sections) instead of a typographical description (in terms of fonts and sizes) [ISO, 1986]. In an electronic environment, the production of a truly physical product can be entirely eliminated, or replaced by a print job on a laser printer in the receivers office. In the user-survey reported in [Coles, 1993], all respondents indicated that they wanted print-on-paper versions of articles of interest; they preferred to restrict reading from the screen to article scanning.

It must therefore be possible to obtain an adequate printed version of electronic articles. This requirement, however, is far more stringent for the comprehensive receiver than for the selective receiver, who does not read the entire article. At least using the current technology, paper is easier to handle than the computer for the reader. It is more pleasant to read from paper than from a computer screen. Also, a paper article is more portable and it can more easily be annotated. And viewing different documents (or parts of documents) simultaneously is more practical if they are spread out over a desk than if they are presented on the screen.

FLEXIBILITY

An electronic journal is more flexible than its paper equivalent. Information represented in an electronic article can be presented in such a way that the receiver can manipulate it. For example, experimental data can be presented in a machine-readable format, integrated with tools for calculation and plotting graphs. In an electronic article, not only the presentation is flexible, but the storage as well. Whereas a printed article is fixed, an electronic article can be changed. In printed articles, effective updating is impossible, because the only instruments are errata, addenda and follow-up articles pointing back. In an electronic environment, various additions can be attached to the original article, such as comments or links pointing forward to later work on the subject. Thus, the correctness and the clarity of articles can be enhanced in an efficient way.

This flexibility can also be used to adapt the system of peer review. The essence of the certification of the information as such does not depend on the technology but on the social and philosophical ideas about science. However, it can be implemented in different ways and at different times. Nowadays, selection takes place before publication and the acceptance in that particular journal forms the certification. On-line electronic publication allows for spontaneous peer review after the article has been published without previous selection.

The comments, made by referees before and after publication, can be attached to the article, giving a specific certification with all necessary nuances, instead of a simple acceptance by some journal. The receiver himself can then filter the information flow, aided by the certification of the articles or the lack thereof. The higher the status of the referee, the more convinced the receiver will be of the scientific quality.

The flip side of flexibility is insecurity. So far, electronically stored documents are less secure than printed documents. Firstly, files can be changed without authorisation. It is important to protect the integrity of the original article, to avoid confusion, e.g. by `watermarking' original copies. This problem does not occur if the information has been stored on a read-only carrier, such as a CD-ROM. Secondly, the electronic information stored on any carrier can become inaccessible if the carrier breaks down or becomes obsolete. Technical and organisational solutions must be found for these problems.

NON-LINEARITY

The electronic media provide us with a distributed storage environment, which allows for a flexible consultation of publication units. On paper, a linear, essay-like one-dimensional presentation of the text is natural: the readers is supposed to begin at the top of the first page and follow the line of the article until the bottom of the final page. The electronic media allow for a non-linear, hypertext presentation. According to [Conklin, 1987, p.36]: People [...] think in terms of ideas, facts and evidence. Hypertext, via the notion of nodes as individual expressions of ideas, provides a vehicle which respects this way of thinking and working.

If the structure of an article and of a larger repository of knowledge is non-linear, it can be organised and presented in such a way that the clarity is enhanced and navigation is facilitated. However, hypertext has a double-edged impact on the clarity of the representation of information. On the one hand, the representation can reflect the structure of the information more closely, and thereby more clearly, if the information is non-linear. On the other hand, the non-linear representation can lead to disorientation, and an increase of the `cognitive load', as the reader has to make an additional effort to know where he is and how to get to the desired location. Therefore, the requirement of clarity is even more crucial in a non-linear presentation than in a linear presentation. Thus, hypertext can provide a tool for the presentation of information in scientific articles, provided that an adequate structure is devised for the organisation of the information. In this thesis, we develop a model for a systematic non-linear structure for scientific articles.

COMMUNICATION CRITERIA FOR ELECTRONIC ARTICLES

In the previous sections, we have discussed the needs of the scientists engaged as senders and receivers in scientific communication, as well as the characteristics of the electronic medium. In this section, we summarise the 'communication criteria' that the electronic scientific article itself, and in particular its structure, must fulfil to satisfy the interactants' needs.

Firstly, the representation of the information has to satisfy the following `retrieval requirement': the representation has to be characterised completely, sufficiently precisely, correctly, clearly and relevantly in order to allow the receiver to locate, by means of complex search operations, the information that satisfies his information needs.

Communication Criteria for the Characterisation:

- Each publication unit has to be precisely and uniquely characterised so that it can be localised by (and so that the receivers are informed of) at least:
  * its domain-oriented content (allowing the receivers to search for units on the desired subject);
  * its genre (allowing them to search for and to filter units with the desired aims, e.g. tutorial, article) and publication status (allowing them to filter unpublished material from published material);
  * its standard bibliographic data.
- The structure of the publication has to be predictable. This allows 1) the searcher who has located a publication unit using its characterisation (during the retrieval process) to find in this publication unit indeed the information that the characterisation led him to expect. This also allows 2) the receiver (during the reading process) to recognise the role of the unit in the discourse.
- The metadata of every unit must be made explicit and grouped in such a way that they can be used to locate the publication and that they can easily be consulted by the receiver during the reading process.

Secondly, once the receiver has obtained the message, that message has to fulfil the requirements of quantity, clarity, quality and relevance. Structuring the article adequately can contribute most to the fulfilment of the quantity and the clarity requirement. In particular, the representation of the information in an article has to satisfy the following 'reading requirements' in order to allow the receiver to assimilate it.

Quantity: The requirement of quantity implies sufficiency and no excessiveness: all information necessary to fulfil the receiver's information need has to be provided, but all unnecessary information must be avoided.

Communication Criteria for the Quantity:

- Each issue that will presumably be considered a separate subject by part of the target audience has to be dealt with in a separate unit.
- Each unit has to be self-contained, so that it can be located, retrieved, consulted, cited and used repeatedly as a separate entity

Clarity: The representation of the information is required to be clearly structured.

Communication Criteria for the Clarity:

- The representation of research information should have a structure reflecting the process of the research itself (reconstructed as a problem-solving process, not as a depiction of the day-to-day proceedings).
- The representation has to contain explicit, precise connections between the related parts of the article and between (parts of) the article and related (parts of) articles, so that:
    * the accounts of subsequent steps in the problem-solving process are connected (for content-oriented coherence: what depends on what);
    * the steps in the line of reasoning are connected (for argumentative or rhetorical coherence);
- The structure of the article in particular, and of the collection of articles in general, must be made explicit in a clear overview.
- The representation of information in a publication unit (or in a coherent collection of units) has to form a 'readable' discourse.

* Receivers must be able to follow the main line without being bogged down in details or background information.
* All details and background information that are necessary for the members of the target audience to understand the discourse have to be made explicitly available. There is tension between the need for full detail and the need for a clear line of discourse mentioned above.
* The discourse has to contain summarising remarks that facilitate the receivers' understanding of large and complicated parts of the discourse.
* The same information should not be unnecessarily repeated in a coherent discourse.

The repetition can be necessary 1) in summaries (following the previous criterion) or 2) to meet the criteria of self-containedness in order to meet the quantity requirement of receivers who do not follow the entire discourse. In the last case, there is tension between the need for repetition by selective receivers and the need for a smooth discourse by comprehensive receivers.

- A distinction has to be made between main points and side issues, and between new information and background information.

Quality: The information is required to be based on adequate grounds for belief, i.e. to be correct given the current state of affairs in science. To guarantee this claim of quality, the information has to be:

- controllable by the receiver;
- Communication criterion: Details about all methods used in the research and about its outcome (in particular about their restrictions) must be made available to the receiver, to justify the reliability of the work.
- certified by an accepted authority (e.g. a referee, a PhD committee). In addition, the authenticity and the integrity must be guaranteed.

Communication Criterion: The certification and authenticity must be expressed in metadata that must be made explicit and grouped for every publication unit in such a way that they can easily be consulted by receivers of the publication.

Relevance: The information represented in the article is required to be relevant to the problem of the article.

Communication Criterion: If the relevance of the information to the problem is not immediately clear, it has to be justified.

Thirdly, the publication format has to fulfil the following authoring requirements.

1. From the authors' perspective, the quantity requirement means that they do not have to do more work than necessary.

   Communication criterion: Information has to be represented in a way that allows for multiple use of the presentation by means of reference to a previous publication.

2. The requirement of clarity implies that the prescribed format has to be clear, so that the author understands how and where he should represent the information.

   Communication Criterion: The format has to be systematic, allowing the author to follow practical guidelines and to get used to it.

3

PUBLISHING

INTRODUCTION

Publishing is the process of production and dissemination of literature or information-the activity of making information available for public view. In some cases, authors may be their own publishers.

Traditionally, the term refers to the distribution of printed works such as books (the "book world") and newspapers. With the advent of digital information systems and the Internet, the scope of publishing has expanded to include electronic resources, such as the electronic versions of books and periodicals, as well as websites, blogs, and the like.

Publishing includes the stages of the development, acquisition, marketing, production-printing (and its electronic equivalents), and distribution of newspapers, magazines, books, literary works, musical works, software and other works dealing with information, including the electronic media. Publication is also important as a legal concept:

(1) as the process of giving formal notice to the world of a significant intention, for example, to marry or enter bankruptcy;

(2) as the essential precondition of being able to claim defamation; that is, the alleged libel must have been published, and

(3) for copyright purposes, where there is a difference in the protection of published and unpublished works.

THE PROCESS OF PUBLISHING

Book and magazine publishers spend a lot of their time buying or commissioning copy. At a small press, it is possible to survive by relying entirely on commissioned material. But as activity increases, the need for works may outstrip the publisher's established circle of writers. Writers often first submit a query letter or proposal.

The majority of unsolicited submissions come from previously unpublished authors. When such manuscripts are unsolicited, they must go through the slush pile, in which acquisitions editors sift through to identify manuscripts of sufficient quality or revenue potential to be referred to the editorial staff. Established authors are often represented by a literary agent to market their work to publishers and negotiate contracts.

Acceptance and Negotiation

Once a work is accepted, commissioning editors negotiate the purchase of intellectual property rights and agree on royalty rates. The authors of traditional printed materials sell exclusive territorial intellectual property rights that match the list of countries in which distribution is proposed (i.e. the rights match the legal systems under which copyright protections can be enforced). In the case of books, the publisher and writer must also agree on the intended formats of publication--mass-market paperback, "trade" paperback and hardback are the most common options.

The situation is slightly more complex if electronic formatting is to be used. Where distribution is to be by CD-ROM or other physical media, there is no reason to treat this form differently from a paper format, and a national copyright is an acceptable approach. But the possibility of Internet download without the ability to restrict physical distribution within national boundaries presents legal problems that are usually solved by selling language or translation rights rather than national rights. Thus, Internet access across the European Union is relatively open because of the laws forbidding discrimination based on nationality, but the fact of publication in, say, France, limits the target market to those who read French.

Having agreed on the scope of the publication and the formats, the parties in a book agreement must then agree royalty rates, the percentage of the gross retail price that will be paid to the author. This is difficult because the publisher must estimate the potential sales in each market and balance projected revenue against production costs.

Editorial Stage

Once the immediate commercial decisions are taken and the technical legal issues resolved, the author may be asked to improve the quality of the work through rewriting or smaller changes, and the staff will edit the work. Publishers may maintain a house style, and staff will copy edit to ensure that the work matches the style and grammatical requirements of each market. Editing may also involve structural changes and requests for more information. Some publishers employ fact checkers.

Prepress

When a final text is agreed upon, the next phase is design. This may include artwork being commissioned or confirmation of layout. In publishing, the word "art" also indicates photographs. This process prepares the work for printing through processes such as typesetting, dust jacket composition, specification of paper quality, binding method and casing, and proofreading.

The activities of typesetting, page layout, the production of negatives, plates from the negatives and, for hardbacks, the preparation of brasses for the spine legend and imprint are now all computerized. Prepress computerization evolved mainly in about the last twenty years of the 20th century. If the work is to be distributed electronically, the final files are saved as formats appropriate to the target operating systems of the hardware used for reading. These may include PDF files.

PUBLISHING AS A BUSINESS

The publisher usually controls the advertising and other marketing tasks, but may subcontract various aspects of the process described above. In smaller companies, editing, proofreading and layout might be done by freelancers. Dedicated in-house salespeople are rapidly being replaced by specialized companies who handle sales to bookshops, wholesalers and chain stores for a fee. This trend is accelerating as retail book chains and supermarkets have centralized their buying.

If the entire process up to the stage of printing is handled by an outside company or individuals, and then sold to the publishing company, it is known as book packaging. This is a common strategy between smaller publishers in different territorial markets where the company that first buys the intellectual property rights then sells a package to other publishers and gains an immediate return on capital invested. Indeed, the first publisher will often print sufficient copies for all markets and thereby get the maximum quantity efficiency on the print run for all.

Some businesses maximize their profit margins through vertical integration; book publishing is not one of them. Although newspaper and magazine companies still often own printing presses and binderies, book publishers rarely do. Similarly, the trade usually sells the finished products through a distributor who stores and distributes the publisher's wares for a percentage fee or sells on a sale or return basis.

The advent of the Internet has therefore posed an interesting question that challenges publishers, distributors and retailers. In 2005, Amazon.com announced its purchase of Booksurge and self sane publishing, a major print on demand operation. This is probably intended as a preliminary move towards establishing an Amazon imprint. One of the largest bookseller chains, Barnes & Noble, already runs its own successful imprint with both new titles and classics-hardback editions of out-of-print former best sellers. Similarly, Ingram Industries, parent company of Ingram Book Group (a leading US book wholesaler), now includes its own print-on-demand division called Lightning Source. Among publishers, Simon & Schuster recently announced that it will start selling its backlist titles directly to consumers through its website.

Book clubs are almost entirely direct-to-retail, and niche publishers pursue a mixed strategy to sell through all available outlets-their output is insignificant to the major booksellers, so lost revenue poses no threat to the traditional symbiotic relationships between the four activities of printing, publishing, distribution and retail.

Academic Publishing

The development of the printing press represented a revolution for communicating the latest hypotheses and research results to the academic community and supplemented what a scholar could do personally. But this improvement in the efficiency of communication created a challenge for libraries which have had to accommodate the weight and volume of literature.

To understand the scale of the problem it can be pointed that approximately two centuries ago the number of scientific papers published annually was doubling every fifteen years. Today, the number of published papers doubles about every ten years. Modern academics can now run electronic journals and distribute academic materials without the need for publishers. Not surprisingly, publishers perceive this emancipation as a serious threat to their business. In reality, the interests of scholars and publishers have long been in conflict.

Today, publishing academic journals and textbooks is a large part of an international industry. The shares of the major publishing companies are listed on national stock exchanges and management policies must satisfy the dividend expectations of international shareholders. Critics claim that these standardized accounting and profit-oriented policies have come to the fore and now constrain more altruistic leanings. In contrast to the commercial model, there is non-profit publishing, where the publishing organization is either organised specifically for the purpose of publishing, such as a university press, or is one of the functions of an organisation such as a medical charity, founded to achieve specific practical goals. An alternative approach to the corporate model is open access, the online distribution of individual articles and academic journals without charge to readers and libraries.

Tie-in Publishing

Technically, radio, television, cinemas, VCDs and DVDs, music systems, games, computer hardware and mobile telephony publish information to their audiences. Indeed, the marketing of a major film often includes a novelization, a graphic novel or comic version, the soundtrack album, a game, model, toys and endless promotional publications.

Some of the major publishers have entire divisions devoted to a single franchise, e.g. Ballantine Del Rey Lucasbooks has the exclusive rights to Star Wars in the United States; Random House UK (Bertelsmann)/Century LucasBooks holds the same rights in the United Kingdom.

The game industry self-publishes through BL Publishing/ Black Library (Warhammer) and Wizards of the Coast (Dragonlance, Forgotten Realms, etc). The BBC has its own publishing division which does very well with long-running series such as Doctor Who. These multimedia works are cross-marketed aggressively and sales frequently outperform the average stand-alone published work, making them a focus of corporate interest.

Independent Publishing Alternatives

Writers in a specialized field or with a narrower appeal have found smaller alternatives to the mass market in the form of small presses and self-publishing. More recently, these options include print on demand and ebook format. These publishing alternatives provide an avenue for authors who believe that mainstream publishing will not meet their needs or who are in a position to make more money from direct sales than they could from bookstore sales, such as popular speakers who sell books after speeches.

DESKTOP PUBLISHING

Desktop publishing (also known as DTP) combines a personal computer and page layout software to create publication documents on a computer for either large scale publishing or small scale local economical multifunction peripheral output and distribution. Users create page layouts with text, graphics, photos and other visual elements using software such as QuarkXPress, Adobe InDesign, the free Scribus, Microsoft Publisher, Apple Pages and (to some extent) any graphics software or word processor that combines editable text with images. For small jobs a few copies of a publication might be printed on a local printer. For larger jobs a computer file can be sent to a vendor for high-volume printing.

The term "desktop publishing" is commonly used to describe page layout skills. However, the skills and software are not limited to paper and books. The same skills and software are often used to create graphics for point of sale displays, promotional items, trade show exhibits, retail package designs, and outdoor signs.

Desktop publishing began in 1985 with the introduction of PageMaker software from Aldus and the LaserWriter printer from Apple Computer for the Apple Macintosh computer. The ability to create WYSIWYG page layouts on screen and then print pages at crisp 300 dpi resolution was revolutionary for both the typesetting industry as well as the personal computer industry. The term "desktop publishing" is attributed to Aldus Corporation founder Paul Brainerd, who sought a marketing catch-phrase to describe the small size and relative affordability of this suite of products in contrast to the expensive commercial phototypesetting equipment of the day.

Often considered a primary skill, increased accessibility to more user-friendly DTP software has made DTP a secondary skill to art direction, graphic design, multimedia development, marketing communications, administrative careers and advanced high school literacy in thriving economies. DTP skill levels range from what may be learned in a few hours (e.g. learning how to put clip art in a word processor) to what requires a college education and years of experience (e.g. advertising agency positions.) The discipline of DTP skills range from technical skills such as prepress production and programming to creative skills such as communication design and graphic image development.

By the standards of today, early desktop publishing was a primitive affair. Users of the PageMaker-LaserWriter-Macintosh 512K system endured frequent software crashes, the Mac's tiny 512 x 342 1-bit black and white screen, the inability to control letter spacing, kerning (the addition or removal of space between individual characters in a piece of typeset text to improve its appearance or alter its fit) and other typographic features, and discrepancies between the screen display and printed output. However, for that moment in time, it was received with considerable acclaim.

Behind-the-scenes technologies developed by Adobe Systems set the foundation for professional desktop publishing applications. The LaserWriter and LaserWriter Plus printers included high quality, scalable Adobe fonts built into their ROM memory. The LaserWriter's additional PostScript capability allowed publication designers to proof files on a local printer then print the same file at DTP service bureaus using optical resolution 600+ ppi PostScript-printers such as those from Linotronic. Later, the Macintosh II was released which was much more suitable for desktop publishing because of its larger, colour screen.

In 1986, the GEM-based Ventura Publisher was introduced for MS-DOS computers. While PageMaker's pasteboard metaphor closely simulated the process of creating layouts manually, Ventura Publisher automated the layout process through its use of tags/style sheets and automatically generated indices and other body matter. This made it suitable for manuals and other long-format documents. Desktop publishing moved into the home market in 1986 with Professional Page for the Amiga, Publishing Partner for the Atari ST, GST's Timeworks Publisher on the PC and Atari ST, Calamus for the Atari TT030, and even Home Publisher, Newsroom, and GEO Publish for 8-bit computers like the Apple II and Commodore 64.

During these early years, desktop publishing acquired a bad reputation from untrained users who created poorly-organized ransom note effect layouts-criticisms that would be levied again against early web publishers a decade later. However, some were able to realize truly professional results. For example,.info (magazine) became the very first desktop-published, full-colour, newsstand magazine in the last quarter of 1986, using a combination of Commodore Amiga computers, Professional Page desktop publishing software, and an Agfagraphics typesetter.

Comparisons with Word Processing

While desktop publishing software still provides extensive features necessary for print publishing, modern word processors now have publishing capabilities beyond those of many older DTP applications, blurring the line between word processing and desktop publishing. In the early days of graphical user interfaces, DTP software was in a class of its own when compared to the fairly spartan word processing applications of the time. Programs such as WordPerfect and WordStar were still mainly text-based and offered little in the way of page layout, other than perhaps margins and line spacing. On the other hand, word processing software was necessary for features like indexing and spell checking, features that are today taken for granted.

As computers and operating systems have become more powerful, vendors have sought to provide users with a single application platform that can meet all needs. Software such as Open Office.org Writer and Microsoft Word offers advanced layouts and linking between documents, and DTP applications have added in common word processor features.

Comparisons with other Electronic Layout

In modern usage, DTP is not generally said to include tools such as TeX or troff, though both can easily be used on a modern desktop system and are standard with many Unix-like operating systems and readily available for other systems. The key difference between electronic typesetting software and DTP software is that DTP software is generally interactive and WYSIWYG in design, while older electronic typesetting software tends to operate in batch mode, requiring the user to enter the processing program's markup language manually without a direct visualization of the finished product. The older style of typesetting software occupies a substantial but shrinking niche in technical writing and textbook publication; however, since much software in this genre is freely available, it can be more cost-effective than the professionally-oriented DTP systems.

There is some overlap between desktop publishing and what is known as Hypermedia publishing (i.e. Web design, Kiosk, CD-ROM). Many graphical HTML editors such as Microsoft FrontPage and Dreamweaver use a layout engine similar to a DTP program. However, some Web designers still prefer to write HTML without the assistance of a WYSIWIG editor and resort to such software, if at all, solely for complex layout that cannot easily be rendered in hand-written HTML code.

ELECTRONIC PUBLISHING

Electronic publishing includes the digital publication of ebooks and electronic articles, and the development of digital libraries and catalogues. Electronic publishing has become common in scientific publishing where it has been argued that peer-reviewed paper scientific journals are in the process of being replaced by electronic publishing. Although network distribution is nowadays strongly associated with electronic publishing, there are many non network electronic publications such as Encyclopedias on CD and DVD, as well as technical and reference publications relied on by mobile users and others without reliable and high speed access to a network.

There is usually a delay of several months after an article is written before it is published in a paper journal and this makes journals not an ideal format for disseminating the latest research. In some fields such as astronomy and some parts of physics, the role of the journal at disseminating the latest research has largely been replaced by preprint databases such as arXiv.org. However, scientific journals still provide an important role in quality control, archiving papers, and establishing scientific credit. In general, the electronic material uploaded to preprint database are still intended for eventual publication in a peer-reviewed journal.

There is an article titled "Online or Invisible?" (see link at end of article) which provides statistical evidence that electronic publishing provides wider dissemination. A number of journals have, while retaining their peer review process, established electronic versions or even moved entirely to electronic publication.

Electronic publishing is increasingly popular in works of fiction as well as with scientific articles. Electronic publishers are able to provide quick gratification for late-night readers, books that customers might not be able to find in standard book retailers (erotica is especially popular in eBook format), and books by new authors that would be unlikely to be profitable for traditional publishers.

Hyponyms are:

- Online publishing
- ePublishing
- Web Publishing

While the term "Electronic Publishing" is primarily used today to refer to the current offerings of online and web-based publishers, the term has a history of being used to describe the development of new forms of production, distribution, and user interaction in regards to computer-based production of text and other interactive media. A good example of this use of the term can be found in the work of Walter Bender and his Electronic Publishing Research Group at the MIT Media Lab.

EDITING

Editing is the process of preparing language, images, or sound for presentation through correction, condensation, organization, and other modifications. A person who edits is called an editor. A peer editor is usually referred to students editing each others work and giving tips for improvement.

Etymology

According to the Oxford English Dictionary, editor comes from the Latin phrase 'e ditus' which means "to put forward". The editor ludorum in Ancient Rome was the person who put on the games. The verb to edit is a back formation from editor.

PRINT MEDIA

There are various levels of editorial positions in publishing. Typically one finds junior editorial assistants reporting to the senior level editorial managers and directors, who themselves report to senior executive editors responsible for project development to final releases. Human editors in the print publishing industry include people who are responsible for:

- Newspapers and wire services; see below.
- Organizing anthologies and other compilations.
- Organizing and publishing a magazine. The top editor may be called editor-in-chief. Those who get the magazine into the hands of readers and subscribers, even, have editorial titles and are called circulation editors. Frequent and esteemed contributors to a magazine may acquire the title editor at-large.
- Producing a definitive edition of a classic author's works-a scholarly editor.
- Organizing and managing contributions to a multi-author book-symposium editor or volume editor.
- Finding marketable ideas and presenting them to appropriate authors-a sponsoring editor.
- Obtaining copy or recruiting authors-such as the acquisitions editor or commissioning editor for a publishing house.
- Improving an author's writing so that they indeed say what they want to say, in an effective manner-a substantive editor. Depending on the writer's skill, this editing can sometimes turn into ghost writing. Substantive editing is seldom a title. Many types of

editors do this type of work, either in-house at a publisher or on an independent basis.

- Correcting spelling, grammar, and matters of house style-a copyeditor. But copy editors at newspapers usually also have greater and higher responsibilities, which may include the design of pages and the selection of news stories for inclusion. At UK newspapers, the term is "sub-editor."
- Choosing the layout of the publication and communicating with the printer-a production editor. This and similar jobs are also called "layout editor," "design editor," "news designer," or-more so in the past-"makeup editor."

The smaller the publication, the more these roles run together. In particular, the substantive editor and copy editor often overlap: Fact-checking and rewriting can be the responsibility of either.

Executive Editor

The top editor sometimes has the title executive editor or editor-in-chief (the former is replacing the latter in the language). This person is generally responsible for the content of the publication. The exception is that newspapers that are large enough usually have a separate editor for the editorials and opinion pages in order to have a complete separation of its news reporting and its editorial content.

The executive editor sets the publication standards for performance, as well as for motivating and developing the staff. The executive editor is also responsible for developing and maintaining the publication budget. In concert with the publisher and the operating committee, the executive editor is responsible for strategic and operational planning.

Newspapers

Editors at newspapers supervise journalists and improve their work. Newspaper editing encompasses a variety of titles and functions. These include:

- Copyeditors
- Department editors
- Managing editors and assistant or deputy managing editors (the managing editor is often second in line after the top editor)
- News editors, who oversee the news desks
- Photo or picture editors
- Section editors and their assistants, such as for business, features, and sports
- Editorial Page Editor who oversees the coverage on the editorial page. This includes chairing the Editorial Board and assigning editorial writing responsibilities. The editorial page editor may also oversee the op-ed page or those duties are assigned to a separate op-ed editor.
- Top editors, who may be called editor in chief or executive editor
- Readers' editors, sometimes known as the ombudsman, who arbitrate complaints
- Wire editors, who choose and edit articles from various international wire services, and are usually part of the copy desk
- Administrative editors (who actually don't edit but perform duties such as recruiting and directing training)

The term city editor is used differently in North America, where it refers to the editor responsible for the news coverage of a newspaper's local circulation area (also sometimes called metro editor), and in the United Kingdom, where (normally with a capital C) it refers to the editor responsible for coverage of business in the City of London and, by extension, coverage of business and finance in general.

Scholarly Books and Journals

Editors of scholarly books and journals are of three types, each with particular responsibilities: the acquisitions editor (or commissioning editor in Britain), who contracts with the author to produce the copy, the project editor or production editor, who sees the copy through its stages from manuscript through bound book and usually assumes most of the budget and schedule responsibilities, and the copyeditor or manuscript editor, who performs the tasks of readying the copy for conversion into printed form. The primary difference between copy editing scholarly books and journals and other sorts of copy editing lies in applying the standards of the publisher to the copy. Most scholarly publishers have a preferred style guide, usually a combination of Merriam-Webster's Collegiate Dictionary and either the The Chicago Manual of Style, the MLA Style Manual, or the APA Publication Manual. Since scholars often have strong preferences, very often a publisher will adopt different styles for different fields. For instance, psychologists prefer the APA style, while linguists might prefer the MLA style. These guidelines offer sound advice on making cited sources complete and correct and making the presentation scholarly.

Technical Editing

Technical editing involves reviewing text written on a technical topic, and identifying errors related to the use of language in general or adherence to a specific style guide.

This activity ensures that documentation is of good quality. In large companies, experienced writers are dedicated to the technical editing function; in organizations that cannot afford dedicated editors, experienced writers typically peer-edit text produced by their relatively less experienced colleagues.

It helps if the technical editor is familiar with the subject being edited, but that is not always essential. The "technical" knowledge that an editor gains over time while working on a particular product or technology does give the editor an edge over another who has just started editing content related to that product or technology. In the long run, however, the skills that really matter are attention to detail, the ability to sustain focus while working through lengthy pieces of text on complex topics, tact in dealing with writers, and excellent communication skills.

COPY EDITING

Copy editing (also copyediting), is the editorial work that an editor does to make formatting changes and improvements to a manuscript; copy (as a noun) refers to written or typewritten text for typesetting, printing, and publication. The editor effecting this is a copy editor; an organization's highest-ranking copy editor, or the supervising editor of a group of copy editors, is the copy chief.

There is no universal form for the job and job title; in magazine and book publishing, it often is one word (copyediting). The newspaper business spells it either as two words (copy editing) or hyphenates it (copy-editing); the hyphenated form is British. Similarly, the term copy editor may be spelled either as a one word-, or a two word-, or as a hyphenated compound term.

Generally, in British newspaper and magazine publishing (but not book publishing), the job is called sub-editing or revise editing (The Times).

Overview

The copy editor's job is summarized in the Five Cs: to make the copy clear, correct, concise, comprehensible, and consistent. Typically, copy editing involves correcting spelling, terminology, punctuation, grammatical, and semantic errors; ensuring that the typescript adheres to the publisher's house style; and adding standardized headers, footers, headlines, etc. These stylistic elements must be addressed and determined before the typesetter can prepare a final proof copy.

The copy editor is expected to ensure that the text flows, that it is sensible, fair, and accurate, and that it will provoke no legal problems for the publisher. Newspaper copy editors are sometimes responsible for choosing which news service wire copy the newspaper will use, and for rewriting it per house style. Often, the copy editor is the only person, other than the author, to read an entire text before its publication. Newspaper editors often regard copy editors as the newspaper's last line of accurate defense.

A copy editor may abridge text, by "cutting" and "trimming" it, to reduce the length of a novel or an article, either to fit broadcast or publishing limits or to improve its meaning. This may involve omitting parts of the text, but sometimes it is necessary to rewrite uncut parts to bridge the missing details and plot; some abridgements are only slightly shorter than the originals, but others may be much abridged, particularly when a literary classic is abridged for the children's market.

Changes in the Profession

Traditionally, the copy editor would read a printed or written manuscript, manually marking it with editor's correction marks. Currently, the manuscript is usually read on a computer display and corrections entered directly; increasingly, the copy editor marks up the text using XML or another code and also prepares the text for online publication and printing.

The diffusion of desktop publishing means that many copy editors do design and layout work that once was province of design production crews in print publications. As a result, the skills needed for editing copy have shifted; technical knowledge sometimes is considered as important as writing ability, particularly in journalism, rather than in book publishing.

Traits, Skills and Training

Besides excellent command of the language, copy editors need broad general knowledge of the world in spotting factual errors, good critical-thinking skill (to recognize inconsistencies), diplomacy for dealing with writers, and a thick skin for when editorial diplomacy fails. Also, they must establish priorities balancing striving for perfection within deadlines. Many copy editors have a college degree, often in journalism, English, or communications. Copy editing often is taught as a college journalism course, though its name varies; news design and pagination also are taught.

In the United States, The Dow Jones Newspaper Fund sponsors internships that include two weeks of training. Also, the American Press Institute, the Poynter Institute, the University of North Carolina at Chapel Hill, and conferences of the American Copy Editors Society offer mid-career training for newspaper copy editors and news editors (news copy desk supervisors).

Most U.S. newspapers and publishers give copy-editing job candidates an editing test or a try-out. These vary widely and often include general items such as acronyms, current events, simple mathematics, and punctuation, and skills such as Associated Press style, headline writing, infographics editing, and journalism ethics.

In the U.K., training is through university publishing courses such as the one at Oxford Brookes University, alongside privately-run seminars, and correspondence courses of the Society for Editors and Proofreaders, and commercial centers.

PROOFREADING

Proofreading traditionally means reading a proof copy of a text in order to detect and correct any errors. Modern proofreading often requires reading copy at earlier stages as well.

Proofreading in Printing and Publishing

A proof copy is a version of a manuscript that has been typeset after copyediting. Proof typescripts often contain typographical errors introduced by mistyping (hence the word typo to refer to misplaced or incorrect characters). Traditionally, a proofreader checks the typeset copy and marks any errors using standard proof correction marks (such as those specified in style manuals, by house style, or, more broadly, by the international standard ISO 5776, or, for English, the British Standard BS-5261:2). The proof is then returned to the typesetter for correction, and in many cases the production of a second proof copy (often known as a revise). The term proofreading is sometimes used incorrectly to refer to copy-editing. This is a separate activity, although there is some overlap between the two. Proofreading consists of reviewing any text, either hard copy (on paper) or electronic copy (on a computer) and checking for typos and formatting errors. This may be done either against an original document or "blind" (without checking against any other source). Many modern proofreaders are also required to take on some light copy-editing duties, such as checking for grammar and consistency issues.

Proofreading in Biology

The term proofreading is used to refer to the error-correcting processes involved in DNA replication. In bacteria, all three DNA polymerases (I, II, and III) have the ability to proofread, using 3'->5' exonuclease activity. In eukaryotes only the polymerases that deal with the elongation (?, d and e) have proofreading ability (3'->5' exonuclease activity).

Controlled Natural Language

Controlled Natural Languages are subsets of natural languages whose grammars and dictionaries have been restricted in order to reduce or eliminate both ambiguity and complexity. Both grammars and dictionaries typically follow either the positive list principle (use only the constructions/words in the list) or the negative list principle (do not use the constructions/words in the list). The purpose behind the development and implementation of a controlled natural language typically is to aid non-native speakers of a natural language in understanding it, or to ease computer processing of a natural language.

Steps in Editing (Proofreading) Your Papers

Identify Typical Errors

Review graded or scored comments on your old papers, and list errors which were marked frequently. Be as specific as possible in gathering your list (for example, problems with introductory commas).

Make a Hierarchy

Determine which of the errors on your list occurred most often and/or cost you the most in points or letter grades. Rank order the items on your list so that the most serious errors are on the top.

Learn Concepts

Make sure that you understand why you made the errors on your list. Do a couple of practice exercises, and talk to a Writing Lab tutor. Using your hierarchy, write rules and sample sentences in your notebook or in the back of your dictionary.

Develop Strategies

Ask a Writing Lab tutor for specific, "quick" strategies you can use to locate these errors in your papers. Refer, if needed, to the OWL handōuts listed above. Write each strategy, step by step, next to its corresponding rule in your notebook or dictionary. Include any relevant key words or phrases.

Write

Write your paper as you normally would, concentrating mainly on your ideas, not on rules or strategies.

Apply your Strategies

When you finish writing, take a break, and then apply the strategies one at a time, using the rules and sample sentences as reminders if you get stuck. Remember that you are looking for specific errors, not reading the paper. Go completely through the paper looking for only one kind of error at a time. You will be able to focus your concentration and energy better that way.

Please Note: Editing is not a substitute for, but a supplement to, reading for meaning. For best results, use both methods.

Proofreading Strategies

No matter how many times you read through a "finished" paper, you're likely to miss many of your most frequent errors. This handout will help you proofread more effectively...

- by giving you some useful general strategies for proofreading well
- by giving you strategies which personalize proofreading so you can identify errors you typically make (You don't need to check for everything. It's more efficient to know

your typical problem areas and make several passes through the paper for them.)

- by giving you specific strategies for finding and correcting those errors.

General Strategies

Begin by taking a break. Allow yourself some time between writing and proofing. Even a five-minute break is productive because it will help get some distance from what you have written. The goal is to return with a fresh eye and mind. The following strategies will help you s l o w d o w n as you read through a paper and will therefore help you catch mistakes that you might otherwise overlook. As you use these strategies, remember to work slowly. If you read at a normal speed, you won't give your eyes sufficient time to spot errors.

Read Aloud

Reading a paper aloud encourages you to read every little word.

Read with a "Cover"

Sliding a blank sheet of paper down the page as you read encourages you to make a detailed, line-by-line review of the paper.

Role-play

Playing the role of the reader encourages you to see the paper as your audience might.

Strategies which Personalize Proofreading

In addition to using the general strategies already listed, you'll need to personalize the proofreading process.

You won't be able to check for everything (and you don't have to), so you should find out what your typical problem areas are and look for each type of error individually. Here's how: Find out what errors you typically make. Review instructors' comments about your writing and/or review your paper(s) with a Writing Lab tutor.

Learn how to fix those errors. Talk with your instructor and/or with a Writing Lab tutor. The instructor and the tutor can help you understand why you make the errors you do so that you can learn to avoid them.

Use specific strategies. Use the strategies detailed on the following pages to find and correct your particular errors in organization and paragraphing, usage and sentence structure, and spelling and punctuation.

To locate and correct errors in your papers, find the strategies on the following pages which correspond to your typical problem areas and follow the step-by-step instructions provided for you. Each strategy is designed to focus your attention on only one particular error, so to be most effective, use only one strategy at a time. (Ask a Writing Lab tutor about any terms you don't understand and/or refer to Lab handouts.)

Organization and Paragraphing

Thesis/Focus/Main Point

1. Find your paper's thesis statement. Copy it on another sheet of paper. If your thesis is not directly stated, write down a possible thesis.
2. Locate the central idea of each paragraph and try to reduce that idea to a word or phrase. If you cannot decide on one phrase, list two or three options.
3. List the paragraph ideas. List these in order under your thesis.
4. Decide whether your paragraphs clearly relate to your thesis. If not, either rewrite your thesis to incorporate the unrelated ideas or eliminate the unrelated paragraphs.

Paragraph Clarity

1. Locate the central idea of each paragraph. Reduce that idea to a word or phrase.
2. Look at each paragraph randomly. Consider only the information in that paragraph.

3. Ask yourself whether you offer enough details in the paragraph to support that word or idea.
4. Decide whether all of your details are relevant.
5. Ask yourself whether all of the information is related enough to be in the same paragraph. Should you create another paragraph or move some of the details to another paragraph?

Overall Coherence

1. See whether you have clear transitions between paragraphs. If not, clarify existing transitions, add new ones, and/or rearrange your paragraphs to make transitions clearer.

Usage and Sentence Structure

Subject/Verb Agreement

1. Find the main verb in each sentence.
2. Match the verb to its subject.
3. Make sure that the subject and verb agree in number.

Pronoun Reference/Agreement

1. Skim your paper, stopping at each pronoun. Look especially at it, this, they, their, and them.
2. Search for the noun that the pronoun replaces. If you can't find any noun, insert one beforehand or change the pronoun to a noun. If you can find a noun, be sure it agrees in number and person with your pronoun.

Parallel Structure

1. Skim your paper, stopping at key words that signal parallel structures.

   Look especially for and, or, not only...but also, either... or, neither...nor, both...and.
2. Make sure that the items connected by these words (adjectives, nouns, phrases, etc.) are in the same grammatical form.

SPELLING AND PUNCTUATION

Spelling

1. Examine each word in the paper individually.

   Move from the end of each line back to the beginning. Pointing with a pencil helps you really see each word.

2. If necessary, check a dictionary to see that each word is spelled correctly.

Compound Sentence Commas

1. Skim for the conjunctions and, but, for, or, nor, so and yet.
2. See whether there is a complete sentence on each side of the conjunction.

If so, place a comma before the conjunction.

Introductory Commas

1. Skim your paper, looking only at the first two or three words of each sentence.
2. Stop if one of these words is a dependent marker, a transition word, a participle, or a preposition.
3. Listen for a possible break point before the main clause.
4. Place a comma at the end of the introductory phrase or clause (which is before the independent clause).

Comma Splices

1. Skim the paper, stopping at every comma.
2. See whether there is a complete sentence on each side of the comma. If so, add a coordinating conjunction after the comma or replace the comma with a semicolon.

Fragments

1. Look at each sentence to see whether it contains an independent clause.
2. Pay special attention to sentences that begin with dependent marker words (such as because) or phrases such as for example or such as.

3. See if the sentence might be just a piece of the previous sentence that mistakenly got separated by a period.

Run-On Sentences

1. Review each sentence to see whether it contains more than one independent clause. Start with the last sentence of your paper, and work your way back to the beginning, sentence by sentence.
2. Break the sentence into two sentences if necessary.

Apostrophes

1. Skim your paper, stopping only at those words which end in "s."
2. See whether or not each "s" word needs an apostrophe. If an apostrophe is needed, you will be able to invert the word order and say "of" or "of the":
   - Mary's hat
   - the hat of Mary

Left-Out Words

1. Read the paper aloud, pointing to every word as you read. Don't let your eye move ahead until you spot each word.
2. Also, make sure that you haven't doubled any words.

Proofreading Your Work

It is always difficult to find errors in one's own work. The words and sentences appear correct on rereading because if the writer had known better, he or she would not have made the errors in the first place. But a careful rereading of a paper aloud before it is turned in helps considerably. Perhaps a checklist of common errors will serve as a guide for you. Keep this list and a grammar book with you as you read your paper over, checking every sentence for these items.

Run-on Sentences and Sentence Fragments

Check each sentence to make sure it has a subject, a verb, and a complete thought. Have you run two sentences together incorrectly without a period, conjunction or semicolon separating them?

Punctuation

Have you ended every sentence with a period, question mark, or exclamation point?

Are your thoughts within sentences broken up correctly by commas for easier understanding?

Have you broken up series with commas?

Have you used a period after abbreviations?

If you are in doubt about the proper punctuation of a sentence, have you asked or looked at our handouts on punctuation.

A or An?

Brought to you by the Purdue University Online Writing Lab

"A" goes before all words that begin with consonants.

- a cat
- a dog
- a purple onion
- a buffalo
- a big apple

with one exception: Use an before unsounded h.

- an honourable peace
- an honest error

"An" goes before all words that begin with vowels:

- an apricot
- an egg
- an Indian
- an orbit
- an uprising

With Two Exceptions: When U makes the same sound as the Y in you, or O makes the same sound as W in won, then a is used.

- a union
- a united front
- a unicorn
- a used napkin
- a U.S. ship
- a one-legged man

Note: The choice of article is actually based upon the phonetic (sound) quality of the first letter in a word, not on the orthographic (written) representation of the letter.

If the first letter makes a vowel-type sound, you use "an"; if the first letter would makes a consonant-type sound, you use "a." So, if you consider the rule from a phonetic perspective, there aren't any exceptions.

Since the 'h' hasn't any phonetic representation, no audible sound, in the first exception, the sound that follows the article is a vowel; consequently, 'an' is used. In the second exception, the word-initial 'y' sound (unicorn) is actually a glide [j] phonetically, which has consonantal properties; consequently, it is treated as a consonant, requiring 'a'.

AVOIDING COMMON ERRORS

Bad or Badly?

When you want to describe how you feel, you should use an adjective (Why? Feel is a sense verb;see rule #3 above). So you'd say, "I feel bad." Saying you feel badly would be like saying you play football badly. It would mean that you are unable to feel, as though your hands were partially numb.

Good or Well?

Good is an adjective, so you do not do good or live good, but you do well and live well.

Remember, though, that an adjective follows sense-verbs and be-verbs, so you also feel good, look good, smell good, are good, have been good, etc. (Refer to rule #3 above for more information about sense verbs and verbs of appearance.) Confusion can occur because well can function either as an adverb or an adjective.

When well is used as an adjective, it means "not sick" or "in good health." For this specific sense of well, it's OK to say you feel well or are well--for example, after recovering from an illness. When not used in this health-related sense, however, well functions as an adverb; for example, "I did well on my exam."

Double-negatives

Scarcely and hardly are already negative adverbs. To add another negative term is redundant, because in English only one negative is ever used at a time

They found scarcely any animals on the island. (not scarcely no...)

Hardly anyone came to the party. (not hardly no one...)

Adjectives with Countable and Uncountable Nouns

Some/Any:

Both modify countable and uncountable nouns.

There is some water on the floor.

There are some Mexicans here.

Do you have any food?

Do you have any apples?

Much/Many:

MUCH modifies only uncountable nouns.

They have much money in the bank.

MANY modifies only countable nouns.

Many Americans travel to Europe.

A lot of/lots of:

These are informal substitutes for MUCH and MANY. They are used with uncountable nouns when they mean MUCH and with countable nouns when they mean MANY.

They have lots of money in the bank.

A lot of Americans travel to Europe.

Little/Few:

LITTLE modifies only uncountable nouns.

He had little food in the house.

FEW modifies only countable nouns.

There are a few doctors in town.

A little bit of:

This phrase is informal and always precedes an uncountable noun.

There is a little bit of pepper in the soup.

Enough:

ENOUGH modifies both countable and uncountable nouns.

There is enough money to buy a car.

I have enough books to read.

Plenty of:

This phrase modifies both countable and uncountable nouns.

They have plenty of money in the bank.

There are plenty of millionaires in Switzerland.

No:

NO modifies both countable and uncountable nouns.

There is no time to finish now.

There are no squirrels in the park.

Independent and Dependent Clauses (Definitions)

When you want to use commas and semicolons in sentences and when you are concerned about whether a sentence is or is not a fragment, a good way to start is to be able to recognize dependent and independent clauses. The definitions offered here will help you with this.

This handout will:

- define independent and dependent clauses
- explain proper ways to punctuate sentences that use them
- note some common errors to avoid

Definitions

Independent Clause (IC): An independent clause is a group of words that contains a subject and verb and expresses a complete thought. An independent clause is a sentence.

Example: Jim studied in the Sweet Shop for his chemistry quiz.(IC)

Dependent Clause (DC): A dependent clause is a group of words that contains a subject and verb but does not express a complete thought. A dependent clause cannot be a sentence. Often a dependent clause is marked by a dependent marker word.

Example: When Jim studied in the Sweet Shop for his chemistry quiz... (DC) (What happened when he studied? The thought is incomplete.)

Dependent Marker Word (DM): A dependent marker word is a word added to the beginning of an independent clause that makes it into a dependent clause.

Example: When Jim studied in the Sweet Shop for his chemistry quiz, it was very noisy. (DM) Some common dependent markers are: after, although, as, as if, because, before, even if, even though, if, in order to, since, though, unless, until, whatever, when, whenever, whether, and while.

Connecting Dependent and Independent Clauses: There are two types of words that can be used as connectors at the beginning of an independent clause: coordinating conjunctions and independent marker words.

Coordinating Conjunction (CC): The seven coordinating conjunctions used as connecting words at the beginning of an independent clause are and, but, for, or, nor, so, and yet. When the second independent clause in a sentence begins with a coordinating conjunction, a comma is needed before the coordinating conjunction:

Example: Jim studied in the Sweet Shop for his chemistry quiz, but it was hard to concentrate because of the noise. (CC)

Independent Marker Word (IM): An independent marker word is a connecting word used at the beginning of an independent clause. These words can always begin a sentence that can stand alone. When the second independent clause in a sentence has an independent marker word, a semicolon is needed before the independent marker word.

Example: Jim studied in the Sweet Shop for his chemistry quiz; however, it was hard to concentrate because of the noise. (IM). Some common independent markers are: also, consequently, furthermore, however, moreover, nevertheless, and therefore.

Proper Punctuation Methods: This table gives some examples of ways to combine independent and dependent clauses and shows how to punctuate them properly.

C. IC.	I went to the store. I didn't buy any bread.
IC; IC.	I went to the store; I didn't buy any bread.
IC, CC IC.	I went to the store, but I didn't buy any bread.
IC; IM, IC.	I went to the store; however, I didn't buy any bread.
DC, IC.	When I went to the store, I didn't buy any bread.
IC DC.	I didn't buy any bread when I went to the store.

Some Common Errors to Avoid

Comma Splices: A comma splice is the use of a comma between two independent clauses. You can usually fix the error by changing the comma to a period and therefore making the two clauses into two separate sentences, by changing the comma to a semicolon, or by making one clause dependent by inserting a dependent marker word in front of it.

Incorrect: I like this class, it is very interesting.

Correct: I like this class. It is very interesting.

(or) I like this class; it is very interesting.

(or) I like this class, and it is very interesting.

(or) I like this class because it is very interesting.

(or) Because it is very interesting, I like this class.

Fused Sentences: Fused sentences happen when there are two independent clauses not separated by any form of punctuation.

This error is also known as a run-on sentence. The error can sometimes be corrected by adding a period, semicolon, or colon to separate the two sentences.

Incorrect: My professor is intelligent I've learned a lot from her.

Correct: My professor is intelligent. I've learned a lot from her.

(or) My professor is intelligent; I've learned a lot from her.

(or) My professor is intelligent, and I've learned a lot from her.

(or) My professor is intelligent; moreover, I've learned a lot from her.

Sentence Fragments: Sentence fragments happen by treating a dependent clause or other incomplete thought as a complete sentence. You can usually fix this error by combining it with another sentence to make a complete thought or by removing the dependent marker.

Incorrect: Because I forgot the exam was today.

Correct: Because I forgot the exam was today, I didn't study.

(or) I forgot the exam was today.

Parallel Structure

Parallel structure means using the same pattern of words to show that two or more ideas have the same level of importance. This can happen at the word, phrase, or clause level. The usual way to join parallel structures is with the use of coordinating conjunctions such as "and" or "or."

1. Words and Phrases

With the-ing form (gerund) of words:

Parallel: Mary likes hiking, swimming, and bicycling.

With Infinitive Phrases:

Parallel: Mary likes to hike, to swim, and to ride a bicycle.

OR

Mary likes to hike, swim, and ride a bicycle.

(Note: You can use "to" before all the verbs in a sentence or only before the first one.)

Do not mix forms.

Example 1

Not Parallel: Mary likes hiking, swimming, and to ride a bicycle.

Parallel: Mary likes hiking, swimming, and riding a bicycle.

Example 2

Not Parallel: The production manager was asked to write his report quickly, accurately, and in a detailed manner.

Parallel: The production manager was asked to write his report quickly, accurately, and thoroughly.

Example 3

Not Parallel: The teacher said that he was a poor student because he waited until the last minute to study for the exam, completed his lab problems in a careless manner, and his motivation was low.

Parallel: The teacher said that he was a poor student because he waited until the last minute to study for the exam, completed his lab problems in a careless manner, and lacked motivation.

2. Clauses

A parallel structure that begins with clauses must keep on with clauses. Changing to another pattern or changing the voice of the verb (from active to passive or vice versa) will break the parallelism.

Example 1

Not Parallel: The coach told the players that they should get a lot of sleep, that they should not eat too much, and to do some warm-up exercises before the game.

Parallel: The coach told the players that they should get a lot of sleep, that they should not eat too much, and that they should do some warm-up exercises before the game. --or--

Parallel: The coach told the players that they should get a lot of sleep, not eat too much, and do some warm-up exercises before the game.

Example 2

Not Parallel: The salesman expected that he would present his product at the meeting, that there would be time for him to show his slide presentation, and that questions would be asked by prospective buyers. (passive)

Parallel: The salesman expected that he would present his product at the meeting, that there would be time for him to show his slide presentation, and that prospective buyers would ask him questions.

3. Lists after a Colon

Be sure to keep all the elements in a list in the same form.

Example 1

Not Parallel: The dictionary can be used for these purposes: to find word meanings, pronunciations, correct spellings, and looking up irregular verbs.

Parallel: The dictionary can be used for these purposes: to find word meanings, pronunciations, correct spellings, and irregular verbs. Proofreading Strategies to try:

- Skim your paper, pausing at the words "and" and "or." Check on each side of these words to see whether the items joined are parallel. If not, make them parallel.
- If you have several items in a list, put them in a column to see if they are parallel.

- Listen to the sound of the items in a list or the items being compared. Do you hear the same kinds of sounds? For example, is there a series of "-ing" words beginning each item? Or do your hear a rhythm being repeated? If something is breaking that rhythm or repetition of sound, check to see if it needs to be made parallel.

Run-ons-Comma Splices-Fused Sentences

The above are all names given to compound sentences that are not punctuated correctly. The best way to avoid such errors is to punctuate compound sentences correctly by using one or the other of these rules.

1. Join the two independent clauses with one of the coordinating conjunctions (and, but, for, or, nor, so, yet), and use a comma before the connecting word.

______________________, and ________________________.

(He enjoys walking through the country, and he often goes backpacking on his vacations.)

2. When you do not have a connecting word (or when you use a connecting word other than and, but, for, or nor, so, or yet between the two independent clauses) use a semicolon (;).

___________________________; ___________________________.

(He often watched TV when there were only reruns; she preferred to read instead.) or

________________________; however,____________________.

(He often watched TV when there were only reruns; however, she preferred to read instead.)

So, run-ons and fused sentences are terms describing two independent clauses which are joined together with no connecting word or punctuation to separate the clauses.

Incorrect: They weren't dangerous criminals they were detectives in disguise.

Correct: They weren't dangerous criminals; they were detectives in disguise.

Incorrect: I didn't know which job I wanted I was too confused to decide.

Correct: I didn't know which job I wanted, so I was too confused to decide.

Sentence Fragments

Fragments are incomplete sentences. Usually, fragments are pieces of sentences that have become disconnected from the main clause.

One of the easiest ways to correct them is to remove the period between the fragment and the main clause. Other kinds of punctuation may be needed for the newly combined sentence. Below are snme examples with the fragments shown in red. Punctuation and/or words added to make corrections are highlighted in blue.

Notice that the fragment is frequently a dependent clause or long phrase that follows the main clause.

Fragment (phrase or dependent clause)	Possible Revision
Purdue offers many majors in engineering. Such as electrical, chemical, and industrial engineering.	Purdue offers many majors in engineering, such as electrical, chemical, and industrial engineering.
Coach Dietz exemplified this behavior by walking off the field in the middle of a game. Leaving her team at a time when we needed her.	Coach Dietz exemplified this behavior by walking off the field in the middle of a game, leaving her team at a time when we needed her.
I need to find a new roommate. Because the one I have now isn't working out too well.	I need to find a new roommate because the one I have now isn't working out too well.
The current city policy on housing is incomplete as it stands. Which is why we believe the proposed amendments should be passed.	Because the current city policy on housing is incomplete as it stands, we believe the proposed ammendments should be passed.

You may have noticed that newspaper and magazine journalists often use a dependent clause as a separate sentence when it follows clearly from the preceding main clause, as in the last example above. This is a conventional journalistic practice, often used for emphasis.

For academic writing and other more formal writing situations, however, you should avoid such journalistic fragment sentences. Some fragments are not clearly pieces of sentences that have been left unattached to the main clause; they are written as main clauses but lack a subject or main verb.

Fragment (incomplete main clause)	Possible Revisions
No main verb A story with deep thoughts and emotions.	*Appositive*: **Gilman's "The Yellow Wallpaper,"** a story with deep thoughts and emotions, **has impressed critics for decades.** *Direct object*: **She told** a story with deep thoughts and emotions.
Toys of all kinds thrown everywhere.	*Complete verb*: Toys of all kinds **were** thrown everywhere. *Direct object*: **They found** toys of all kinds thrown everywhere.
A record of accomplishment beginning when you were first hired.	*Direct object*: **I've noticed** a record of accomplishment beginning when you were first hired. *Main verb*: A record of accomplishment **began** when you were first hired.
No subject With the ultimate effect of all advertising is to sell the product.	*Remove preposition*: The ultimate effect of all advertising is to sell the product.
By paying too much attention to polls can make a political leader unwilling to propose innovative policies.	*Remove preposition*: Paying too much attention to polls can make a political leader unwilling to propose innovative policies.
For doing freelance work for a competitor got Phil fired.	*Remove preposition*: Doing freelance work for a competitor got Phil fired. *Rearrange*: **Phil got fired** for doing freelance work for a competitor.

These last three examples of fragments with no subjects are also known as mixed constructions, that is, sentences constructed out of mixed parts.

They start one way (often with a long prepositional phrase) but end with a regular predicate. Usually the object of the preposition (often a gerund, as in the last two examples) is intended as the subject of the sentence, so removing the preposition at the beginning is usually the easiest way to edit such errors.

While active voice helps to create clear and direct sentences, sometimes writers find that using an indirect expression is rhetorically effective in a given situation, so they choose passive voice. Also, as mentioned above, writers in the sciences conventionally use passive voice more often than writers in other discourses.

Passive voice makes sense when the agent performing the action is obvious, unimportant, or unknown or when a writer wishes to postpone mentioning the agent until the last part of the sentence or to avoid mentioning the agent at all. The passive voice is effective in such circumstances because it highlights the action and what is acted upon rather than the agent performing the action.

Changing Active to Passive

If you want to change an active-voice sentence to passive voice, consider carefully who or what is performing the action expressed in the verb, and then make that agent the object of a "by the..." phrase.

Make what is acted upon the subject of the sentence, and change the verb to a form of be + past participle. Including an explicit "by the..." phrase is optional.

Don't trust the grammar-checking programs in word-processing software. Many grammar checkers flag all passive constructions, but you may want to keep some that are flagged. Trust your judgement, or ask another human being for their opinion about which sentence sounds best.

Irregular Verbs

Present	Past	Past Participle
be	was, were	been
become	became	become
begin	began	begun
blow	blew	blown
break	broke	broken
bring	brought	brought
build	built	built
burst	burst	burst
buy	bought	bought
catch	caught	caught
choose	chose	chosen
come	came	come
cut	cut	cut
deal	dealt	dealt
do	did	done
drink	drank	drunk
drive	drove	driven
eat	ate	eaten
fall	fell	fallen
feed	fed	fed
feel	felt	felt
fight	fought	fought
find	found	found
fly	flew	flown
forbid	forbade	forbidden
forget	forgot	forgotten
forgive	forgave	forgiven
freeze	froze	frozen
get	got	gotten
give	gave	given
go	went	gone
grow	grew	grown
have	had	had
hear	heard	heard
hide	hid	hidden

hold	held	held
hurt	hurt	hurt
keep	kept	kept
know	knew	known
lay	laid	laid
lead	led	led
leave	left	left
let	let	let
lie	lay	lain
lose	lost	lost
make	made	made
meet	met	met
pay	paid	paid
quit	quit	quit
read	read	read
ride	rode	ridden
ring	rang	rung
rise	rose	risen
run	ran	run
say	said	said
see	saw	seen
seek	sought	sought
sell	sold	sold
send	sent	sent
shake	shook	shaken
shine	shone	shone
sing	sang	sung
sit	sat	sat
sleep	slept	slept
speak	spoke	spoken
spend	spent	spent
spring	sprang	sprung
stand	stood	stood
steal	stole	stolen
swim	swam	swum
swing	swung	swung
take	took	taken
teach	taught	taught

tear	tore	torn
tell	told	told
think	thought	thought
throw	threw	thrown
understand	understood	understood
wake	woke (waked)	woken (waked)
wear	wore	worn
win	won	won
write	wrote	written

LIE versus LAY

Present	Past	Past Participle
lie, lying (to tell a falsehood)	I lied to my mother.	I have lied under oath.
lie, lying (to recline)	I lay on the bed because I was tired.	He has lain in the grass.
lay, laying (to put, place)	I laid the baby in her cradle.	We have laid the dishes on the table.

After laying down his weapon, the soldier lay down to sleep. Will you lay out my clothes while I lie down to rest?

SIT versus SET

Present	Past	Past Participle
sit (to be seated or come to resting position)	I sat in my favorite chair.	You have sat there for three hours.
set (to put or place)	I set my glass on the table.	She has set her books on my desk again.

Let's set the table before we sit down to rest.

RISE versus RAISE

Present	Past	Past Participle
rise (steady or customary upward movement)	The balloon rose into the air.	He has risen to a position of power.
raise (to cause to rise)	They raised their hands because they knew the answer.	I have raised the curtain many times.

The boy raised the flag just before the sun rose.

Sequence of Tenses

Strictly speaking, in English, only two tenses are marked in the verb alone, present (as in "he sings") and past (as in "he sang"). Other English language tenses, as many as thirty of them, are marked by other words called auxiliaries. Understanding the six basic tenses allows one to recreate much of the reality of time in his writing. The six are

Simple Present: They walk

Present Perfect: They have walked

Simple Past: They walked

Past Perfect: They had walked

Future: They will walk

Future Perfect: They will have walked

Problems in sequencing tenses usually occur with the perfect tenses, all of which are formed by adding an auxiliary or auxiliaries to the past participle, the third principal part.

ring, rang, rung

walk, walked, walked

The most common auxiliaries are forms of "be," "can," "do," "may," "must," "ought," "shall," "will," "has," "have," "had," and they are the forms we shall use in this most basic discussion.

Present Perfect

The present perfect consists of a past participle (the third principal part) with "has" or "have." It designates action which began in the past but which continues into the present or the effect of which still continues.

1. Betty taught for ten years. (simple past)

2. Betty has taught for ten years. (present perfect)

The implication in (1) is that Betty has retired; in (2), that she is still teaching.

1. John did his homework. He can go to the movies.

2. If John has done his homework, he can go to the movies.

Infinitives, too, have perfect tense forms when combined with "have," and sometimes problems arise when infinitives are used with verbs such as "hope," "plan," "expect," and "intend," all of which usually point to the future (I wanted to go to the movie. Janet meant to see the doctor.)

The perfect tense sets up a sequence by marking the action which began and usually was completed before the action in the main verb.

1. I am happy to have participated in this campaign!
2. John had hoped to have won the trophy.

Thus the action of the main verb points back in time; the action of the perfect infinitive has been completed.

The past perfect tense designates action in the past just as simple past does, but the action of the past perfect is action completed in the past before another action.

1. John raised vegetables and later sold them. (past)
2. John sold vegetables that he had raised. (past perfect)

The vegetables were raised before they were sold.

1. Renee washed the car when George arrived (simple past)
2. Renee had washed the car when George arrived. (past perfect)

In (1), she waited until George arrived and then washed the car. In (2), she had already finished washing the car by the time he arrived.

In sentences expressing condition and result, the past perfect tense is used in the part that states the condition.

1. If I had done my exercises, I would have passed the test.
2. I think George would have been elected if he hadn't sounded so pompous.

Notice: There can be only one "would have" action group in a sentence.

Future Perfect Tense

The future perfect tense designates action that will have been completed at a specified time in the future.

1. Saturday I will finish my housework. (simple future)
2. By Saturday noon, I will have finished my housework. (future perfect)

Review

1. Judy saved thirty dollars. (past)
2. Judy will save thirty dollars. (future)
3. Judy has saved thirty dollars. (present perfect)
4. Judy had saved thirty dollars by the end of last month. (past perfect)
5. Judy will have saved thirty dollars by the end of this month. (future perfect)

Controlling Shifts in a Paragraph or Essay: General guideline: Establish a primary tense for the main discourse, and use occasional shifts to other tenses to indicate changes in time frame.

Hints:

- Rely on past tense to narrate events and to refer to an author or an author's ideas as historical entities (biographical information about a historical figure or narration of developments in an author's ideas over time).
- Use present tense to state facts, to refer to perpetual or habitual actions, and to discuss your own ideas or those expressed by an author in a particular work. Also use present tense to describe action in a literary work, movie, or other fictional narrative. Occasionally, for dramatic effect, you may wish to narrate an event in present tense as though it were happening now. If you do, use present tense consistently throughout the narrative, making shifts only where appropriate.
- Future action may be expressed in a variety of ways, including the use of will, shall, is going to, are about to, tomorrow and other adverbs of time, and a wide range of contextual cues.

Using Other Tenses in Conjunction with Simple Tenses: It is not always easy (or especially helpful) to try to distinguish perfect and/or progressive tenses from simple ones in isolation, for example, the difference between simple past progressive ("She was eating an apple") and present perfect progressive ("She has been eating an apple"). Distinguishing these sentences in isolation is possible, but the differences between them make clear sense only in the context of other sentences since the time-distinctions suggested by different tenses are relative to the time frame implied by the verb tenses in surrounding sentences or clauses.

Example 1: Simple past narration with perfect and progressive elements

On the day in question...

By the time Tom noticed the doorbell, it had already rung three times. As usual, he had been listening to loud music on his stereo. He turned the stereo down and stood up to answer the door. An old man was standing on the steps. The man began to speak slowly, asking for directions.

In this example, the progressive verbs had been listening and was standing suggest action underway at the time some other action took place. The stereo-listening was underway when the doorbell rang. The standing on the steps was underway when the door was opened. The past perfect progressive verb had been listening suggests action that began in the time frame prior to the main narrative time frame and that was still underway as another action began.

If the primary narration is in the present tense, then the present progressive or present perfect progressive is used to indicate action that is or has been underway as some other action begins. This narrative style might be used to describe a scene from a novel, movie, or play, since action in fictional narratives is conventionally treated as always present. For example, we refer to the scene in Hamlet in which the prince first speaks (present) to the ghost of his dead father or the final scene in Spike Lee's Do the Right Thing, which takes place (present) the day after Mookie has smashed (present perfect) the pizzeria window. If the example narrative above were a scene in a play, movie, or novel, it might appear as follows.

Example 2: Simple present narration with perfect and progressive elements

In this scene...

By the time Tom notices the doorbell, it has already rung three times. As usual, he has been listening to loud music on his stereo. He turns the stereo down and stands up to answer the door. An old man is standing on the steps. The man begins to speak slowly, asking for directions.

In this example as in the first one, the progressive verbs has been listening and is standing indicate action underway as some other action takes place. The present perfect progressive verb has been listening suggests action that began in the time frame prior to the main narrative time frame and that is still underway as another action begins. The remaining tense relationships parallel those in the first example.

In all of these cases, the progressive or-ing part of the verb merely indicates ongoing action, that is, action underway as another action occurs. The general comments about tense relationships apply to simple and perfect tenses, regardless of whether there is a progressive element involved.

It is possible to imagine a narrative based on a future time frame as well, for example, the predictions of a psychic or futurist. If the example narrative above were spoken by a psychic, it might appear as follows.

Example 3: Simple future narration with perfect and progressive elements

Sometime in the future...

By the time Tom notices the doorbell, it will have already rung three times. As usual, he will have been listening to loud music on his stereo. He will turn the stereo down and will stand up to answer the door. An old man will be standing on the steps. The man will begin to speak slowly, asking for directions.

In this example as in the first two, the progressive verbs will have been listening and will be standing indicate ongoing action. The future perfect progressive verb will have been listening suggests action that will begin in the time frame prior to the main narrative time frame and that will still be underway when another action begins. The verb notices here is in present-tense form, but the rest of the sentence and the full context of the narrative cue us to understand that it refers to future time. The remaining tense relationships parallel those in the first two examples.

General Guidelines for use of Perfect Tenses

In general the use of perfect tenses is determined by their relationship to the tense of the primary narration. If the primary narration is in simple past, then action initiated before the time frame of the primary narration is described in past perfect. If the primary narration is in simple present, then action initiated before the time frame of the primary narration is described in present perfect. If the primary narration is in simple future, then action initiated before the time frame of the primary narration is described in future perfect.

Past primary narration corresponds to Past Perfect (had + past participle) for earlier time frames

Present primary narration corresponds to Present Perfect (has or have + past participle) for earlier time frames

Future primary narration corresponds to Future Perfect (will have + past participle) for earlier time frames

The present perfect is also used to narrate action that began in real life in the past but is not completed, that is, may continue or may be repeated in the present or future. For example: "I have run in four marathons" (implication: "so far... I may run in others"). This usage is distinct from the simple past, which is used for action that was completed in the past without possible continuation or repetition in the present or future. For example: "Before injuring my leg, I ran in four marathons" (implication: "My injury prevents me from running in any more marathons").

Time-orienting words and phrases like before, after, by the time, and others--when used to relate two or more actions in time--can be good indicators of the need for a perfect-tense verb in a sentence.

By the time the Senator finished (past) his speech, the audience had lost (past perfect) interest.

By the time the Senator finishes (present: habitual action) his speech, the audience has lost (present perfect) interest.

By the time the Senator finishes (present: suggesting future time) his speech, the audience will have lost (future perfect) interest.

After everyone had finished (past perfect) the main course, we offered (past) our guests dessert.

After everyone has finished (present perfect) the main course, we offer (present: habitual action) our guests dessert.

After everyone has finished (present perfect) the main course, we will offer (future: specific one-time action) our guests dessert.

Long before the sun rose (past), the birds had arrived (past perfect) at the feeder.

Long before the sun rises (present: habitual action), the birds have arrived (present perfect) at the feeder.

Long before the sun rises (present: suggesting future time), the birds will have arrived (future perfect) at the feeder.

Sample Paragraphs: The main tense in this first sample is past. Tense shifts are inappropriate and are indicated in bold.

The gravel crunched and spattered beneath the wheels of the bus as it swung into the station. Outside the window, shadowy figures peered at the bus through the darkness. Somewhere in the crowd, two, maybe three, people were waiting for me: a woman, her son, and possibly her husband. I could not prevent my imagination from churning out a picture of them, the town, and the place I will soon call home. Hesitating a moment, I rise from my seat, these images flashing through my mind. (adapted from a narrative) Inappropriate shifts from past to present, such as those that appear in the above paragraph, are sometimes hard to resist. The writer becomes drawn into the narrative and begins to relive the event as an ongoing experience.

The inconsistency should be avoided, however. In the sample, will should be would, and rise should be rose. The main tense in this second sample is present. Tense shifts--all appropriate--are indicated in bold. A dragonfly rests on a branch overhanging a small stream this July morning. It is newly emerged from brown nymphal skin. As a nymph, it crept over the rocks of the stream bottom, feeding first on protozoa and mites, then, as it grew larger, on the young of other aquatic insects. Now an adult, it will feed on flying insects and eventually will mate. The mature dragonfly is completely transformed from the drab creature that once blended with underwater sticks and leaves. Its head, thorax, and abdomen glitter; its wings are iridescent in the sunlight. (adapted from an article in the magazine Wilderness)

This writer uses the present tense to describe the appearance of a dragonfly on a particular July morning. However, both past and future tenses are called for when she refers to its previous actions and to its predictable activity in the future.

TWO-PART (PHRASAL) VERBS (IDIOMS)

Many verbs in English are followed by an adverb or a preposition (also called a particle), and these two-part verbs, also called phrasal verbs, are different from verbs with helpers. The particle that follows the verb changes the meaning of the phrasal verb in idiomatic ways:

VERB	MEANING	EXAMPLE
drop off	decline gradually	The hill dropped off near the river.
drop off(2)	fall asleep	While doing his homework, he dropped off.
drop off(3)	stop and give something to someone	Would you drop this off at the post office?
drop out	cease to participate	After two laps, the runner dropped out.

Some particles can be separated from the verb so that a noun and pronoun can be inserted, and some particles can't be separated from the verb. In addition, some phrases are intransitive, meaning they cannot take a direct object.

Separable	add up (meaning: to add)	Correct: She **added up** the total on her calculator.
		Correct: She **added** it **up** on her calculator.
Inseparable	get around (meaning: to evade)	Correct: She always **gets around** the rules.
		Incorrect: She always **gets** the rules **around** (This construction makes no sense in English.)
Intransitive	catch on (meaning: to understand)	Correct: After I explained the math problem, she began to **catch on**.
		Incorrect: She began to **catch on** the math problem. (*catch on* cannot take a direct object in this meaning.)
		Correct: She began to **catch on** to the math problem. (the word *to* makes *the math problem* an indirect object, which is acceptable in this meaning.)

Unfortunately, there is usually no indicator whether an idiomatic phrase is separable, inseparable, or intransitive. In most cases the phrases must simply be memorized. Below is a partial list of each kind of phrase.

Separable

add up-add

back up-cause to move backwards; support; blow up; cause to explode; destroy by explosives

break down-analyze; list the parts of separately

break into-go into a house or room forcibly; suddenly; begin; bring about-cause to happen

bring off-accomplish

bring on-cause

bring out-publish; emphasize

bring over-bring

bring to-revive

bring up-raise; care for from childhood

brush out-brush the inside of

burn down-destroy by burning

burn up-consume by fire

buy out-by the other person's share of a business

buy up-buy the whole supply of

call off-cancel; order away

call up-telephone; summon for military service

calm down-become calm

carry on-continue

carry out-fulfill; complete; accomplish; perform

carry over-carry; continue at another time or place

cheer up-cause to become cheerful

chew up-chew thoroughly

chop up-chop into small pieces

clean off-clean the surface of

clean out-clean the inside of

clean up-clarify; tidy

clear out-clear the surface of

clear up-clear the inside of

close down-close permanently

close up-close temporarily

count in-include

count out-exclude

count up-calculate; count; add to a total

cross out-eliminate

cut off-interrupt; sever; amputate

cut out-eliminate; delete

cut down-reduce in quantity

draw up-write; compose (a document)

dress up-put clothes on; adorn

dust out-dust the inside of

eat up-eat completely

figure out-interpret; understand

figure up-compute

fill in-complete (a printed form)

fill out-complete (a printed form)

fill up-fill completely (a container)

find out-discover

fix up-repair; arrange in a suitable manner

get across-cause to be understood

give back-return

give out-distribute; announce

give up-surrender something

hand down-deliver; pronounce formally; leave as an inheritance

hand over-yield control of

hang up-suspend

have on-be dressed in

have over-entertain someone informally at one's home

hold off-delay; restrain

hold up-delay; rob; threaten with a weapon

keep up-continue; keep the same pace

leave out-omit

let down-disappoint

let out-release from confinement; make larger (in sewing)

light up-light; illuminate thoroughly

live down-live in such a way as to cause something to be forgotten make over-remake

move over-move to the side

pass out-distribute

pass up-not take advantage of (as an opportunity)

pass on-transmit

pay back-repay

pay off-discharge a debt completely; give someone his final pay

pick up-come to meet an escort; lift with hands or fingers; learn casually;

initiate an association publicly

play down-minimize

play up-emphasize

point out-indicate

pull down-pull in a downward direction; raze

push across-cause to be understood or accepted

put off-postpone

put on-dress in; deceive or fool

put up-preserve (food); receive as an overnight guest

quiet down-be quiet

ring up-the telephone

rinse off-rinse the surface of

rinse out-rinse the inside of

rule out-eliminate

run down-trace; disparage; hit with a vehicle

run off-cause to depart; reproduce mechanically

save up-accumulate

see through-complete; in spite of difficulties

see off-accompany someone to the beginning of a trip

send back-send to a place where formerly located

send over-send to where someone is

set up-arrange

show off-exhibit ostentatiously

shut off-cause to cease functioning

slow up-cause to move more slowly

spell out-enumerate; state in detail

stand up-fail to keep an appointment with

sweep out-sweep the inside of

take back-return; retract a statement

take down-remove from a high position; write from dictation

take in-understood; fool; deceive; make smaller (in sewing)

take over-take; assume command of

tear down-destroy

tear up-tear into small pieces

tell off-scold; reprimand

think over-consider

think through-consider from beginning to end

think up-create; invent

throw away-discard

throw over-reject

tie up-tie securely or tight

tire out-cause to be exhausted

touch up-repair

try on-put on a garment to verify the fit

try out-test

turn down-refuse; lower the volume

turn out-produce; force into exile, extinguish (a light)

wash off-wash the surface of

wash out-wash the inside of

wear out-use until no longer usable; tire greatly

wind up-finish, tighten the spring of a watch or machine

wipe off-wipe the surface of

wipe out-wipe the inside of; decimate

work out-solve

write down-record

write out-write down every detail; spell out

write up-compose; prepare (a document)

Inseparable

back out of-desert; fail to keep a promise

bear down on-lean on; browbeat

bear on-have to do with

bear up under-endure

break in on-interrupt

break into-interrupt

call for-come to get; require

care for-like; guard; supervise; maintain

carry on with-continue

catch up with-cover the distance between oneself and

check up on-examine; verify

come across-find accidentally

come along with-accompany; make progress

come by-find accidentally

come down with-become ill with

come out with-utter; produce

come up with-utter; produce

count on-rely on

cut in on-interrupt

disagree with-cause illness or discomfort to

do away with-abolish

do without-deprive oneself of

drop in at/on-visit casually without planning

drop out of-leave; quit

face up to-acknowledge

fall behind in-lag; not progress at required pace

fall back on-use for emergency purpose

fall out with-quarrel with

fill in for-substitute for

get ahead of-surpass; beat

get around-evade; avoid

get away with-do without being caught or punished

get by with-manage with a minimum of effort

get down to-become serious about; consider

get in-enter (a vehicle)

get off-descend from; leave

get on-enter (a vehicle); mount

get on with-proceed with

get through with-terminate, finish

go back on-desert; fail to keep (a promise)

go for-like a great deal

go in for-be interested in; participate in

go on with-continue

go over-review

go with-harmonize with; look pleasing together

go without-abstain from

hang around-remain idly in the vicinity of

hear from-receive a communication from

hear of-learn about (sometimes accidentally)

hit on-discover accidentally

hold on to-grasp tightly

hold out against-resist

keep at-persevere at

keep to-persist in; continue

keep up with-maintain the pace of

lie down on-evade; fail to do

live on-support or sustain oneself by means of

live up to-maintain the standard demanded of

look after-take care of

look back on-remember nostalgically

look down on-feel superior to

look forward to-anticipate

look up to-respect; admire

make up for-compensate for

pass on-transmit

pick on-tease; bully

play up to-flatter for personal advantage

put up with-tolerate

read up on-search out information on

run against-compete against in an election

run away with-leave; escape from

run for-campaign for

see about-consider; arrange

see to-arrange; supervise

settle on-decide on; choose

stand for-represent; permit

stand up for-support; demand

stand up to-resist

stick to-persist

stick up for-support; defend

take after-resemble

talk back to-answer impolitely

talk over-discuss

tell on-report misbehaviour to authority

touch on-mention briefly

turn into-become

wait on-serve

wait up for-not go to bed while waiting for

watch out for-be careful for

Intransitive

back down-retreat from a position in an argument

back out-desert; fail to keep a promise

back up-move backwards

bear up-endure

blow in-drop in to visit unexpectedly

blow over-pass without doing harm

blow up-explode; lose one's temper

call up-telephone

calm down-become calm

carry on-continue as before; misbehave

catch on-understand

catch up-cover the distance between oneself and a moving goal

check up-investigate

check out-leave; pay one's bill

cheer up-become cheerful

clear out-leave

clear up-become clear

close down-close permanently

close up-close temporarily

came about-happen

come along-accompany; make progress

come back-return

come by-visit someone in his home

come out-appear; make a social debut

come over-come to someone's house, to where someone is

come through-succeed

come to-regain consciousness

cut in-interrupt

die away-fade; diminish

die down-fade; diminish

die off/out-disappear; become extinct

dress up-don fancy or unusual clothes

drive back-return by car

drop in-visit someone casually without planning

drop out-abandon some organized activity; leave; quit

drop over-visit someone casually

fall behind-not progress at required pace

fall off-decrease; lose weight

fall through-fail; not be accomplished

fill in-substitute

find out-learn

fly back-return by air

fly over-fly to where someone is

get ahead-make progress

get along-have a friendly relationship

get around-circulate; move about

get away-escape

get by-manage; either just barely or with a minimum of effort

get in-enter

get off-descend from leave

get on-enter (a vehicle); mount (a horse, etc.)

get on/along-progress; be compatible

get up-rise

get through-finish

give out-become exhausted

give up-surrender; fail to finish

go back-return

go off-explode

go on-happen; continue

go out-stop burning; leave one's residence

go over-go; succeed

grow up-mature

hang around-remain idly; dawdle

hang up-replace a telephone receive on its hook

hold on-grasp tightly; persevere; wait while telephoning

hold out-continue to resist; persevere; persist

keep on-continue

keep up-maintain the required pace or standard; continue

let up-diminish in intensity

lie down-recline

look on-be a spectator

make out-progress; succeed

make up-become reconciled

move over-move to the side

pan out-turn out well; be successful

pass out-become unconscious

pass on-die

pick up-grow; increase

pull in-arrive

pull out-deport

pull through-survive (barely)

ride over-ride to where someone is

run away-escape; leave; leave quickly without permission

run down-slowly lose power so as to stop functioning

run off-depart running; drain

sell out-sell the ownership or responsibility

settle up-pay one's bills or debts

show off-boast by words or actions

show up-arrive; appear unexpectedly

shut up-stop talking

slow up-reduce speed

stand by-wait; be prepared to assist

stand up-stand; rise from sitting; last; endure

stay over-remain at someone's house overnight or longer

step aside-move to one side

take off-leave the ground

take over-assume command

talk back-answer impolitely

throw up-vomit

turn around-turn so that one is facing another direction

turn in-go to bed

turn out-succeed; come; appear, as at a public meeting

turn up-arrive; be found unexpectedly

wait up-remain awake in anticipation

wake up-awaken

walk back-return on foot to where one was

walk over-walk to where someone is

wash out-fade or disappear from washing

watch out-be careful

wear off-fade; disappear through use or time

wear out-become unusable through use; become used up

work out-be successful

4

ONE-, TWO-, AND THREE-POINT EDITING TECHNIQUES

INTRODUCTION

This chapter covers the various methods for editing your source footage into your timeline, so I should probably cover some other time-saving techniques. You do not have to always use all four editing marks to edit a shot into your timeline (the in and out points on the source side and the in and out points on the record side):

One-point Editing

This usually is done during a rough-cutting session. If you are just trying to add clips to your timeline without setting in and out points, you can use the playback indicator as your single mark. Just place the playback indicator anywhere in your timeline and click one of the edit buttons (Insert or Overlay, depending on what else exists in your timeline). The playback indicator acts as the in point in your timeline and carries the full duration of the clip in your Source monitor down into the timeline (because there are no marks in the Source monitor).

Two-point Editing

This technique is usually used to match up two points-one in the Source monitor and one in the timeline. Two points work well when you're trying to match up a starting point in the Source monitor and a starting point in the timeline (or in the Edit monitor). The rest of the duration, from the mark in point in the Source monitor until where the clip ends, is added to the timeline when you click the Insert or Overlay edit button.

Three-point Editing

This is the most common method of editing that I have seen editors use. It is quick and convenient (faster than measuring where to put the fourth edit point) while still giving you the accuracy to determine the exact starting and ending frames for either the source clip or the timeline. Premiere automatically edits in the fourth point. Therefore, you can mark any combination of the source clip's in point or out point and the in point or out point in your timeline. With experience you'll learn which circumstances determine which marks to use.

FILM EDITING

Film editing is the connecting of one or more shots to form a sequence, and the subsequent connecting of sequences to form an entire movie. Film editing, by definition, is the only art that is unique to cinema and which defines and separates filmmaking from almost all other art forms (such as: photography, theater, dance, writing, and directing).

The job of an editor isn't merely to mechanically put pieces of a film together, nor to just cut off the film slates, nor merely to edit dialogue scenes. Film editing is an art form which can either make or break a film. A film editor works with the layers of images, the story, the music, the rhythm, the pace, shapes the actors' performances, "re-directing" and often re-writing the film during the editing process, honing the infinite possibilities of the juxtaposition of small snippets of film into a creative, coherent, cohesive whole.

THE DEVELOPMENT OF FILM EDITING PROCESSES

Film editing evolved from the process of a film editor physically cutting and taping together pieces of film, using a splicer and threading the film on a machine with a viewer such as a Moviola, or "flatbed" machine such as a Kem or Steenbeck.

Before the widespread use of non-linear editing systems, the initial editing of all films was done with a positive copy of the film negative called a film workprint. Today, most films are edited digitally (on systems such as Avid or Final Cut Pro) and bypass the film positive workprint altogether. In the past, the use of a film positive (not the original negative) allowed the editor to do as much experimenting as he or she wished, without the risk of damaging the original.

When the film workprint had been cut to a satisfactory state, it was then used to make a negative cutting list. The negative cutter referred to this list while processing the negative, splitting the shots into rolls, which were then contact printed to produce the final film print. Today, production companies have the option of to bypass negative cutting altogether. With the advent of digital intermediate or "DI," the physical negative does not necessarily need to be physically cut and hot spliced together; rather the negative is optically scanned into computer(s) and a cut list is conformed by a DI editor.

Film Editor

A film editor is a person who practices film editing by assembling footage into a coherent film. Film editors often are responsible for pulling together all of the elements of story, dialogue, music, sound effects, visual effects, rhythm and pace of a film. In the making of a film, the editors usually play a dynamic and creative role.

POST-PRODUCTION

The Editor's Cut

There are several editing stages and the editor's cut is the first. An editor's cut (sometimes referred to as the "assembly edit" or "rough cut") is normally the first pass of what the final film will be when it reaches picture lock.

The film editor usually starts working while principal photography (shooting) starts. In the first stage of editing the film editor will usually work alone (save for his or her own team of assistant editors, associate or co-editors and/or visual effects and music editors). Likely, prior to cutting, the editor and director will have seen and/or discussed "dailies" (raw footage shot each day) as shooting progresses. Screening dailies gives the editor a ballpark idea of the director's intentions.

Because it is the first pass, the editor's cut might be somewhat longer than the final film. The editor continues to refine the cut while shooting continues, and often the entire editing process goes on for many months and sometimes more than a year, depending on the film.

The Director's Cut

When shooting is finished, the director can then turn his or her full attention to collaborating with the editor and further refining the cut of the film. This is the time that is set aside where the film editor's first cut is molded to fit the director's vision, and before the studio and/or producers are generally allowed to have input. Under DGA rules directors receive a minimum of ten weeks after completion of principal photography to prepare their first cut.

While collaborating on what is referred to as the "director's cut," the director and the editor go over the entire movie with a fine tooth comb; scenes and shots are re-ordered, removed, shortened and otherwise tweaked. Often it is discovered that there are plot holes, missing shots or even missing segments which might require that new scenes be filmed.

Because of this time working closely and collaborating-a period that is normally far longer, and far more intimately involved, than the entire production and filming-most directors and editors form a unique artistic bond.

THE PRODUCERS VS. THE DIRECTOR

Often after the director has had his or her chance to oversee a cut, the subsequent cuts are supervised by one or more producers, who represent the production company and/ or movie studio. At times, the final cut of films produced by the major studios is the one that most closely represents what the studio wants from the film and not necessarily what the director wants. Because of this, there have been several conflicts in the past between the director and the studio, sometimes leading to the use of the "Alan Smithee" credit signifying disownership or the aforementioned "director's cut" re-issues in subsequent years after the original theatrical releases.

Some directors are also the producers of their films, and, with the approval of the funding studio, have a much tighter grip on what makes the final cut than other directors. The most well-known example of a director who lorded over all aspects of his films, with little studio intervention, and worked completely outside of the Hollywood system is Stanley Kubrick. On the other hand, Orson Welles is an example of a director constantly dogged by studio supervision and many times had films taken away from him. Independent directors who work outside of the "studio system" are usually more free to have a final cut; thus independent films often take more risks and have more creative rewards than studio films.

CONTINUITY

Often a film editor is blamed for improper continuity. For example, cutting from a shot where the beer glass is empty to one where it is full. Continuity is, in fact, very nearly last on a film editor's list of important things to maintain. Continuity is typically the business of the script supervisor and film director, who are together responsible for preserving continuity and preventing errors from take to take and shot to shot. Generally speaking, the editor utilizes the script supervisor's notes during post-production to log and keep track of the vast amounts of footage and takes that a director might shoot. However, to most editors what is more important than continuity is the editing of emotional and storytelling aspects of any given film-something that is much more abstract and harder to judge-which is why films often take much longer to edit than to shoot.

METHODS OF MONTAGE

In motion picture terminology, a montage (from the French for "putting together" or "assembly") is a film editing technique.

There are at least three senses of the term:

1. In French film practice, "montage" has its literal French meaning and simply identifies a movie's editor.
2. In Soviet filmmaking of the 1920s, "montage" was a method of juxtaposing shots to derive new meaning that did not exist in either shot alone.
3. In classical Hollywood cinema, a "montage sequence" is a short segment in a film in which narrative information is presented in a condensed fashion. This is the most common meaning among laymen.

Soviet Montage

Lev Kuleshov was among the very first to theorize about the relatively young medium of the cinema in the 1920s. For him, the unique essence of the cinema-that which could be duplicated in no other medium-is editing. He argues that editing a film is like constructing a building. Brick-by-brick (shot-by-shot) the building (film) is erected. His often-cited Kuleshov Experiment established that montage can lead the viewer to reach certain conclusions about the action in a film. Montage works because viewers infer meaning based on context.

Although, strictly speaking, U.S. film director D.W. Griffith was not part of the montage school, he was one of the early proponents of the power of editing-mastering cross-cutting to show parallel action in different locations, and codifying film grammar in other ways as well. Griffith's work in the teens was highly regarded by Kuleshov and other Soviet filmmakers and greatly influenced their understanding of editing.

Sergei Eisenstein was briefly a student of Kuleshov's, but the two parted ways because they had different ideas of montage. Eisenstein regarded montage as a dialectical means of creating meaning. By contrasting unrelated shots he tried to provoke associations in the viewer, which were induced by shocks.

Montage Sequence

A montage sequence consists of a series of short shots that are edited into a sequence to condense narrative. It is usually used to advance the story as a whole (often to suggest the passage of time), rather than to create symbolic meaning. In many cases, a song plays in the background to enhance the mood or reinforce the message being conveyed. Classic examples are the training montages in Sylvester Stallone's Rocky series of movies.

EDITING TECHNIQUES

Stanley Kubrick noted that the editing process is the one phase of production that is truly unique to motion pictures. Every other aspect of filmmaking originated in a different medium than film (photography, art direction, writing, sound recording), but editing is the one process that is unique to film. In Alexander Walker's Stanley Kubrick Directs, Kubrick was quoted as saying, "I love editing. I think I like it more than any other phase of filmmaking. If I wanted to be frivolous, I might say that everything that precedes editing is merely a way of producing film to edit." In his book, On Film Editing, Edward Dmytryk stipulates seven "rules of cutting" that a good editor should follow:

- "Rule 1. Never make a cut without a positive reason.
- "Rule 2. When undecided about the exact frame to cut on, cut long rather than short" (Dmytryk, 23).
- "Rule 3: Whenever possible cut 'in movement'" (Dmytryk, 27).
- "Rule 4: The 'fresh' is preferable to the 'stale'" (Dmytryk, 37).
- "Rule 5: All scenes should begin and end with continuing action" (Dmytryk, 38).
- "Rule 6: Cut for proper values rather than proper 'matches'" (Dmytryk, 44).
- "Rule 7: Substance first-then form" (Dmytryk, 145).

According to Walter Murch, when it comes to film editing, there are six main criteria for evaluating a cut or deciding where to cut. They are (in order of importance, most important first):

- emotion-Does the cut reflect what the editor believes the audience should be feeling at that moment?
- story-Does the cut advance the story?
- rhythm-Does the cut occur "at a moment that is rhythmically interesting and 'right'" (Murch, 18)?
- eye-trace-Does the cut pay respect to "the location and movement of the audience's focus of interest within the frame" (Murch, 18)?
- two-dimensional place of the screen-Does the cut respect the 180 degree rule?
- three-dimensional space of action-Is the cut true to the physical/spatial relationships within the diegesis?

Murch assigned notional percentage values to each of the criteria. Emotion, with 51%, outweighed the combined value of all the other criteria.

FLATBED EDITOR

A flatbed editor is a type of machine used for the editing of a motion picture film. The two most common brands, Steenbeck and K.-E.-M. (Keller-Elektro-Mechanik), were invented in Germany in the 1930's. There are also the Italian Prévost, the Dutch Oude Delft or Oldelft, and the French Atlas as well as Moritone flatbeds. To round it off, the U K has LEM, and America its Moviola flatbed issue.

All these machines have a rotating prism rather than the "Maltese Cross" or geneva drive intermittent mechanism used by the American Moviola editing machine. The rotating prism allows to move the film smoothly and continuously, reducing mechanical noise and damage to the film. It also makes high-speed operation feasible, and some machines can move the film at up to ten times standard speed. The trade-off for these advantages is a slight smearing of the image compared to the American Moviola.

The use of multiple sound tracks, up to three separate tracks, and multiple picture heads, up to three, is also a feature of the "table", which has a modular construction. Flatbeds also made it easy to view ten or even twenty minutes of film at a time. With the "armed" Moviola one could manage a thousand-foot eleven-minute 35mm reel, but with difficulty because it did not have high-speed operation.

European flatbeds came into more common use in the United States during the 1970's, although never completely replacing the Moviola.

By the mid-1990's, flatbeds were in turn becoming replaced by electronic non-linear systems such as Avid and Lightworks.

As of 2007, flatbed editors are still used in many film schools for their educational value. Feature films in the United States use electronic non-linear systems almost exclusively.

180 Degree Rule

The 180° rule is a basic film editing guideline that states that two characters (or other elements) in the same scene should always have the same left/right relationship to each other. If the camera passes over the imaginary axis connecting the two subjects, it is called crossing the line. The new shot, from the opposite side, is known as a reverse angle.

Examples

In the example of a dialogue, if Ted is on the left and Bob is on the right, then Ted should be facing right at all times, even when Bob is off the edge of the frame, and Bob should always be facing left. Shifting to the other side of the characters on a cut, so that Bob is now on the left side and Ted is on the right, will disorient the viewer, and break the flow of the scene.

In the example of an action scene, such as a car chase, if a vehicle leaves the right side of the frame in one shot, it should enter from the left side of the frame in the next shot. Leaving from the right and entering from the right will create a similar sense of disorientation as in the dialogue example.

An excellent example of sustained use of the 180 degree rule occurs throughout much of The Big Parade, a drama about World War One directed by King Vidor. In the sequences leading up to the battle scenes, the American forces (arriving from the west) are always shown marching from left to right across the screen, while the German troops (arriving from the east) are always shown marching from right to left. After the battle scenes, when the weary troops are staggering homeward, the Americans are always shown crossing the screen from right to left (moving west) and the Germans from left to right (moving east). The audience's viewpoint is therefore always from a consistent position, in this case southward of the action.

Problems Caused and Solutions

Avoiding crossing the line is a problem that those learning filmcraft can struggle with. In the above example with the car chase, a possible solution is to begin the second cut with the car driving into frame from the "wrong" side. Although this may be wrong in the geographic sense on set, it looks more natural to the viewer. Another possibility is to insert a "buffer shot" of the subject head-on (or from behind) to help the viewer understand the camera movement.

STYLE

In professional productions, the 180° rule is an essential element of a style of film editing called continuity editing. The rule is not always obeyed. Sometimes a filmmaker will purposely break the line of action in order to create disorientation. Stanley Kubrick was known to do this. The Wachowski Brothers and directors Tinto Brass, Yasujiro Ozu, Wong Kar-Wai and Jacques Tati sometimes ignored this rule also. The British TV presenters Ant & Dec extend this continuity to almost all their appearances, with Ant almost always on the left and Dec on the right.

Some filmmakers state that the fictional axis created by this rule can be used to plan the emotional strength of a scene. The closer you place the camera to the axis, the more emotionally involved the audience will be.

In the Japanese animated picture Paprika, two of the main characters discuss crossing the line and demonstrate the disorienting effect of actually performing the action.

Use in TV Sports

Sporting events that are covered with several cameras often use cameras on the other side of the line in order to obtain an optimal view of an incident that is blocked by the main shots. In order to prevent confusion, reverse angle shots are used sparingly and with some kind of graphic (e.g. "REVERSE ANGLE" on screen) to explain the change of viewpoint.

CONTINUITY EDITING

Continuity editing is the predominant style of film editing practiced by most Hollywood editors. The goal of continuity editing is to make the work of the editor as invisible as possible. The viewer should not notice the cuts, and shots should flow together naturally. Hence, the sequence of shots should appear to be continuous.

COMMON CONVENTIONS

Establishing Shot

In film and television, an establishing shot sets up, or "establishes", a scene's setting and/or its participants.

It might be a shot at the beginning of a scene indicating where the remainder of the scene takes place. For example, an exterior shot of a large building on a rainy night, followed by an interior shot of a couple talking, implies that the conversation is taking place inside that building. (Of course the conversation may in fact have been filmed on a studio set far from the actual location, because of budget, permits, time limitations, etc.)

For example, the TV show, Seinfeld, often uses a "Restaurant" establishing shot-an exterior shot of a restaurant that is followed by interior shots of the characters inside.

Or an establishing shot might just be a long shot of a room that shows all the characters from a particular scene. For example, a scene about a murder in a college lecture hall might begin with a shot that shows the entire room-including the lecturing professor and the students taking notes. Establishing shots are not required for every scene in a film or TV program.

In fact, they were more common during the classical era of filmmaking than they are now. Contemporary filmmakers tend to skip the establishing shot in order to move the scene along more quickly. In addition, scenes in mysteries and the like often wish to obscure the setting and its participants and thus avoid clarifying them with an establishing shot. An establishing shot may also establish a concept, rather than a location. For example, opening with a martial arts drill visually establishes the theme of martial arts.

Shot Reverse Shot

Shot reverse shot (or shot/countershot) is a film technique wherein one character is shown looking (often off-screen) at another character, and then the other character is shown looking "back" at the first character. Since the characters are shown facing in opposite directions, the viewer unconsciously assumes that they are looking at each other (the 180 degree rule). However, shot reverse shot is also often combined with creative geography to create the sense that two characters are facing each other, when in fact they may be being filmed in completely different locations or at completely different times.

These techniques are all features of the "classical" Hollywood style of continuity editing, which deemphasizes transitions between shots such that the audience perceives one continuous action that develops linearly, chronologically, and logically.

By comparison, an alternating sequence shows the systematic intertwining of actions or motifs occurring in a single diegetic space, and therefore involves cutting back and forth from one action or character to another, but does not necessarily imply that the subjects of the shots are interacting directly with one another

Eyeline Match

An eyeline match is a popular editing technique associated with the continuity editing system. It is based on the premise that the audience will want to see what the character on-screen is seeing. The eyeline match begins with a character looking at something off-screen, then there will then be a cut to the object or person that he is looking at. For example, a man is looking off-screen to his left, and then the film cuts to a television that he is watching.

30 Degree Rule

The 30° rule is a basic film editing guideline that states the camera must make at least 30° movements around the axis of movement while still respecting the 180° rule. These 30° of movement avoid the creation of a jump cut, or cutting at the same angle, making the subject appear to "jump" in the frame. Moving the camera at least 30° between shots seems to soften the effect of changing distance such as changing from a medium shot to a close-up.

Cutting on Action

Cutting on action or matching on action refers to a film editing technique where the editor cuts from one shot to another view that "matches" the first shot's action and energy. Although the two shots may have actually been shot hours apart from each other, cutting on action gives the impression of continuous time when watching the edited film. By having a subject begin an action in one shot and carry it through to completion in the next, the editor creates a visual bridge which distracts the viewer from noticing the cut or noticing any slight continuity error between the two shots. A variant of cutting on action is a cut in which the subject exits the frame in the first shot and then enters the frame in the subsequent shot. The entrance in the second shot must match the screen direction and motive rhythm of the exit in the first shot.

Some films, like Alain Resnais's Last Year at Marienbad play with this technique to connect scenes playing in different places together. For example, there is a shot of a large hall in which somebody turns her head, then the film cuts to the same person finishing the head turn, but standing in a completely different room. In this case, the edit creates an atmosphere where the spatial and temporal relationship between scenes become blurred.

Footage

In film and video, footage is the raw, unedited material as it has been recorded by the camera, which usually must be edited to create a motion picture, video clip, television show or similar completed work. More loosely, footage can also refer to all sequences used in film and video editing, such as special effects and archive material (for special cases of this, see stock footage and B roll). Since the term originates in film, footage is only used for recorded images, such as film stock, videotapes or digitized clips-on live television, the signals from the cameras are called sources instead.

The origin of the term "footage" is that 35mm film has traditionally been measured in feet and frames; the fact that film was measured by length in cutting rooms, and that there are exactly 16 4-perf frames in a foot of 35mm film which roughly represented 1 second of silent film, made footage a natural unit of measure for film. The term then became used figuratively to describe moving image material of any kind.

Television footage, especially news footage, is often traded between broadcasting organizations, but good footage usually commands a high price. The actual sum depends on duration, age, size of intended audience, duration of licensing and other factors. Amateur video footage of current events can also often fetch a high price on the market-scenes shot inside the World Trade Center during the September 11, 2001 attacks were reportedly sold for US$45,000. Sometimes film projects will also sell or trade footage, usually second unit material not used in the final cut. For example, the end of the non-director's cut version of Blade Runner used landscape views that were originally shot for The Shining before the script was modified after shooting had finished.

Found Footage

Found footage is a filmmaking term which describes a method of compiling films partly or entirely of footage which has not been created by the filmmaker, and changing its meaning by placing it in a new context. It should not be mistaken for documentary or compilation films. It is also not to be mistaken with stock footage. The term refers to the "found object" (objet trouvé) of art history.

Experimental Film

The American collage artist Joseph Cornell produced one of the earliest found films with his reassembly of East of Borneo, combined with pieces of other films, into a new work he titled Rose Hobart after the leading actress. His film is notable for its Surrealist form and influence on later filmmakers.

In contrast to Cornell's use, structural film or "Materialfilm" (German) often demands that the artist only uses material of preferably unknown origin, not very defined content, and poor physical condition. This material might be treated in any way the artist chooses, even completely untreated, as long as he ignores any meaning or content of the source material. Other notable users of this technique are Craig Baldwin in his films "Spectors of the Spectrum," Tribulation 99" and "O No Coronado." Bill Morrisson uses found footage lost and neglected in film archives in his 2002 work "Decasia." Another remarkable entry in the found footage cannon is Peter Delpeut's "Lyrical Nitrate."

Commercial Cinema

Another common use of found footage searches for material with recognisable content, which is edited into more or less narrative structures. Through means of editing, sound, voice-over, subtitles and/or inserts, the filmmaker tweaks the interpretation of the audience in a way that it accepts the new "truth" of the footage. Normally the source footage is of unknown origin, however, if footage with recognisable content (like historical or well-known commercial footage) is used the result can be made a parody or a political statement. A term which describes this genre is "mockumentary".

One of the first examples in mainstream cinema is Orson Welles' "F for Fake" (1974), which masterfully plays with truth and fiction and seems to be able to proof each of its statements. Another example of the use of found footage is in Woody Allen's first film, "What's Up Tiger Lily" in which Allen took a Japanese spy film by Senkichi Taniguchi, completely re-edited it and wrote a new soundtrack comprised of his own dialogue for comic effect.

A third meaning of found footage came up with the invention of TV formats which featured odd films and videos, mostly done by amateurs, combined with outtakes of film and video professionals, as well as stunts and accidents from sports shows.

MUSIC VIDEO AND VJING

A certain style of music video makes extensive use of found footage, mostly found on TV, like news, documentaries, old (and odd) films etc. Prominent examples are videos of bands like Public Enemy and Coldcut. The latter also project video material during their stage show, which includes live mixing of video footage. Many artists already work in this new field of "VJing"", but not all of them work with found footage. Those who do extensively mine the internet for new material, dig through archives like the famous Prelinger archive, or trade material among artists

Axial Cut

An axial cut is a type of jump cut, where the camera suddenly moves closer to or further away from its subject, along an invisible line drawn straight between the camera and the subject. While a plain jump cut typically involves a temporal discontinuity (an apparent jump in time), an axial cut usually does not.

An axial cut can be made with the use of a zoom lens, or physically moving the camera with a crane or Camera dolly. The intervening footage (as the camera moves or zooms) is then removed while editing the film. Since footage is discarded, this technique works better for static shots. If action is required, several takes will be required to get the necessary footage.

Alternately, a multi-camera setup can be used, with the cameras showing the subject at different sizes. The footage from both cameras is then edited together to create the effect. As the cameras cannot occupy the same space, there will always be a slight deviation from the axis. Moving the cameras further away from the subject and using telephoto lenses can reduce the deviation.

B-ROLL

B-roll or B roll is unrelated talk during an interview.

This technique of using the cutaway is common to hide zooms in documentary films: the visuals may cut away to B roll footage of what the person is talking about while the A camera zooms in, then cut back after the zoom is complete. The cutaway to B roll footage can also be used to hide verbal or physical tics that the editor and/or director finds distracting: with the audio separate from the video, the filmmakers are free to excise "uh"s, sniffs, coughs, and so forth. Similarly, a contextually irrelevant part of a sentence or anecdote can be removed to construct a more effective, to-the-point delivery. This can also be used to change the meaning of the speaker to fit the view of the producer. In fiction film, the technique can be used to indicate simultaneous action or flashbacks, usually increasing tension or revealing information. "B roll" also refers to footage provided free of charge to broadcast news organizations as a means of gaining free publicity. For example, an auto maker might shoot a video of its assembly line, hoping that segments will be used in stories about the new model year. "B roll" sometimes makes its way into stock footage libraries.

B-Rolls in EDLs

In an Edit decision list (EDL), b-rolls have an entirely different meaning. Linear editing systems are unable to dissolve between clips on the same tape. Therefore, the EDL can mark such clips as "b-roll" to indicate that they should be dubbed onto another tape to make the dissolve possible,

INSERT (FILM)

In film, an insert is a shot of part of a scene as filmed from a different angle and/or focal length from the master shot.

Inserts cover action already covered in the master shot, but emphasize a different aspect of that action due to the different framing. An insert is different from a cutaway in that the cutaway is of action not covered in the master shot.

There are more exact terms to use when the new, inserted shot is another view of actors: close-up, head shot, knee shot, two shot. So the term "insert" is often confined to views of objects--and body parts, other than the head. Thus: CLOSE-UP of the gunfighter, INSERT of his hand quivering above the holster, TWO SHOT of his friends watching anxiously, INSERT of the clock ticking. Often inserts of this sort are done separately from the main action, by a second-unit director using stand-ins.

Inserts and cutaways can both be vexatious for directors, as care must be taken to preserve continuity by keeping the objects in the same relative position as in the main take, and having the lighting the same.

The 1975 movie Inserts directed by John Byrum about a pornographic film production, which starred Richard Dreyfuss and was originally released with an X rating, took its name from the double meaning that "insert" both refers to this film technique (often used in pornographic filmmaking) and to sexual intercourse.

CUTAWAY (FILM)

In film, a cutaway is the interruption of a continuously-filmed action by inserting a view of something else. It is usually followed by a cutback to the first shot, but not always.

Generally, cutaways are divided into two types: related and unrelated. Related cutaway is a shot which is juxtaposing in between the shots without disturbing the meaning of the scene and it enhance the mood of the scene but unrelated cutaway used in where the continuity breaks between the shots generally editors should avoid the unrelated cutaways in film it will disturb the audience. Probably its most common uses in dramatic films are to adjust the pace of the main action, to conceal the deletion of some unwanted part of the main shot, or to allow the joining of parts of two versions of that shot. For example, a scene may be improved by cutting a few frames out of an actor's pause; a brief view of some listener can help conceal the break. Or the actor may fumble some of his lines in a group shot; rather than discarding a good version of the shot, the director may just have the actor repeat the lines "in one" and cut to that solitary view when necessary--some actors have fumbled their lines deliberately to get that treatment. These are journeyman techniques. Cutaways can also be used for reasons of art.

One example of a cutaway being used deliberately to break continuity, for comic effect, appears in Shoot the Piano Player (Tirez sur le pianiste), by François Truffaut: the pianist and his female companion are being followed; she opens her compact and uses it to show him the two gangsters behind them, impossibly large in the reflection. On television, The Simpsons and Family Guy both used cutaways widely to introduce brief gags before returning to the episode's main storyline. The Simpsons writers cut back on cutaways around the time the technique was adopted by Family Guy.

Cross Cutting is a Series of Cutaways and Cutbacks

In news and documentary work, the cutaway is used much as it would be in fiction. On location, there is usually just one camera to film an interview, and it's usually trained on the interviewee. Often there is only one microphone. After the interview, the interviewer will usually repeat his questions while he himself is being filmed, with pauses as he pretends to listen to the answers. (The comedy Micki and Maude shows this process quite accurately.) These shots can be used as cutaways. They may be necessary just to ensure that the audience can hear the questions correctly.

KEYING (GRAPHICS)

In graphics and visual effects, keying is an informal term for compositing two full frame images together, by discriminating the visual information into values of colour and light.

Chroma Key

A chroma key is the removal of a colour from one image to reveal another "behind" it.

Luma Key

A luma key similarly replaces colour from an image which falls into a particular range of brightness. This technique is less controllable, but can be used on graphic elements. It is particularly useful for realistic fire keying, and was also used for on-screen text, such as programme titles and credits, before the advent of digital compositing.

Difference Key

A difference key uses a background plate of the scene that the foreground object is being keyed out of and the software then assesses the source video and any pixels that don't match the grid are obviously meant to be keyed out.

For example, if your subject is standing in front of a wall, a photo taken from the camera of the same wall, is used. This must be taken from the same camera angle, focus & distance. The software then compares the video to be keyed with the original photo and generates a mask based upon that difference, hence the name explain well.

Matte Key

A matte key uses three images: the two images that will be composited, and a black-and-white third image (called "mask") that dictates the blending of the two, with white revealing one image, black the other, and grey revealing a blend of the two together.

Generally, the "bottom" image is called the beauty, the image that appears on top is the fill and the discriminating element (chroma, luma or matte) is called the key or matte.

Downstream Key

A downstream key (or DSK) is a method of Matte keying, so you use three image or video signals. You have the base signal, where the fill signal is keyed on to, using the key signal to control the opacity of the fill signal. This results in a new signal, that you can use as an input for another DSK. This technique is used in television production, where you show the station name in a corner (DSK 1), and need a name title for a guest (DSK 2), while showing subtitles for translation of his/her speech (DSK 3).

KULESHOV EFFECT

The Kuleshov Effect is a montage effect demonstrated by Russian filmmaker Lev Kuleshov in about 1918.

Kuleshov edited a short film in which shots of the face of Ivan Mozzhukhin (a Tsarist matinee idol) are alternated with various other shots (a plate of soup, a girl, an old woman's coffin). The film was shown to an audience who believed that the expression on Mozzhukhin's face was different each time he appeared, depending on whether he was "looking at" the plate of soup, the girl, or the coffin, showing an expression of hunger, desire or grief respectively. Actually the footage of Mozzhukhin was identical, and rather expressionless, every time it appeared. Vsevolod Pudovkin (who later claimed to have been the co-creator of the experiment) described in 1929 how the audience "raved about the acting.... the heavy pensiveness of his mood over the forgotten soup, were touched and moved by the deep sorrow with which he looked on the dead woman, and admired the light, happy smile with which he surveyed the girl at play. But we knew that in all three cases the face was exactly the same." [Pudovkin, "Naturshchik vmesto aktera", in Sobranie sochinenii, volume I, Moscow: 1974, p.184].

Kuleshov used the experiment to indicate the usefulness and effectiveness of film editing. The implication is that viewers brought their own emotional reactions to this sequence of images, and then moreover attributed those reactions to the actor, investing his impassive face with their own feelings.

The effect has also been studied by psychologists, and is well-known among modern film makers. Alfred Hitchcock refers to the effect in his conversations with François Truffaut, using actor Jimmy Stewart as the example. The experiment itself was created by assembling fragments of pre-existing film from the Tsarist film industry, with no new material. Mozzhukhin had been the leading romantic "star" of Tsarist cinema, and familiar to the audience.

Kuleshov demonstrated the necessity of considering montage as the basic tool of cinema art. In Kuleshov's view, the cinema consists of fragments and the assembly of those fragments, the assembly of elements which in reality are distinct. It is therefore not the content of the images in a film which is important, but their combination. The raw materials of such an art work need not be original, but are pre-fabricated elements which can be deconstructed and re-assembled by the artist into new juxtapositions.

The montage experiments carried out by Kuleshov in the late 1910s and early 1920s formed the theoretical basis of Soviet montage cinema, culminating in the famous films of the late 1920s by directors such as Sergei Eisenstein, Vsevolod Pudovkin and Dziga Vertov, among others. These films included The Battleship Potemkin, October, Mother, The End of St. Petersburg, and The Man with a Movie Camera.

Soviet montage cinema was suppressed under Stalin during the 1930s as a dangerous example of Formalism in the arts, and as being incompatible with the official Soviet artistic doctrine of Socialist Realism.

L Cut

An L cut, also known as a split edit, is a transition from one shot to another in film, where the picture transition does not occur coincidentally with the audio transition. This is often done to enhance the aesthetics or flow of the film (for example--a conversation between two people can feel like a tennis match without L cuts. L cuts allow the audience to see the reactionary impulse to speak, or the aftermath of speaking rather than simply the act of speaking.) L cuts are also used to hide transitions between scenes. An prominent example of an L cut occurs in the film The Silence of the Lambs when Clarice is leaving her first interview with Dr. Lecter. She has just been humiliated and remembers her father arriving home from work one day when she was a child; after he picks her up and spins her around, the camera pans over to a passing truck and tilts up to the sky. Then we hear Clarice's sobs and cut back to her outside the mental institution, leaning on her car and crying.

The name of the cut refers to the shape of the cut pieces of the film-the audio track is cut somewhat after (or before) the last frame of video, resulting in roughly L-shaped film ends, as the video and audio parts of film are in tracks, one below, one above, on the film itself.

MASTER SHOT

A master shot is a filmic recording of an entire dramatized scene, from start to finish, from an angle that keeps all the players in view. It is often a long shot and can sometimes perform a double function as an establishing shot. Usually, the master shot is the first shot checked off during the shooting of a scene-it is the foundation of what is called camera coverage, other shots that reveal different aspects of the action, groupings of two or three of the actors at crucial moments, close-ups of individuals, insert shots of various props, and so on.

Historically, the master shot was arguably the most important shot of any given scene. All shots in a given scene were somehow related to what was happening in the master shot. This is one reason why some of the films from the 1930s and 1940s are considered "stagey" by today's standards. By the 1960s and 1970s, the style of film shooting and editing shifted to include radical angles that conveyed more subjectivity and intimacy within the scenes (Ascher, 227). Today, the master shot is still an extremely important element of film production, but scenes are not built around the master shot in the same way that they were in the 1930s.

Montage Sequence

A montage sequence is a technique in film editing in which a series of short shots is edited into a sequence to condense narrative. It is usually used to advance the story as a whole (often to suggest the passage of time), rather than to create symbolic meaning as it does in Soviet montage theory. In many cases, a song plays in the background to enhance the mood or reinforce the message being conveyed.

Many films are well known for their montage scenes. Examples include:

- the training regimen montages in Sylvester Stallone's Rocky series of movies
- Dirty Dancing
- Flashdance
- several of director Sam Raimi's films
- Ghostbusters
- Scarface's montage showing Tony Montana's rise to power, set to the song "Scarface (Push It to the Limit)"
- Groundhog Day's repeated courtship sequence
- the satirical self-referential montages in the South Park episode "Asspen", the film Team America: World Police and the Buffy the Vampire Slayer episode "Once More with Feeling" (featuring a duet between Buffy and Giles).

In nearly all of these examples, the montages are used to compress narrative time and show the main character learning or improving skills that will help achieve the ultimate goal. The song "Montage"-from "Asspen" and Team America-describes this perfectly:

Show a lot of things happening at once

Remind everyone of what's going on

And with every shot you show a little improvement

To show it all would take too long

That's called a montage

Oh we want montage

The sports training montage

The sports training montage is a standard explanatory montage. It originated in American cinema but has since spread to modern martial arts films from East Asia. Originally depicting a character engaging in physical or sports training, the form has been extended to other activities or themes.

CONVENTIONS AND CLICHES

The standard elements of a sports training montage include a build-up where the potential sports hero confronts their failure to train adequately. The solution is a serious, individual training regimen. The individual is shown engaging in physical training through a series of short, cut sequences. An inspirational song (usually fast-paced rock music) typically provides the only sound. At the end of the montage several weeks have elapsed in the course of just a few minutes and the hero is now prepared for the big competition. One of the most well-known examples is the training sequence in the 1976 movie Rocky, which culminates in Rocky's run up the steps of the Philadelphia Museum of Art.

The simplicity of the technique and its over-use in American film vocabulary has led to its status as a film cliché. A notable parody of the sports training montage appears in the South Park episode, "Asspen", noted above. When Stan Marsh must become an expert skier quickly, he begins training in a montage where the inspirational song explicitly spells out the techniques and requirements of a successful sports training montage sequence as they occur on screen:

In any sport, if you want to go

From just a beginner to a pro

You'll need a montage!

Use in Japanese and Hong Kong cinema

In films from Japan and Hong Kong, particular emphasis is placed on the suffering of the trainee, often with the breakthrough in training being a change in perspective rather than physical capability. More importance is often placed on the master passing down knowledge to their student, rather than the self-discovery of American film.

A classic use of the sports training montage in Hong Kong cinema is The 36th Chamber of Shaolin (Shao Lin san shi liu fang). In The 36th Chamber the student displays an arrogance and unwillingness to learn. The student develops through a process of suffering, towards self-mastery in learning, finally achieving triumph in realising that he controls his ability to learn. This training sequence is much closer to Zen Buddhist ideas regarding teaching practice, or Sufi learning concepts, than the individualistic American model used above.

MOTION PICTURE EDITORS GUILD

The Motion Picture Editors Guild (MPEG) is the guild that represents freelance and staff motion picture film and television editors and other post-production professionals and story analysts throughout the United States. The Motion Picture Editors Guild (Union Local 700) is a part of the 500 affiliated local unions of IATSE (International Alliance of Theatrical Stage Employees), a national labor organization with a nearly 65-year history of bargaining for better wages and working conditions for its 104,000-plus members. Currently there are as more than 6,000 members of the 100-plus year old Editors Guild.

The MPEG negotiates collective bargaining agreements (union contracts) with producers and major motion picture movie studios and enforces existing agreements with employers involved in post-production. The MPEG provides assistance for securing better working conditions, including but not limited to salary, medical benefits, safety (particularly "turnaround time") and artistic (assignment of credit) concerns.

History

The Society of Motion Picture Film Editors was created in 1937 by I. James Wilkinson, Ben Lewis and Philip Cahn when film editors earned a mere $100 per week. Initial membership totaled 571.

In 1938 the first contract talks garnered a 10% wage increase. In 1943 film editors and assistant editors are offered their own local by the International Alliance of Theatrical Stage Employees (IATSE). Many Society members sought to align themselves with this larger national organization, hoping for greater negotiating clout. The Screen Directors Guild of America (DGA) also made overtures, but offered only to admit picture editors (not assistant editors), and only to grant them diluted voting rights. The editors and assistant editors opted to join IATSE instead. In 1944, the Society of Motion Picture Film Editors underwent a name change and became the Motion Picture Editors Guild, Local 776 of the IATSE. In 1998, the two IA editorial locals (776 in Los Angeles and 771 in New York) merged to form one national Editors Guild, now Local 700. Also in 1998, members of IATSE Local 695 are transferred to the Editors Guild consisting of Re-Recording Mixers, Maintenance Engineers, Sound Recordists and Studio Projectionists. In 2000, the Story Analysts, formerly Local 854, also join the Editors Guild.

Non-linear Editing System

A non-linear editing system (NLE) is a video editing (NLVE) or audio editing (NLAE) system which can perform random access on the source material.

5

Non-linear Editing

INTRODUCTION

Non-linear editing for film and television postproduction is a modern editing method which involves being able to access any frame in a video clip with the same ease as any other. This method is similar in concept to the "cut and glue" technique used in film editing from the beginning. However, when working with film, it is a destructive process, as the actual film negative must be cut. Non-linear, non-destructive methods began to appear with the introduction of digital video technology. Video and audio data are first digitized to hard disks or other digital storage devices.

The data is either recorded directly to the storage device or is imported from another source. Once imported they can be edited on a computer using any of a wide range of software. For a comprehensive list of available software, see List of video editing software, whereas Comparison of video editing software gives more detail of features and functionality. In non-linear editing, the original source files are not lost or modified during editing.

Professional editing software records the decisions of the editor in an edit decision list (EDL) which can be interchanged with other editing tools. Many generations and variations of the original source files can exist without needing to store many different copies, allowing for very flexible editing.

It also makes it easy to change cuts and undo previous decisions simply by editing the edit decision list (without having to have the actual film data duplicated). Loss of quality is also avoided due to not having to repeatedly re-encode the data when different effects are applied. Compared to the linear method of tape-to-tape editing, non-linear editing offers the flexibility of film editing, with random access and easy project organization. With the edit decision lists, the editor can work on low-resolution copies of the video. This makes it possible to edit both broadcast quality and high definition quality very quickly on normal PCs which do not have the power to do the full processing of the huge full-quality high-resolution data in real-time. The costs of editing systems have dropped such that non-linear editing tools are now within the reach of home users.

Some editing software can now be accessed free as web applications, some, like Cinelerra (focused on the professional market), can be downloaded free of charge, and some, like Microsoft's Windows Movie Maker or Apple Computer's iMovie, come included if you buy the appropriate operating system. A computer for non-linear editing of video will usually have a video capture card for capturing analog video or a FireWire connection for capturing digital video from a DV camera, as well as video editing software. Modern web based editing systems can take video directly from a camera phone over a GPRS or 3G mobile connection, and editing can take place through a web browser interface, so strictly speaking a computer for video editing does not require any installed hardware or software beyond a web browser and an internet connection.

Various editing tasks can then be performed on the imported video before it is exported to another medium, or MPEG encoded for transfer to a DVD.

HISTORY

The first truly non-linear editor, the CMX 600, was introduced in 1971 by CMX Systems, a joint venture between CBS and Memorex. It recorded & played back black-and-white analog video recorded in "skip-field" mode on modified disk pack drives the size of washing machines. These were commonly used to store data digitally on mainframe computers of the time. The 600 had a console with 2 monitors built in. The right monitor, which played the preview video, was used by the editor to make cuts and edit decisions using a light pen.

The editor selected from options which were superimposed as text over the preview video. The left monitor was used to display the edited video. A Digital PDP-11 computer served as a controller for the whole system. Because the video edited on the 600 was in black and white and in low-resolution "skip-field" mode, the 600 was suitable only for offline editing. Various approximations of non-linear editing systems were built in the '80s using computers coordinating multiple laser discs, or banks of VCRs. One example of these tape & disc-based systems was Lucasfilm's EditDroid, which used several laserdiscs of the same raw footage to simulate random-access editing (a compatible system was developed for sound post production by Lucasfilm called SoundDroid--one of the earliest digital audio workstations).

The term "nonlinear editing" or "non-linear editing" was formalized in 1991 with the publication of Michael Rubin's "Nonlinear: a handbook for electronic film and video editing" (Triad, 1991)--which popularized this terminology over other language common at the time, including "real time" editing, "random-access" or "RA" editing, "virtual" editing, "electronic film" editing, and so on. The handbook has remained in print since 1991, currently in its 4th edition (Triad, 2000).

Computer processing advanced sufficiently by the end of the '80s to enable true digital imagery, and has progressed today to provide this capability in personal desktop computers.

An example of computing power progressing to make non-linear editing possible was demonstrated in the first all-digital non-linear editing system to be released, the "Harry" effects compositing system manufactured by Quantel in 1985. Although it was more of a video effects system, it had some non-linear editing capabilities. Most importantly, it could record (and apply effects to) 80 seconds (due to hard disk space limitations) of broadcast-quality uncompressed digital video encoded in 8-

bit CCIR 601 format on its built-in hard disk array. Non-linear editing with computers as we know it today was first introduced by Editing Machines Corp. in 1989 with the EMC2 editor; a hard disk based non-linear off-line editing system, using half-screen resolution video at 15 frames per second. A couple of weeks later that same year, Avid introduced the Avid/1, the first in the line of their Media Composer systems. It was based on the Apple Macintosh computer platform (Macintosh II systems were used) with special hardware and software developed and installed by Avid. The Avid/1 was not the first system to introduce modern concepts in non-linear editing, however, such as timeline editing and clip bins--both of which were pioneered in Lucasfilm's EditDroid in the early 1980s.

The video quality of the Avid/1 (and later Media Composer systems from the late 80s) was somewhat low (about VHS quality), due to the use of a very early version of a Motion JPEG (M-JPEG) codec. But it was enough to be a very versatile system for offline editing, to revolutionize video and film editing, and quickly become the dominant NLE platform.

In October 1990 NewTek introduced Video Toaster, a hardware and software solution for the Commodore Amiga 2000 computer system, taking advantage of the video-friendly aspects of that system's hardware to deliver the product at an unusually low cost ($1499). The hardware component was a full-sized card which went into the Amiga's unique single video expansion slot rather than the standard bus slots, and therefore could not be used with the A500 and A1000 models. The card had several BNC connectors in the rear, which accepted four video input sources and provided two outputs (preview and program). This initial generation system was essentially a real-time four-channel video switcher.

For the second generation NewTek introduced the Video Toaster Flyer. The Flyer was a much more capable Non-linear editing system. In addition to just processing live video signals, the Flyer made use of hard drives to store video clips as well as audio and allow complex scripted playback. The Flyer was capable of simultaneous dual-channel playback, which allowed the Toaster's Video switcher to perform transitions and other effects on Video clips without the need for rendering.

The hardware component was again a card designed for the Amiga's Zorro 2 expansion slot, and was primarily designed by Charles Steinkuehler. The Flyer portion of the Video Toaster/ Flyer combination was a complete computer of its own, having its own Microprocessor and Embedded software, which was written by Marty Flickinger. Its hardware included three embedded SCSI controllers. Two of these SCSI buses were used to store video data, and the third to store audio. The hard drives were thus connected to the Flyer directly and used a proprietary filesystem layout, rather than being connected to the Amiga's buses and were available as regular devices using the included DOS driver. The Flyer used a proprietary Wavelet compression algorithm known as VTASC, which was well regarded at the time for offering better visual quality than comparable Motion JPEG based non-linear editing systems.

Until 1993, the Avid Media Composer could only be used for editing commercials or other small content projects, because the Apple Macintosh computers could access only 50 gigabytes of storage at one time. In 1992, this limitation was overcome by a group of industry experts lead by a Digital Video R&D team at the Disney Channel. By February 1993, this team had integrated a long form system which gave the Avid Media Composer Apple Macintosh access to over 7 terabytes of digital video data. With instant access to the shot footage of an entire movie, long form non-linear editing (Motion Picture Editing) was now possible. The system made its debut at the NAB conference in 1993, in the booths of the three primary sub-system manufacturers, Avid, SGI and Sony. Within a year, thousands of these systems replaced a century of 35mm film editing equipment in major motion picture studios and TV stations world wide, making Avid the undisputed leader in non-linear editing systems for over a decade.

Although M-JPEG became the standard codec for NLE during the early 1990s, it had drawbacks. Its high computational requirements ruled out software implementations, leading to the extra cost and complexity of hardware compression/playback cards. More importantly, the traditional tape workflow had involved editing off tape, often in a rented facility. When the editor left the edit suite he could take his confidential video tapes with him. But the M-JPEG data rate was too high for systems like Avid on the Mac and Lightworks on PC to store the video on removable storage, so these used fixed hard discs instead. The tape paradigm of keeping your (confidential) content with you was not possible with these fixed discs. Editing machines were often rented from facilities houses on a per-hour basis, and some productions chose to delete their material after each edit session, and then redigitize it again the next day, in order to guarantee the security of their content. In addition, each NLE system had storage limited by its hard disc capacity.

These issues were addressed by a small UK company, Eidos plc (which later became famous for its Tomb Raider video game series). Eidos chose the new ARM-based computers from the UK and implemented an editing system, launched in Europe in 1990 at the International Broadcasting Convention. Because it implemented its own compression software designed specifically for non-linear editing, the Eidos system had no requirement for JPEG hardware and was cheap to produce. The software could decode multiple video and audio streams at once for real-time effects at no extra cost. But most significantly, for the first time, it allowed effectively unlimited quantities of cheap removable storage. The Eidos Edit 1, Edit 2, and later Optima systems allowed the editor to use any Eidos system, rather than being tied down to a particular one, and still keep his data secure. The Optima software editing system was closely tied to Acorn hardware, so when Acorn stopped manufacturing the Risc PC in the late 1990s, Eidos stopped selling the Optima system; by this time Eidos had become predominantly a games company.

In the early 1990s a small American company called Data Translation took what it knew about coding and decoding pictures for the US military and large corporate clients and threw $12m into developing a desktop editor which would use its proprietary compression algorithms and off-the-shelf parts.

Their aim was to 'democratize' the desktop-and take some of Avid's market. In August 1993 Media 100 entered the market and thousands of would-be editors had a low-cost, high-quality platform to use. Inspired by the success of Media 100, members of the Premiere development team left Adobe to start a project called "Keygrip" for Macromedia. Difficulty raising support and money for development lead the team to take their non-linear editor to NAB. After various companies made offers, Keygrip was purchased by Apple as Steve Jobs wanted a product to compete with Adobe Premiere in the desktop video market. At around the same time, Avid-now with Windows versions of its editing software-was considering abandoning the Macintosh platform. Apple released Final Cut Pro in 1999, and despite not being taken seriously at first by professionals, it has evolved into a serious competitor to Avid.

Another leap came in the late 1990s with the launch of DV-based video formats for consumer and professional use. With DV came IEEE 1394 (FireWire/iLink), a simple and inexpensive way of getting video into and out of computers. The video no longer had to be converted from an analog signal to digital data-it was recorded as digital to start with-and FireWire offered a straightforward way of transferring that data without the need for additional hardware or compression. With this innovation, editing become a more realistic proposition for standard computers with software-only packages. It enabled real desktop editing producing high-quality results at a fraction of the cost of other systems.

More recently the introduction of highly compressed HD formats such as HDV has continued this trend, making it possible to edit HD material on a standard computer running a software-only editing application.

Avid is still considered the industry standard, with the majority of major feature films, television programs, and commercials created with its NLE systems. Avid products were used in the creation of every film nominated in the Best Picture, Directing, Film Editing, Sound Editing, Sound Mixing, Visual Effects, and Animated Feature categories of the 2005 Academy

Awards. Avid systems were also the overwhelming NLE choice of the 2004-2005 Primetime Emmy Award nominees, being used on more than 50 shows in eleven major categories. Final Cut Pro continues to develop a strong following, and the software received an Technology & Engineering Emmy Award in 2002.

Avid has held on to its market-leading position, but faces growing competition from other, cheaper software packages, notably Adobe Premiere in 1992, and later Final Cut Pro in 1999. These three competing products by Avid, Adobe, and Apple are the foremost NLEs, often referred to as the A-Team.

QUALITY

One of the primary concerns with non-linear editing has always been picture and sound quality. The need to compress and decompress video leads to some loss in quality. While improvements in compression techniques and disc storage capacity have reduced these concerns, they still exist. Most professional NLEs are able to edit uncompressed video with the appropriate hardware.

With the more recent adoption of DV formats, quality has become an issue again: DV's compression means that manipulation of the image can introduce significant degradation. However this can be partially avoided by rendering DV footage to a non-compressed intermediary format, thereby avoiding quality loss through recompression of the modified video images. Ultimately it depends on what changes are made to the image, simple edits should show no degradation, however effects that alter the colour, size or position of parts of the image will have a more negative effect. The range of user-friendly editing tools has given inexperienced people access to editing at high quality for the first time.

POINT OF VIEW SHOT

A point of view shot (also known as POV shot or a subjective camera) is a short film scene that shows what a character (the subject) is looking at (represented through the camera). It is usually established by being positioned between a shot of a character looking at something, and a shot showing the character's reaction (see shot reverse shot). The technique of POV is one of the foundations of film editing. A POV shot need not be the strict point-of-view of an actual single character in a film. Sometimes the point-of-view shot is taken over the shoulder of the character (third person), who remains visible on the screen.

Sometimes a POV shot is "shared" ("dual" or "triple"), i.e. it represents the joint POV of two (or more) characters. There is also the "nobody POV", where a shot is taken from the POV of a non-existent character. This often occurs when an actual POV shot is implied, but the character is removed. Sometimes the character is never present at all, despite a clear POV shot, such as the famous "God-POV" of birds descending from the sky in Alfred Hitchcock's film, The Birds. Another example of a POV shot is in the movie Doom, which contains a fairly long POV shot which resembles a heads-up display in a first-person shooter video game, with the viewer watching through a character who is venturing through hallways shooting and killing aliens.

A POV shot need not be established by strictly visual means. The manipulation of diegetic sounds can be used to emphasize a particular character's POV. It makes little sense to say that a shot is "inherently" POV; it is the editing of the POV shot within a sequence of shots that determines POV. Nor can the establishment of a POV shot be isolated from other elements of filmmaking-mise en scene, acting, camera placement, editing, and special effects can all contribute to the establishment of POV. With some POV shots when an animal is the chosen character, the shot will look distorted or black and white.

LEADING ACTOR POV

Subjective viewpoint is what it is called when the leading actor is the subject of the POV. The audience sees events through the leading actor's eyes, as if they were experiencing the events themselves. Some films are partially or totally shot using this technique,

One of the first films to use this technique was Rouben Mamoulian's Dr. Jekyll and Mr. Hyde. Everything is seen through Jekyll's eyes, as he leaves his house to go to the medical lecture.

Then, as he begins to speak, Jekyll is seen for the first time. When Jekyll first transforms himself into Hyde, Mamoulian once again uses the subjective camera to record his agonized reaction to the drug that he drinks. In the film noir Dark Passage, the protagonist has plastic surgery, and when his bandages are removed, he is revealed to be Humphrey Bogart. But until that moment, everything is seen through his eyes and the viewer has no idea what he looks like.

In another film noir, Lady in the Lake, directed by and starring Robert Montgomery as Raymond Chandler's detective Philip Marlowe, the entire film is shot from a subjective viewpoint, and Montgomery's face is seen only when he looks in a mirror. The film was not a critical or popular success.

LONG TAKE

A long take is an uninterrupted shot in a film which lasts much longer than the conventional editing pace either of the film itself or of films in general, usually lasting several minutes. It can be used for dramatic and narrative effect if done properly, and in moving shots is often accomplished through the use of a dolly or Steadicam.

Some films, such as Timecode and Russian Ark are filmed in one single take; others, such as Rope, Before Sunset, Elephant, and Irréversible are composed entirely from a series of long takes, while others, such as Goodfellas, Children of Men, Boogie Nights, Touch of Evil, The Player and Brazil, are well-known for a specific long take or two within otherwise more conventionally edited films. The term "long take" is used because it avoids the ambiguous meanings of "long shot", which can refer to the framing of a shot, and "long cut", which can refer to either a whole version of a film or the general editing pacing of the film. However, these two terms are sometimes used interchangeably with "long take".

SEQUENCE SHOT

A sequence shot involves both a long take and sophisticated camera movement; it is sometimes called by the French term plan-séquence. Jean Renoir's movie La Grande Illusion illustrates the use of the sequence shot effectively throughout the film. The use of the sequence shot allows for realistic and dramatically significant background and middle ground activity. Actors range about the set transacting their business while the camera shifts focus from one plane of depth to another and back again. Significant off-frame action is often followed with a moving camera, characteristically through a series of pans within a single continuous shot.

Talking Head

Talking head can refer to:

- In Sex Toys, the Talking Head™ Vibrator is a rabbit vibrator with MP3 playback and voice recording capability.
- In broadcasting, slang for interview footage shot in a locked down medium shot of the subject's head and shoulders. It also refers to an anchor, pundit, or other personality on news television.
- In music, the group Talking Heads gets its name from the second definition. The phrase can also refer to one of the individual members of the band. There is also a song by Motörhead called "Talking Head"
- In legend and mythology, a magical talking head giving advice is a recurring motif (see Mimir, Baphomet, Pope Silvester II).
- In computer graphics, a computer-generated character that talks. The topic is a subset of computer facial animation with focus on visual speech synthesis.
- Talking head, a film by Mamoru Oshii.

Wipe

Wipe has several meanings:

- Wipe (transition) is a gradual transition in film editing.
- In roleplaying games, especially MMORPGs, a wipe can refer to a situation where an entire group or party is killed by hostile units. It is sometimes also called Total Party Kill.
- File wiping is the process of thoroughly deleting a file on computers.
- In networking, wipe is short for a "server wipe," in which an administrator inadvertently removes a server from the network.
- Wiping, a process in which old television and radio recordings were erased or destroyed.
- Wiping is also a process of cleansing the anus after defecation.

AUDIO EDITING

Audio editing is the process of taking recorded sound and changing it directly on the recording medium. It was a new technology that developed in the middle part of the 20th century with the advent of magnetic tape recording. Originally, editing was done on reel-to-reel tape machines and edits were made with straight razors and special tape to connect pieces of tape that had been cut. Audio editors would listen to recorded tapes at low volumes, and then located specific sounds using a process called scrubbing, which is the slow rocking back and forth of the tape reels across the playback heads of the tape deck.

With the development of microcomputer technology, Sound Recordists were able to digitize their recordings and edit them as files on a computer's hard disk. The computer programs responsible for this task are known as digital audio editors. The earliest program to become widely used in this application was a wave editor called Sound Designer in the late 1980s and early 1990s. Sound Designer was created by a company called Digidesign who achieved early industry dominance. In recent years, however, that dominance has been challenged by a number of companies attempting to grab a portion of Digidesign's market share. In recent years, with the growing popularity of GNU/Linux, a number of Open Source software projects have sprung up in order to develop an open source audio editing program. This movement has been bolstered recently by the development of ALSA, and the Linux low latency kernel patch, which allow the GNU/Linux Operating System to achieve audio processing performance equal to that of commercial operating systems. The multi-platform package Audacity is currently the most fully-featured free software audio editor.

SOUND RECORDING AND REPRODUCTION

Sound recording and reproduction is the electrical or mechanical transcription and re-creation of sound waves, usually used for the voice or for music. The two main classes of sound recording technology are analog recording and digital recording.

The Cylinder Phonograph

The first practical sound recording and reproduction device was the mechanical cylinder phonograph, invented by Thomas Edison in 1877 and patented in 1878, and in some ways resembled the phonoautograph patented by Edouard-Leon Scott de Martinville in 1857. The invention soon spread across the globe and over the next two decades the commercial recording, distribution and sale of sound recordings became a growing new international industry, with the most popular titles selling millions of units by the early 1900s. The development of mass-production techniques enabled cylinder recordings to become a major new consumer item in industrial countries and the cylinder was the main consumer format from the late 1880s until around 1910.

The Disc

The next major technical development was the invention of the gramophone disc, generally credited to Emile Berliner and commercially introduced in the United States in 1889. Discs were easier to manufacture, transport and store, and they had the additional benefit of being louder (marginally) than cylinders, which by necessity, were single-sided. Sales of the Gramophone record overtook the cylinder ca. 1910, and by the end of World War I the disc had become the dominant commercial recording format. In various permutations, the audio disc format became the primary medium for consumer sound recordings until the end of the 20th century, and the double-sided 78rpm shellac disc was the standard consumer music format from the early 1910s to the late 1950s.

Although there was no universally accepted speed, and various companies offered discs that played at several different speeds, the major recording companies eventually settled on a de facto industry standard of 78 revolutions per minute, which gave the disc format its common nickname, the "seventy-eight". Discs were made of shellac or similar brittle plastic like materials, played with metal needles, and had a distinctly limited life.

ELECTRICAL RECORDING

Sound recording began as a mechanical process and remained so until the 1920s (with the exception of the 1898 Telegraphone) when a string of groundbreaking inventions in the field of electronics revolutionised sound recording and the young recording industry. These included sound transducers such as microphones and loudspeakers, and various electronic devices such as the mixing desk, designed for the amplification and modification of electrical sound signals.

After the Edison phonograph itself, arguably the most significant advances in sound recording were the electronic systems invented by two American scientists between 1900 and 1924.

In 1906 Lee De Forest invented the "Audion" triode vacuum-tube, electronic valve, which could greatly amplify weak electrical signals, (one early use was to amplify long distance telephone in 1915) which became the basis of all subsequent electrical sound systems until the invention of the transistor. The valve was quickly followed by the invention of the Regenerative circuit, Super-Regenerative circuit and the Superheterodyne receiver circuit, all of which were invented and patented by the young electronics genius Edwin Armstrong between 1914 and 1922. Armstrong's inventions made higher fidelity electrical sound recording and reproduction a practical reality, facilitating the development of the electronic amplifier and many other devices; after 1925 these systems had become standard in the recording and radio industry. Armstrong's groundbreaking inventions (including FM radio) also made possible the broadcasting of long-range, high-quality radio transmissions of voice and music. The importance of Armstong's Superheterodyne circuit cannot be under-estimated--it was the central component of almost all analog amplification and radio-frequency transmitter and receiver devices of the 20th century.

Beginning during World War One, experiments were undertaken in the United States and Great Britain to reproduce among other things, the sound of a Submarine (u-boat) for training purposes. The acoustical recordings of that time proved entirely unable to reproduce the sounds, and other methods were actively sought. Radio had developed independently to this point, and now Bell Laboritories sought a marriage of the two disparate technologies, greater than the two separately. The first experiments were not very promising, but by 1920 greater sound fidelity was achieved using the electrical system than had ever been realized acoustically. One early recording made without fanfare or announcement was the dedication of the Tomb of the Unknown Soldier at Arlington Cemetery. By early 1924 such dramatic progress had been made, that Bell Labs arranged a demonstration for the leading recording companies, Victor Talking Machine, and Columbia Phonograph Co's.

Columbia, always in financial straits, could not afford it, and Victor, essentially leaderless since the Mental collapse of Founder E. Johnson, left the demonstration without comment. English Columbia, by then a separate Company, got a hold of a test pressing from these sessions, and realized the immediate and urgent need to have the new system. Bell was only offering its method to United States Companies, and to circumvent this, Managing Director Louis Sterling of British Columbia, bought his once parent company, and signed up for electrical recording.

When Victor Talking Machine was apprised of the Columbia deal, they too quickly signed. Columbia made its first electrical recordings on February 25, 1925 with Victor following a few weeks later. The two then agreed privately to "be quiet" until November 1925, by which time enough electrical repretory would be available.

OTHER RECORDING FORMATS

This period also saw several other historic developments including the introduction of the first practical magnetic sound recording system, the magnetic wire recorder, which was based on the work of Danish inventor Valdemar Poulsen. Magnetic wire recorders were effective, but the sound quality was poor, so between the wars they were primarily used for voice recording and marketed as business dictating machines.

In the 1930s radio pioneer Guglielmo Marconi developed a system of magnetic sound recording using steel tape. This was the same material used to make razor blades, and not surprisingly the fearsome Marconi-Stille recorders were considered so dangerous that technicians had to operate them from another room for safety. Because of the high recording speeds required, they used enormous reels about one metre in diameter, and the thin tape frequently broke, sending jagged lengths of razor steel flying around the studio.

The other major invention in sound recording in this period was the optical sound-on-film system, also generally credited to Lee De Forest. Although famous early "Talkies" like The Jazz Singer used a sound-on-disc system, the film industry eventually adopted the optical sound-on-film system and it revolutionised the movie industry in the 1930s, ushering in the era of 'talking pictures'. Optical sound-on-film, based on the photoelectric cell, became the standard film audio system throughout the world until it was superseded in the 1960s.

Magnetic Tape

The other major inventions of this period were magnetic tape and the tape recorder(Telegraphone). Paper-based tape was first used but was soon superseded by polyester and acetate backing due to dust drop and hiss. Acetate was more brittle than polyester and snapped easily. This technology, the basis for almost all commercial recording from the 1950s to the 1980s, was invented by German audio engineers in the 1930s, who also discovered the technique of AC biasing, which dramatically improved the frequency response of tape recordings. Tape recording was perfected just after the war by American audio engineer John T. Mullin, whose pioneering recorders were based on captured German recorders, and the Ampex company produced the first commercially available tape recorders in the late 1940s.

Magnetic tape brought about sweeping changes in both radio and the recording industry. Sound could be recorded, erased and re-recorded on the same tape many times, sounds could be duplicated from tape to tape with only minor loss of quality, and recordings could now be very precisely edited by physically cutting the tape and rejoining it.

Within a few years of the introduction of the first commercial tape recorder, the Ampex 200 model, launched in 1948, American musician-inventor Les Paul had invented the first multitrack tape recorder, bringing about another technical revolution in the recording industry. Tape made possible the first sound recordings totally created by electronic means, opening the way for the bold sonic experiments of the Musique Concrète school and avant garde composers like Karlheinz Stockhausen, which in turn led to the innovative pop music recordings of artists such as Frank Zappa, The Beatles and The Beach Boys.

Tape enabled the radio industry for the first time to pre-record many sections of program content such as advertising, which formerly had to be presented live, and it also enabled the creation and duplication of complex, high-fidelity, long-duration recordings of entire programs. It also, for the first time, allowed broadcasters, regulators and other interested parties to undertake comprehensive logging of radio broadcasts. Innovations like multitracking and tape echo enabled radio programs and advertisements to be pre-produced to a level of complexity and sophistication that was previously unattainable and tape also led to significant changes to the pacing of program content, thanks to the introduction of the endless-loop tape cartridge.

The vinyl microgroove record was introduced in the late 1940s, and the two main vinyl formats--the 7-inch single turning at 45 rpm and the 12-inch LP (long-playing) record turning at 33? rpm--had totally replaced the 78 rpm shellac disc by the end of the 1950s. Vinyl offered improved performance, both in stamping and in playback, and came to be generally played with polished diamond styli, and when played properly (precise tracking weight, etc.) offered longer life. Vinyl records were, over-optimistically, advertised as "unbreakable". They were not, but were much less brittle and breakable than shellac. Nearly all were tinted black, but some were coloured, as red, swirled, translucent, etc.

Stereo and Hi-fi

Magnetic tape also enabled the development of the first practical commercial sound systems that could record and reproduce high-fidelity stereophonic sound. Experiments with stereo dated back to the 1880s and during the 1930s and 1940s there were many attempts to record in stereo using discs, but these were hampered by problems with synchronization.

The first major breakthrough in practical stereo sound was made by Bell Laboratories, who in 1937 demonstrated a practical system of two-channel stereo, using dual optical sound tracks on film. Major movie studios quickly developed three-track and four-track sound systems, and the first stereo sound recording in a commercial film was made by Judy Garland for the MGM movie Listen, Darling in 1938. The first commercially-released movie with a full stereo soundtrack was Walt Disney's Fantasia, released in 1940.

German audio engineers working on magnetic tape are reported to have developed stereo recording by 1943, but it was not until the introduction of the first commercial two-track tape recorders by Ampex in the late 1940s that stereo tape recording became commercially feasible. However, despite the availability of multitrack tape, stereo did not become the standard system for commercial music recording for some years and it remained a specialist market during the 1950s. This changed after the late 1957 introduction of the "Westrex stereo phonograph disc".

Most pop singles were mixed into monophonic sound until the mid 1960s, it was common for major pop releases to be issued in both mono and stereo until the early 1970s. Many Sixties pop albums now available only in stereo were originally intended to be released only in mono, and the so-called "stereo" version of these albums were created by simply separating the two tracks of the master tape. In the mid Sixties, as stereo became more popular, many mono recordings (such as The Beach Boys' Pet Sounds) were remastered using the so-called "fake stereo" method, which spread the sound across the stereo field by directing higher-frequency sound into one channel and lower-frequency sounds into the other.

The Fifties and Beyond

Magnetic tape transformed the recording industry, and by the late-1950s the vast majority of commercial recordings were being mastered on tape. The electronics revolution that followed the invention of the transistor brought other radical changes, the most important of which was the introduction of the world first "personal music device", the miniaturized transistor radio, which became a major consumer luxury item in the 1960s, transforming radio broadcasting from a static group experience into a mobile, personal listening activity. The first multitrack recording made using magnetic tape was "How High the Moon" by Les Paul, on which Paul played eight overdubbed guitar tracks. In the 1960s Brian Wilson of The Beach Boys, Frank Zappa and The Beatles (with producer George Martin) were among the first popular artists to explore the possibilities of multitrack techniques and effects on their landmark albums Pet Sounds, Freak Out! and Sgt. Pepper's Lonely Hearts Club Band.

The next important innovation was the compact cassette, introduced by the Philips electronics company in 1964. The cassette became a major consumer audio format and advances in microelectronics eventually led to the development of the Sony Walkman, introduced in the 1970s, which gave a major boost to the mass distribution of music recordings. Cassettes became the first successful consumer recording/re-recording medium as opposed to the gramophone record, which was a pre-recorded playback medium.

A key advance in audio fidelity came with the Dolby A noise reduction system, invented by Ray Dolby and introduced in 1966. Dolby's noise reduction system, which greatly improved the sound of cassette tape recordings, also found wide application in the recording and film industries. Dolby A was crucial to the popularisation and commercial success of the compact cassette as a domestic recording and playback medium, and became a part of the booming "hi-fi" market of the 1970s and beyond.

The multitrack audio cartridge was in wide use in the radio industry, from the late 1950s to the 1980s, but in the 1960s the pre-recorded 8-track cartridge was launched as a consumer audio format. Aimed particularly at the automotive market, they were the first practical, affordable car hi-fi systems, and they offered superior sound quality to the compact cassette. However the smaller size and greater durability--augmented by the ability to create home-recorded music "compilations"--saw the cassette become the dominant consumer fórmat for portable audio devices in the 1970s and 1980s.

There had been experiments with multi-channel sound for many years--usually for special musical or cultural events--but the first commercial application of the concept came in the early 1970s with the introduction of Quadraphonic sound. This spin-off development from multitrack recording used four tracks (instead of the two used in stereo) and four speakers to create a 360-degree audio field around the listener. Following the release of the first consumer 4-channel hi-fi systems, a number of popular albums were released in the Quadraphonic format; among the best known are Mike Oldfield's Tubular Bells and

Pink Floyd's The Dark Side of the Moon. Quadraphonic sound was not a commercial success, and it eventually faded out in the late 1970s, although this early venture paved the way for the eventual introduction of domestic Surround Sound systems, which have gained enormous popularity since the introduction of the DVD.

The replacement of the thermionic valve(vacuum tube) by the smaller, cooler and less power-hungry transistor also accelerated the sale of consumer high-fidelity "hi-fi" sound systems from the 1960s onward. In the 1950s most record players were monophonic and relatively low fidelity in sound quality, and few consumers could afford high-quality stereophonic sound systems. In the 1960s American manufacturers introduced a new generation of "modular" hi-fi components--turntables, integrated amplifiers, tape recorders and other ancillary equipment (like the graphic equaliser), which could be connected together to create a complete home sound system. These developments were rapidly taken up by the Japanese electronics companies, which soon flooded the world market with relatively cheap, high-quality components. By the 1980s, corporations like Sony had become world leaders in the music recording and playback industry.

Digital Recording

The invention of digital sound recording and the compact disc in 1983 brought significant improvements in the durability of consumer recordings. The CD initiated another massive wave of change in the consumer music industry, with vinyl records effectively relegated to a small niche market by the mid-1990s.

The most recent and revolutionary developments have been in digital recording, with the invention of purely electronic consumer recording formats such as the WAV digital music file and the compressed file type, the MP3. This generated a new type of portable solid-state computerised digital audio player, the MP3 player. Another invention, by Sony, was the minidisc player, using ATRAC compression on small, cheap, re-writeable discs. This was in vogue in the 1990s, and is still popular, especially in a newer, longer playing and higher fidelity version. New technologies such as Super Audio CD, DVD-A, Blu ray Disc and HD DVD continue to set very high standard in evolution of digital audio storage. This technology spreads across various associated fields, from hi-fi to professional audio, internet radio and podcasting.

Technological developments in recording and editing have transformed the record, movie and television industries in recent decades. Audio editing became practicable with the invention of magnetic tape recording, but the use of computers has made editing operations faster and easier to execute, and the use of hard-drives for storage has made recording cheaper. We now divide the process of making a recording into tracking, mixing and mastering. Multitrack recording makes it possible to capture sound from several microphones, or from different 'takes' to tape or disc with maximum headroom and quality, allowing maximum flexibility in the mixing and mastering stages for editing, level balancing, compressing and limiting, and the addition of effects such as reverberation, equalisation, flanging and many more.

In the 1920s, the first talkies came out, featuring the new sound-on-film technology which used photoelectric cells to record and reproduce sound signals that were optically recorded directly onto the movie film. The advent of talkies, spearheaded by The Jazz Singer in 1927, saw the rapid demise of live cinema musicians and orchestras, which were replaced with pre-recorded soundtracks, causing the loss of many jobs. The American Federation of Musicians took out ads in newspapers, protesting the replacement of real musicians with mechanical playing devices, especially in theatres.

Voice to Note

Voice-to-note refers to the capability of personal computers to be able to recognize notes that are sung, hummed, or whistled into a microphone. The pitch and duration of the notes are then calculated and converted into MIDI music files.

6

A New Structure of News Editing

INTRODUCTION

Ideally a computational approach could assist in the human-intensive tasks associated with selecting and presenting timely, relevant information, i.e., news editing. At present this goal is difficult to achieve because of the paucity of effective machine-understanding systems for news. A structure for news that affords a fluid interchange between human and machine-derived expertise is a step toward improving both the efficiency and utility of on-line news. This paper examines a system that employs richer representations of texts within a corpus of news. These representations are composed by a collection of experts who examine news articles in the database, looking at both the text itself and the annotations placed by other experts. These experts employ a variety of methods ranging from statistical examination to natural-language parsing to query expansion through specific-purpose knowledge bases. The system provides a structure for the sharing of knowledge with human editors and the development of a class of applications that make use of article augmentation.

> *A news editor fine-tunes and prioritizes information based on criteria that include timeliness, importance, and relevance to the audience.* —*Jack Driscoll*

News editing is an exacting problem. Many factors contribute to making the selection and presentation of timely, relevant information a task as daunting as it is necessary. People want to be kept informed of events and occurrences that affect them, but at the same time they do not want to wade through the tens of thousands of news articles available every day to find what they need. And it is not just a matter of deciding which articles may be of interest.

How much is enough and how much is too much is a delicate balance to strike. One Elián Gonzales article a week might be interesting-fifty might not be. A person's source of news needs to express what is new rather than just what has happened. However, if someone has relatives in Pakistan, then every article about a revolution that occurs there may be of interest. The amount of time that the average person can spend on the news each day is more or less fixed. Consequently, many personal and situational interests compete for this time.

Decisions must be made as to what to present, in what order, and in what way. It requires understanding on the editor's part of not only what a given article is about, but also what the context is, or how the particular article relates to other articles that are available, as well as how it relates to the reader. The task of an editor, then, is to examine the news for a given day and try to find the meaning in it-that is, not only to understand the article, but also to understand its context. What is new or timely? What is of importance? What is of high general interest? What does the reader need to know about? What would the reader like to know about? What informs, educates, guides, or entertains? How many articles on a topic are appropriate, and, if the answer is not "all of them," then what should be kept and what discarded?

ADVANTAGES OF A HUMAN EDITOR

When considering an on-line newspaper as a primary news source, it makes sense to consider what editors do, what issues they face, and what their strengths are, as well as their weaknesses.

"In today's Journal of the American Medical Association... " There is a need to integrate multiple sources of news, since not all articles of interest come from the same source. In fact, unless someone's interests are exactly aligned with the focus of a particular publication, the reader probably will need to consult several sources of information each day to find what he or she needs. For example, the televised weather report in the morning, the newspaper on the bus ride to work, the radio for the outcome of the afternoon baseball game, and an on-line news service for up-to-date stock information: each of these sources presents information in a different format and, if a unified presentation is to be made, all need to be understood and considered together.

Editors do not work in isolation. They receive feedback from the community they serve in a number of ways: direct letters, telephone calls, or electronic mail to the editor; comments from their colleagues; focus and market surveys; and simple hard numbers like newsstand sales when a particular headline is run. This feedback allows the editor to better serve the needs of the community. Note that none of this feedback is actively solicited from the readership. Rather, these are observations that are made passively or as a result of user-initiated comments. There is something to be said for assuming that, if there are no complaints, then something is going right and need not be modified.

On your doorstep. One other aspect of the "real world" editorial process is that there is no waiting. When one reaches for the newspaper there is no delay. The fact that a newspaper may represent a 24-hour production cycle, thousands of person-hours of preparation, and a variety of news sources is inconsequential. When you want the news, there it is. This is especially important when contemplating on-line editorial approaches that require significant processing time. It may seem obvious, but the right time to think about the news is not the first time someone asks for a copy of the newspaper.

The On-Line Times? When we type a query into a search engine, we are making a request that such an engine consider a large number of possible articles and select and present some of those articles for our consideration. This is nothing more nor less than an editorial process. Many search engines return results that would be considered poorly edited. Sometimes they return nothing, providing no explanation of how the request was too restrictive. Other times they return far too many results, swamping the user with a plethora of information to wade through and decide on. Neither of these alternatives is particularly attractive to an end user. Little wonder then that most individuals would be unwilling to accept an on-line computer-generated newspaper when they have the opportunity to read a traditional one, where the selection is done by human editors.

I do not know what I want! Defining searches is a difficult task. It is even more difficult when trying to define what the search should be about. One of the reasons a reader may subscribe to a newspaper is that he or she trusts the editors will provide needed information. An on-line newspaper should provide users with some reasonable starting point, even if they themselves do not know what that is.

I want what he has! One role a newspaper fills is that of providing a sense of community and shared world view. The conversation that starts with "Did you see the front page of the newspaper?" is absent in a world where each newspaper is custom-made for an individual. The common context provided by a shared information source is important, for without it, individuals lack a common reference point with which to engage in discussion.

News as a product/news as a service. Ideally a computational approach could alleviate the human-intensive tasks associated with news editing. At present this goal is difficult to achieve because of the paucity of effective machine-understanding systems for news. A structure for news that affords a fluid interchange between human and machine-derived expertise is a step toward improving both the efficiency and the utility of on-line news. This structure reflects a reorganizing of on-line news distribution around both a production model and a services model. The on-line news product is a reflection of the traditional paper offering.

On-line services include:

(1) identifying, contrasting, and relating;

(2) analyzing, positioning, and verifying;

(3) localizing, augmenting, and remembering;

(4) contextualizing, connecting, and associating;

(5) expressing, storytelling, and transcoding;

(6) learning, interacting, and constructing; and

(7) marketing, observing, and transacting.

Each of these services contributes to the whole but also has value when offered as a component service. In a distributed but structured architecture, each of these services can be developed and deployed with relative autonomy.

THE ZWRAP SYSTEM

This chapter examines an approach by which a computer system, ZWrap, can develop rich structure for a corpus of news. Beyond developing an understanding of each news item, the system attempts to find context for each article, examining how it fits into the larger picture of the news. (In this paper, we consider the understanding of an article to be the result of examining the article and identifying features within it.

These features may be as simple as the individual words that appear or as complex as the actors and actions they perform in an article or even the bias with which a particular article was written.

"Context" refers to how features relate to each other, especially the way in which they tend to occur in a large number of articles.

This includes, for example, both the co-occurrence of features and their associations and implications.) The ZWrap system considers what technologies are needed to keep this context current in the face of a changing external world. It examines ways in which users who are not information retrieval experts can share their understanding with the system and act as a source of common sense for it.

Background

Ideally, the ZWrap system should be easy to assemble, easy to maintain, and easy to improve. It should perform the task of developing and discovering meaning in a reasonably efficient and interesting manner. More specifically, it should assist, simplify, and automate the types of editorial decisions that a human editor must face and resolve, in a way that is amenable for use in an on-line news environment.

The news editing task embodies information retrieval, in that searching for relevant articles within a corpus is part of the problem being addressed. But a news editing system must span multiple corpora and multiple domains; it must accommodate feedback from multiple sources; it must be capable of continuous updating; it must facilitate the dynamic redefinition of relevance while maintaining high precision and recall; it must support automatic query generation; and it must be the host for a shared context across a varied audience.

The ZWrap approach to news editing is to provide a structure for interoperation of multiple components rather than attempt to design an algorithm that is optimized along the many constraints of the problem. Components were chosen with little regard to employing the best practice within a particular subfield. Those components (e.g., a classifier or a router) that are found most useful are candidates for optimization.

While the field of information retrieval is well populated, the space of projects similar to the ZWrap system is rather sparse. Examples include Apple Computer's Sherlock** (with its "pluggable" search and selection algorithms), IBM's Lotus Notes** (with its loadable experts and integration framework), the UNIX** shell (that allows many processes to interoperate through pipes), the World Wide Web (if viewed as a single system and when considering CGI [common gateway interface] programs as plug-ins), integrated development environments (such as Metrowerks' Code Warrior**), the Emacs editor (in its guise as an electronic mail reader, spell checker, development environment, document authoring tool, and overall "kitchen sink"), and the Media Bank (with its distributed architecture and community of viewers). All of these approaches seek to perform a higher-level task by marshaling a number of conceptually lower-level operations. The ZWrap system might best be described as an attempt to serve the function of information retrieval within the domain of exploring, selecting, and presenting news.

Paper Organization

In this chapter, we address the task of news selection for an on-line environment. Our approach is to create a symbiotic relationship between computer and human editors and human consumers. .Ve accomplish this within the framework of a blackboard structure that manages the simultaneous execution of multiple experts. We conclude with a discussion of the efficiencies gained by this approach, in particular, the advantages of article selection through use of precognition, the use of modular, domain-specific experts, and an augmented presentation.

In the following sections, these topics are discussed:

(1) blackboard systems and the overall architecture,

(2) data representation and management,

(3) networking, distribution, and parallel computation,

(4) searching and sorting in an augmented database,

(5) statistical examinations,

(6) user interface and presentation,

(7) implementation, and

(8) evaluation and conclusion.

Blackboard Systems

Blackboard systems are an old idea, proposed by Newell in 1962. Roughly speaking, a blackboard system is one that employs a collection of experts that independently look at a blackboard. There is one piece of chalk and when an expert has something to contribute to the understanding of a problem, the expert takes the chalk and writes the contribution on the board. Experts are generally not allowed to talk to each other; all communication is done via the blackboard. Each of the experts sitting in front of the blackboard is assumed to have a specialized area of knowledge, but may make use of observations written on the blackboard by other experts. Creating a piece of code to represent an expert is fairly simple. The expert needs to be able to read the blackboard, take the chalk, and write observations on the blackboard. Since all communication is done via the blackboard, no other interexpert protocols are necessary.

Since the experts do not interact with each other except via the blackboard, adding, removing, or changing an expert has minimal impact on the overall system (although, if one expert depends on the work of another, some complications can arise). This allows the development and improvement of experts to be an ongoing process. Since experts do not need to interact except through the blackboard they can all "think" about the problem simultaneously. This opens the possibility of parallel cognition processes. From a theoretical standpoint, this architecture allows for the development of a "society of agents," as suggested by Minsky, with a number of specialized experts contributing their observations about a problem in the hope of developing some kind of understanding about it. Each of these experts can evolve independently; new ones can be added at any time; and those that are found to be less useful can be dropped.

Despite all these benefits, blackboard systems have fallen into disrepute. Perhaps the biggest difficulty with this architecture is its problems with efficiency. It has been observed that in general, most experts wait on the actions of another expert. If Expert B needs to look at Expert A's observations, then until Expert A makes those observations, Expert B can do nothing but wait. The necessity of a single piece of chalk with atomic locking makes writing to the blackboard somewhat expensive: when more than one expert has something to say there is conflict over the chalk; and when one expert writes with the chalk, the other experts are obligated to reconsider the blackboard in light of whatever is written. It has been observed that blackboard systems perform less efficiently than many alternative architectures, e.g., a pipeline.

Why is efficiency such an issue, given that a blackboard system can help to reduce development time, sometimes dramatically? Blackboards have been applied to problems such as speech processing, sonar contact analysis, and fighter aircraft intercept evaluation, all cases where there is a single or small number of problems being considered and there is an element of time pressure (necessitating efficient processing). These applications highlight both the strengths and weaknesses of blackboard systems.

Blackboards and News

Developing understanding of news is a problem that shares many elements with the traditional blackboard problems-it is a complex problem where it makes sense for many experts to work on several different approaches simultaneously. There are, however, a number of key differences that make news an appropriate environment for using blackboards. In the traditional blackboard case, there is a single (or perhaps a small number) of problems being considered, while in news applications, on the order of 10000 articles arrive daily, thus the number of "problems" is quite large; and unlike the case where a single problem might be relevant for only a matter of minutes or hours, news articles often retain their relevance for days or weeks.

In the context of news, the blackboard architecture can be modified. Instead of several dozen experts standing around a single blackboard, one can instead imagine a room with thousands of blackboards, one for each article. Several dozen experts wander around the room, making observations on each of the problems in process. If a blackboard has an expert standing in front of it, then another expert can just pass it by, coming back to it later when it is free. If each expert has a different colour chalk, then those experts that depend on the work of others can just visit blackboards that already have the appropriate coloured marks on them. In short, most of the problems with the original blackboard architecture either do not arise or can be avoided in the case of news systems. The blackboard architecture is amenable to the news-as-a-service model described earlier. Experts can be designed to process the news by contrasting and relating article features and by identifying associations between articles.

Implementation

The ZWrap system uses a blackboard architecture for developing its in-frame representation of articles. Experts watch a variety of news sources. Whenever an article arrives, a new blackboard is created, the article is posted, and the blackboard is then visited by a number of experts.

In the ZWrap system, one group of experts examines the articles for purely structural elements. These experts extract the headline, the dateline, the author, the body text, the time the article was posted, etc., and place this information on the blackboard, mitigating the problem that different news sources provide news utilizing different structures. These experts ensure that all articles will have more or less the same article elements broken out (e.g., body, headline, date, etc.) and tagged for later processing by other experts.

A second group of experts performs information extraction, parsing, and evaluation on the uniform article elements extracted above. These experts perform tasks such as proper-noun identification, word stemming, date and time spotting, parsing to find references to places, spotting country names, etc. These derived features are written back onto the blackboard representing the article.

A third group of experts uses the derived features to perform high-level augmentation. For example, the person spotter looks at the list of proper nouns and decides (through a simple heuristic) which proper nouns are the names of persons. The geography expert uses a list of rules applied to the country feature to decide which regions and continents are being discussed in an article. Also included in this group are experts that use these derived features to produce more features. For example, the Media Lab expert looks at the people feature to search for the names of Media Laboratory professors. It also looks for "MIT Media Lab" in the proper noun feature.

Ultimately, this parade of experts takes an article as an initial, monolithic piece of text and transforms it into a richly annotated structure of identified high-level features.

These features are used for three different purposes:

(1) search engines use them for selecting articles;

(2) clustering and data-mining techniques use them for finding patterns and trends in the articles; and

(3) display engines use them for presenting articles to the user in context.

About Dependency

One design issue with blackboard-type systems is information-dependency management. The person expert can do no work until the proper-noun expert has visited the article. This leads to inefficiency if the person expert keeps checking blackboards to see if they have been processed. The ZWrap system supports a simple directed, acyclical graph (DAG) of expert dependency. It does so by maintaining a list (called a dependency scratch space) of which articles have been visited by which nodes in the DAG. A "downstream" node can examine this list to identify which articles have been visited by every expert it depends on.

If a key/value pair that some other key depends on changes, how does the system know to go back and address the resulting inconsistency? In the current implementation of the ZWrap system, inconsistencies are not repaired. This limitation is being addressed in follow-on work.

Data Representation

The use of a blackboard system simplifies the question of data representation, since the only well-defined representation needed is that of the blackboard. This representation needs to support several actions efficiently: the reading of the contents of a particular blackboard, the addition of a note or notes to a given blackboard, and the search of all blackboards for particular notes or types of notes. The requirements of both flexibility and speed of access argue for the use of frames as the data storage medium. A frame is a collection of key/value pairs, known as terminals, that describe a particular object or concept (in this case, a news article).

Frames have a number of advantages, not the least of which is their flexibility. New key/value pairs can be liberally added and clients looking for a particular datum can ignore those terminals that they do not understand or need. The ability for experts to ignore what they do not understand or need in a frame is important, since it allows the addition of arbitrary experts without the need to modify any other experts in the system.

A feature borrowed from FramerD, a persistent database of frames (framestore) developed at the Media Laboratory, is the use of a universally unique identification number (called an object ID or OID) for each frame. This 64-bit number allows the frame to be referred to in a succinct, unambiguous manner. Since OIDs are never recycled, they can be used as pointers to articles, and it is assured that the articles being pointed to will never change.

In the blackboard context, each blackboard is represented by a frame. Experts examine the frame to see what observations have been made and make their own observations by adding terminal nodes to the frame. A mechanism exists (inherited from FramerD) to allow a blackboard to be locked while an expert is looking at it. When an article enters the system, a frame is allocated and the article is entered as the only terminal, under the key Text. As experts examine the frame in turn, they add terminals, with successive terminals containing increasingly higher-level information about the article.

Network Protocol

Given that the ZWrap system uses a framestore to represent its blackboards, the question arises as to how the experts will communicate with the framestore to read the blackboards and write their annotations. There are characteristics this communication system should have-some implied by the previously made assumptions and others that simply enhance usability:

- *Atomic Framestore Access*: Experts must be able to "grab the chalk" while they are writing on the blackboard.
- *Efficient Framestore Access*: In many cases, the time taken for framestore access will not be the bottleneck for programs augmenting the articles. Because experts tend to be computationally expensive, extremely fast access is probably unnecessary.
- *Lightweight Framestore Access*: The primary concern of someone coding an expert should not be how that expert gets its data. Also, the computation and memory associated with access should be minimal.
- *Concurrent Framestore Access*: The blackboard system gains much of its performance through allowing many experts to access the framestore simultaneously. The extension to multiple blackboards suggests that there be a mechanism for multiple experts to work on different blackboards in the store at the same time.

Taken as a group, these characteristics suggest that the central framestore repository be provided as a service. An expert connecting to the service expects the service provider to worry about issues of concurrent access. This lightens the load on experts and those who author them.

Given the prevalence of network-computing environments, it makes sense to consider that such a service might be provided over a network connection. A network approach also allows computationally intensive experts to run on different computers, allowing for load distribution and for more efficient use of available resources. A side benefit of a network solution is that any program that can obtain a network connection and use the framestore protocol can operate as an expert. Thus, experts can be written in whatever language is appropriate for the processing they perform and run on whatever hardware or operating system is best for their execution.

All that is needed to utilize a networked framestore server is a protocol by which clients can read from, write to, and lock frames. Such a protocol should be:

- *Easy to Implement*: Encoding messages to go over the network and decoding the response should be simple for the programmer. The easier it is to implement an expert, the more likely it is that many experts will be developed.
- *Low Computational Overhead*: The computational load on the expert should be biased toward the task at hand, not toward frame access.
- *Low Bandwidth*: The percentage of bandwidth dedicated to the protocol should be low. Ideally using this protocol will not slow the expert down.
- *Extensibility*: New commands and structures should be easy to add, without the need to rewrite existing experts.
- *Expressiveness*: It is key that experts be able to write nearly any kind of observation into the framestore. The protocol should support arbitrary nesting and combination and extensions of the basic data set.
- *Human Readability*: While not strictly necessary, the existence of a text representation is extremely useful. It facilitates debugging and documenting the protocols.
- *Robustness*: A protocol that works well in light of the peculiarities of packet transport, dropouts, concurrent connections, etc., is important.

A protocol meeting almost all of these criteria existed at the inception of the ZWrap system in the form of Dtypes. Dtypes comprise a simple network protocol for exchanging LISP-like objects. They were designed for situations where there is routine use of data structures with complex interconnections. They include basic elements such as numbers and text arrays, as well as extensions to special-purpose data types. Dtypes were originally developed by Abramson, later extended by Dienes, and subsequently formalized and extended by Haase and Gruhl. The resulting protocol meets all of the above criteria and serves as the underlying communication system for ZWrap. The Dtypes library has been implemented under IBM AIX (Advanced Interactive Executive), DEC Ultrix, Sun Solaris, Linux, NeXT Operating System, Apple Macintosh Operating System, and Microsoft's Windows NT, Windows 95, and Windows 98. Versions exist in the Java language, Perl, C, C++, Scheme, and LISP.

The impact of Dtypes on the ZWrap system is subtle but important. It serves as the lingua franca for the various components of the system, allowing them to communicate with each other in an unprescribed manner. This results in components of the system being used in ways that were not originally intended. (For example, in the MyZWrap application, a weighted search is implemented as a series of calls to an index server.)

There are other protocols that would allow this kind of interaction as well (e.g., XML [Extensible Markup Language]). What is important is not that the communication protocol be Dtypes per se, but that it support arbitrary and nonpremeditated interactions.

Expert Distribution

In the ZWrap system, experts can run on any machine that supports the Dtypes protocol, allowing them to be implemented in the environment most practical for the tasks they will undertake.

The use of the Dtypes protocol facilitates the types of distributed, concurrent interactions needed to implement blackboard systems. This approach allows the development of experts in an incremental manner without incurring a performance penalty.

The ability to run experts on multiple midrange commercial computers allows the use of many computationally expensive experts without the need to resort to expensive special-purpose, supercomputing solutions.

The distribution of experts over a network allows the simultaneous pursuit of very different approaches to representation, increasing the chance that the system will be able to develop interesting and relevant observations for every article.

SEARCHING IN AUGMENTED FRAMESTORES

The approach to searching used in the ZWrap system has an advantage over more traditional approaches in that a host of augmentations are available to help direct the search. In this section, the adaptation of traditional approaches to database searching in the ZWrap environment is discussed.

Boolean searches. Boolean searches are a baseline for many search engines (e.g., AltaVista**, Lexis-Nexis**, Gopher, etc.). Searches of this type examine articles to evaluate a Boolean expression describing the presence of certain words. For example, the Boolean expression ("Bill" OR "Hillary") AND "Clinton"

seeks articles that mention the word Bill or the word Hillary and also mention the word Clinton. The ZWrap system implements this type of search using the operators AND, OR, and NAND. However, the ZWrap system operates on terminals when searching, not words. Since the set of proper nouns is written back into the frame, the above search (in the ZWrap system) is implemented as ((PROPER_NOUN."Bill_Clinton") OR (PROPER_NOUN."Hillary_Clinton"))

But proper noun is not the only feature in the frame of an article. As an example, consider what can be done with the output of three experts. One of the ZWrap experts spots types of food and notes the occurrence under the "food" terminal. A number of experts are inherited from FishWrap (an on-line news system that is a precursor to the ZWrap system), one of which spots morbid news stories, e.g., articles where death, serious injury, or grievous harm occur. A geography expert places information on continents mentioned implicitly in an article into the frames.

These can be used together as ((FOOD."beer") OR (FOOD."wine")) AND (FISHWRAP_TOPIC."morbid") AND (CONTINENT."Europe") which finds (mostly) articles about drunken driving in Europe. With a fairly detailed knowledge of what experts are in the system and some clever authoring of search expressions, reasonably complex concepts can be expressed with just Boolean operations on article features.

There are two problems with this approach. First, there is a considerable onus on the user to understand the details of the system, such as what features are being spotted and what their typical values are. Second, there is no concept of how well an article fits a particular topic. It either matches the search expression or it does not. There is very little that can be passed along, for example, to the display engine to help it decide how the articles should be presented.

Weighted searches. A weighted search, such as that used by AltaVista, introduces the concept of "must" (by prepending a "+" to a search term) and "must not" (by prepending a ""), allowing a simple notion of query weighting. Some features are designated more important than others but once all of the "must" conditions have been met, other terms contribute to the fitness of an article for selection. For example +Bill Hillary+ClintonChelsea

finds articles that contain the words "Bill" and "Clinton" but do not contain the word "Chelsea." From this set, articles that also mention "Hillary" are considered a better match than those that do not. Search results are sorted by their ranking. Of course, as before, in the ZWrap system the search terms can be any of the derived features.

Activation/evidential Searches

The term "activation search" comes from imagining a database of all the terminals with connections to all of the articles that mention a particular feature. A search is performed by activating the stated concepts and selecting those articles that are in turn sufficiently activated through these connections.

The presence or absence of a feature contributes to or detracts from an article's score for selection, as shown in these examples (from explanations generated by ZWrap):

The presence of the PROPER_NOUN "Kosovo" strongly supports selection.

The presence of the STEMMED_WORD "Albanian" does support selection.

The presence of the PROPER_NOUN "NATO" may support selection.

The presence of the PROPER_NOUN "United Nations" may support selection.

To increase readability by the users, a fuzzy mapping to words is used instead of numeric weights, but this is an arbitrary assignment. A very large weighting (i.e., certainty) is used to allow selected features to be "stop" features; selection is prevented if they occur. Activation-style searches are fully weighted searches. The result of this type of search is a list of articles that can be ranked by their level of activation.

RELEVANCE FEEDBACK

The ease of construction from examples suggests that relevance feedback might be a useful approach for designing searches: the user performs an initial search to identify articles similar to the ones he or she is seeking; the system looks for similarities between these articles and uses this as search criteria; the user examines the results of this new search and identifies articles that seem most relevant. The user iterates through this process until articles of the sought-after class are found. Relevance-feedback searches need not be explicit. If the system can observe the user interactions and infer something about which articles were of interest, then this approach can be used to refine news channels without explicit formulation of rankings.

Multiple Algorithms

Ng has found that in some contexts a weighted average of the recommendations of several algorithms almost always performs better than a single algorithm for search tasks, i.e., weighing is better than picking. The ZWrap system is well suited to multiple-algorithm approaches.

News Channels

The ZWrap system borrows the concept of channels for news presentation from NewsPeek, PointCast, and MyExcite. All of the articles in a channel are part of a specific and hopefully well-defined topic. In general, articles are selected for a channel by searching. In the ZWrap system, any search performed by the user is a candidate for redefining as a channel. This allows a user to apply any search skills he or she might have toward automating the editing of his or her newspaper.

Experts

Searching need not be a one-time event. Once a means of finding a particular type of information is developed, it can be turned into a standing request for information (as a channel). From here, there is a clear evolution toward developing an expert. First, a simple query might be developed. Over time, that query might be refined. Commonalities between queries might be formalized into subqueries. If a subquery is sufficiently useful, then it becomes a candidate for being turned into an expert.

Statistics

The ZWrap system makes use of the relationships among frames through a variety of statistical examinations of the corpus, looking for patterns and trends that develop among high-level features.

Developing good searches by hand is effortful. This is compounded by the tendency for topics to "drift" over time. As explained in the previous section, the ZWrap system seeks to capture this work by allowing searches to be turned into news channels, where they can be used for an extended period of time. Statistics can augment search techniques by flagging unusual events, drawing attention to them for further consideration by experts, human editors, or the user.

In order to apply statistical and pattern-recognition techniques to the task of retrieving articles, some mapping is needed between the articles and a vector of features that represent the article. The common mapping is one that takes words that appear in the article and maps them to individual elements in the vector. These vectors are collected into a single matrix, known as a "word document matrix," that represents the corpus (or at least a training set).

When features carry information in addition to words, techniques that work well on word sets work even better on augmented frames. In the ZWrap system, by the time an article is to be examined statistically, additional features have been spotted, computed, or otherwise added to the frame, making it possible to use a "feature document matrix." It is this matrix that is used by experts to provide context for individual articles and to find associations and differences among multiple articles.

Statistical Techniques

Each article in the ZWrap system is represented as a vector of features, where ai is the feature vector for article i and ai(n) the nth entry of that vector.

The mapping of features to entry is arbitrary but fixed for the corpus. For reasons of efficiency, features with insufficient support may be dropped from this mapping (if a feature occurs only once it is not of much help in classification) and, likewise, overly common features may also be dropped (a feature is equally useless if it occurs all the time). For simplicity, the ZWrap system uses Boolean values to represent features. This means that feature vectors are filled with ones and zeros, representing the presence or absence of a feature in a given article.

CLUSTERING

One task that statistical methods perform well is clustering. There are many different clustering algorithms available, ranging from simple K-means to the more complicated simulated annealing. The goal of these algorithms is to take a large number of items and divide them into groups. They often require that the number of groups is fixed initially or modified by a heuristic during the analysis. Some of the algorithms are described here:

- *Simple a Priori Occurrence Expectation*: A priori occurrence is a simple but powerful statistical technique. It looks at a domain (e.g., a channel or the entire corpus) and develops a priori statistics on feature occurrence. For example, let be the normalized, average article in a channel. A 2 or cos(A o A) is then a measure of how "distant" a particular article is from what is typical for the channel. The set of As for all channels represent the typical or expected articles for those channels and a new article is compared to these stereotypical articles in order to decide which channel to place it in.
- *Relat d Articles*: It would be expected that articles covering the same topic would have similar features. Thus, a simple distance metric like cosine angle between the normalized feature vectors would give some sense of how related articles are. This nearest-neighbor analysis allows automatic identification of related articles. It also can be used to find near-duplicate articles, for related articles that are close, but not too close. This is especially true for news streams that tend to repeat stories with small changes from hour to hour. In these cases, just presenting the most recent article is probably sufficient.
- *Association-rule Data Mining*: The next step up from simple occurrence is co-occurrence, determining what features occur together frequently in the same article. Association-rule data mining seeks to find the associations between groups of features, for example that A B C, where A, B, and C are particular features in the corpus.
- *K-means*: An augmented framestore can be used to explain K-means clusters. K-means is run on a set of LSI (latent semantic indexing) dimensionality-reduced vectors generated from the stemmed-word document vectors through singular-value decomposition. The ZWrap system gives the user an indication of why a cluster has been created by revealing those high-level features that are in common among the articles within the cluster.

- *Presentation*: Clustering is used to decide what articles to present to a user. If several dozen articles are candidates for presentation within a particular topic, one approach is to cluster them and select the representative articles from each cluster for presentation. The user asks the system to select an article to indicate that he or she is interested in its associated cluster.
- *Cluster Management*: Most clustering algorithms operate on a fixed number of clusters. This is a difficult number to determine if there is no a priori reason to suspect how many clusters there are in a set. There are several heuristics that can be applied to determine when a cluster should be split (when there appear to be two or more strong subclusters within it) or when two clusters need to be joined (there is not much difference between them). These heuristics can also be used to examine when channels might warrant being split or joined, by examining the features of those articles they contain.
- *Dimensionality Reduction*: Dimensionality reductions (such as those achieved through LSI, PCA [principal-component-analysis], or SVD [singular-value-decomposition] techniques) seek to map a given feature space to a space of much lower dimensionality through projection, where as much as possible of the important information is preserved. The hope is that operations such as finding the nearest neighbor or clustering can be performed much more efficiently in vector space of lower dimensionality. Unfortunately, the vectors in the reduced-dimensionality space tend to be opaque to a user; thus dimensionality reduction is at odds with the design goal of sharing everything with the user. In the ZWrap system, dimensionality reduction needs to be used carefully-never as the main feature in an expert.

USER INTERFACE

The ZWrap system seeks to share its representation with the user at all times-it often uses less than mathematically optimal approaches in the interest of eliciting feedback from the user. The ZWrap system considers the user a resource that may be periodically employed and in general will have more "common sense" than the system does. ("Mathematically optimal" means doing the most with the information the system has. A technique that elicits additional user input may perform better than one that tries to make do with only existing information, since user input represents more information entering the system.)

To the extent possible, all information is stored internally in a form that is human-understandable. Having gone to this trouble, it only makes sense to then share as much of this information as possible with the user. This affords the possibility that the user will notice when the system is "confused" and take steps to address it.

One goal in sharing information with the user is to fill in gaps in the user's understanding. If 15 cities in eastern Europe are mentioned in an article, a map might be used to present this information. If an unusual word appears, perhaps a dictionary definition would be useful. For individuals, a short biographic sketch can be provided. This type of augmentation requires a knowledge base and specialized experts, as in Elo's PLUM, which uses augmentation to localize FishWrap articles about natural disasters.

One of the more frustrating features of many information-retrieval services is how hard it is to figure out why a particular document was selected for presentation. This is not just a trivial annoyance. Without understanding why a search engine produced an unwanted result, it is very difficult to modify an errant query to remedy the problem. The ZWrap system provides an explanation of how each article is selected for presentation.

Collections of articles are easier to skim if similar articles are grouped together. Traditional newspapers use sections such as "Sports" or "Living" to group their articles. An on-line newspaper can be more flexible; the ZWrap system allows users to define their own channels.

A World Wide Web page is not the only delivery mechanism for on-line news. There are also the printed page, pagers, electronic mail, telephones, instant messaging, audio alerts, LED (light-emitting diode) signs, etc. Restructuring of the presentation to use these various media is facilitated by the ZWrap internal structure.

It remains an open question how best to present an augmented news article. One truism about the user interface is that the more a system knows about both the news and the user, the better job it can do in presenting the users with the information they need. The ZWrap system addresses the news-representation half of this equation, but it must await an equally rich user-modeling system, e.g., DOPPELGÄNGER, before its user interface develops further.

Implementation

The ideas set out in the previous sections have been explored in two implementations. The first implementation, MyZWrap, is a general-purpose on-line news system developed and run at the MIT Media Laboratory. It obtains most of its news from the wire services (Associated Press World Stream, Associated Press State 50, Reuters, The New York Times), although it does get some from the Web (The Onion as well as various sources of weather, comics, and sports). MyZWrap is designed to serve as a primary news source for individuals, providing news on a variety of general topics.

Panorama, the second system, was designed and implemented at the IBM Almaden Research Center. It is a more focused on-line news system, designed to serve the needs of an electronics design engineer. Rather than employing wire services, Panorama obtains most of its news from the World Wide Web and Internet news and internal discussion sites. Since it is a more focused application, it utilizes domain-specific understanding (in the domain of the electronics industry) at the expense of a somewhat narrower understanding of the world at large.

In both of the projects, the same basic system was implemented. The general flow of information is as follows. Articles enter the system through the news streams, having been acquired from a variety of sources. The articles are reformatted into frames and placed in a framestore. The experts examine the frames and augment them when appropriate. Statistical examination occurs in the background (trends that are observed are used in a number of ways, including the augmentation of the knowledge bases used by the experts). Searches are performed directly on the framestore and through various indexes that are computed. All of these features are exploited by the user interface to provide an augmented presentation.

Experts

MyZWrap and Panorama both use a large collection of experts to develop understanding. These experts connect to the framestore, request a frame, examine it, and add terminals to reflect their observations. As noted earlier, the experts talk to the framestore using the Dtype network protocol-they are written in whatever language is convenient. There is no constraint on how much an expert can "think." There is also no constraint on the use of human experts. For example, an editor might fine-tune the list of articles suggested by a channel server. Following is a list of some of the experts currently running:

- *Structure*: This is typically the first expert to run against an article. It uses a wide variety of heuristics to identify the various structural elements. For example, the word "by" followed by a proper noun is likely an indication of authorship if it appears in the first few lines of an article.
- *Stemmer*: The list of stemmed words is stored in the frame to facilitate word-based searches.
- *Proper Noun*: A simple heuristic is used to identify proper nouns in an article.
- *Noun/verb*: Noun/verb pairs are identified in an article and included as features in the frame.
- *Time Spotter*: References to time intervals, ages, and dates are identified in an article. These references are converted to UNIX-style date/time.

- *Place Spotter*: This expert identifies places mentioned in an article.
- *Country Spotter*: Using a list of known countries drawn at run time from the CIA World On-Line Factbook, this expert spots country names.
- *Region Spotter*: This expert uses the country feature to identify those regions that are mentioned in an article, for example Middle East or South East Asia.
- *People Spotter*: Using a list of known first names, this expert examines all the proper nouns and identifies persons who are mentioned in an article.
- *Reading Level*: This expert makes use of an automated readability index to guess the "grade level" needed to comprehend an article.
- *Media Lab Faculty*: A filter on the people feature is used to identify a Media Laboratory professor mentioned in an article.
- *FishWrap Topics*: All of the FishWrap keyword topics are run and their matches written back into the frame.

This list is by no means exhaustive. Rather, it gives an idea of the span from the very general to the very specific, and illustrates how experts can work with each other.

PRESENTATION AND USER INTERFACE

MyZWrap is a skewed project, with a disproportionately small amount of effort spent in exploring how articles are presented. Some issues have been examined in enough detail to merit mention:

- *Top-level Presentation*: MyZWrap presents its information in channels. Each channel is focused on a specific topic and the channel list is, in general, shared among users. MyZWrap places these channels in a three-column format. A graphical user interface is provided to allow simple channel selection as well as page-layout management.

- *Searches vs Repurposed Information*: MyZWrap is nonprescriptive regarding the implementation of channel servers. Not all channels perform searches on the news pool to generate their content. (Weather channels and comics acquire their news using other mechanisms, yet their presentation is wholly integrated with the other channels.)
- *Channel Creation*: Repurposed news aside, the majority of MyZWrap channels are the results of searches. Since the system cannot anticipate all possible searches, some mechanism must be provided to enable channel creation. At the moment, the only "user friendly" channel-creation mechanism is an interface similar to AltaVista's that allows a search to be turned into a named channel. The "search explanation" feature in the ZWrap system allows existing channels to be fine-tuned or used as a basis for new channel creation.
- *Channel Analysis*: MyZWrap provides some simple tools for channel analysis. The first is an examination of which features have recently appeared in articles that have been selected for a channel. By examining frequency of occurrence, the channel maintainer can identify active features and perhaps change the channel definition to account for them.
- *New-feature Alerts*: Another category of tool is the "new feature" alert, of which WordWatch is a good example. WordWatch mimics a "word-of-the-day" list. It creates its entries by examining the words that enter the system every day and finding "differences." These new words are filtered through a copy of the Oxford English Dictionary to rule out misspellings and the results are presented with definitions linked to the articles that triggered them. In general, bringing information to the attention of the user only when something new occurs minimizes the necessity for channel monitoring.

A few high-level engineering observations about the ZWrap approach to user interface are:

(1) it allows complex real-time information-understanding and presentation architectures to be constructed out of simple pieces;

(2) it allows the parts of the system to be distributed to arbitrary numbers of arbitrary types of machines for scalability;

(3) it encourages development by allowing new components to be added without adversely impacting the existing system;

(4) it encourages incremental improvement of existing components, since the system does not care how a component accomplishes its task; and

(5) by involving users in channel creation and maintenance, the number of system administrators is kept to a minimum.

Results

There are formal methods of evaluation for many of the individual components of the ZWrap system. However, since the system is designed to readily incorporate new or improved components, their individual evaluation is not particularly significant. It is more interesting to examine the system performance as a whole. The ZWrap system is an interactive information-retrieval system and, as such, it is difficult to construct a repeatable protocol for giving quantitative results.

Side effects, such as users gaining familiarity with the task, differences between users, etc., create a system where an on-going interaction is difficult to characterize. One way to evaluate these systems is to have a large number of typical users work with the system and examine their interactions and opinions of the system.

Such studies are expensive and often inconclusive. Another approach, becoming popular, is to release the system to the Internet and allow its merit to be determined by the number of hits. Some qualitative observations can, however, be made regarding how the ZWrap system fulfills its goal of multiple functionality.

Blackboard Approach

Blackboard systems were initially developed to take advantage of their ease of development as well as opportunities for parallelism. Unfortunately, as noted, this approach fell somewhat into disfavour in the late 1980s due to the performance limitations resulting from the serialization of experts.

The ZWrap system is a validation of the blackboard architecture in the context of news. The system handles on the order of 10000 articles a day; this translates to approximately one gigabyte of text per month. In eight months, the system accumulated approximately 10 gigabytes in the total corpus of news. The ZWrap system can keep augmentations fully integrated to within approximately 20 minutes of the time that news enters the system. Finally, the current system is distributed across five desktop machines. That the system can maintain the approximate 20-minute performance on understanding with five machines working together argues that the multiple blackboard approach allows processing that is efficient enough to warrant its application to real systems.

Flexibility

The strength of a blackboard system is in the ease with which new components can be added to the system, and existing ones can be upgraded and improved upon. Two pieces of anecdotal evidence support this observation.

First, when developing the Panorama system, a full version of the system was implemented in roughly five days. This included the central blackboard, experts to post articles to the blackboard, a single augmentation expert (the stemmer) to test this portion, and the graphical user interface and article-selection structure. The speed with which enough of the system was developed for experimentation to begin was encouraging as it indicates that even on smaller projects, the overhead of including a blackboard approach should not be too burdensome.

The next observation is the ease with which new experts can be added to the system. While developing the technologies used by an expert to understand things may very well be a life's work, actually grafting them into the system is quite painless. A "food spotter" expert was created that, aside from problems in getting an account on the machine, took an afternoon to integrate. Likewise, a "colour spotter" expert was implemented in less than an hour. This low overhead for including specialized understanding experts is heartening, as it encourages their development whenever a particular observation is needed to select articles correctly.

Scalability

The ability to add more hardware as needed is one feature that makes blackboard architectures attractive. Since all the components of the ZWrap system communicate over a network, adding more computational resources is accomplished by adding additional hosts to the network and reassigning services from one host to another. In general, changing hosts caused little impact.

At some point, it becomes impossible to realize performance improvements simply by segregating tasks to machines-the system becomes bound by the performance of the slowest expert running on a single machine. In these cases, it is usually possible to run more than one instance of an agent. Then the bottleneck moves to the database. Fortunately, extensive work has been done on allowing databases to handle large numbers of transactions, including multiple-node (e.g., Beowulf-type) structures and serial-storage architectures.

These considerations aside, a five-machine cluster easily handles the loads discussed here and is sufficient to allow research on much larger dynamic real-time corpora than are traditionally contemplated.

Precognition

One constraint on any system that interacts with users is the need for short response times. This requirement limits the amount of computation that can be done while servicing a request and thus would seem to limit the complexity of the understanding that can be attempted.

The ZWrap system addresses this constraint by precognition, i.e., "thinking" about the articles before requests arrive. (Cognition here is meant to be the processing associated with human or machine augmentation. These "thoughts" are stored along with the article and can be quickly recalled as needed. Since much of the work is precomputed, complex operations can be executed without an adverse impact on response time.

Machine Understanding in Support of Statistics

There is extensive literature on feature spotting as an adjunct to traditional information-retrieval methods. The ZWrap system extends this, allowing domain-specific "spotters" to be added to the mix whenever it appears they will be helpful. New features can be added when required by the task at hand. (In the ZWrap system, all cases are treated as special cases if they are sufficiently important.) As is the case with most traditional information-retrieval methods, the ZWrap system can simply ignore those annotations (tokens) that are not helpful, although they may cause small amounts of confusion for limited corpora.

The Reuters-21578 dataset was used in an experiment to evaluate the impact of feature augmentation on statistical classification as implemented in the ZWrap system. A typical set of activation-channel-selection rules for a ZWrap topic were created using both augmented and unaugmented articles as a training set and the results compared. An experiment was performed to evaluate the impact of machine understanding informing statistics. The experimental procedure was to:

(1) construct a dictionary of all terms in the training set;

(2) construct a normalized vector for the entire training corpus;

(3) construct a normalized vector for the training set;

(4) identify the ten terms whose presence is most indicative of the training set as compared to the corpus norm;

(5) identify the ten terms whose presence is most indicative of the corpus norm as compared to the training set;

(6) use a projection onto these 20 dimensions to generate a cosine distance between each test article and both the "corpus-norm" point and the "training-norm" point, assigning each test article to the bin associated with whichever point is closest (i.e., select for topic or not).

The results of an experiment that was tuned for a South American topic are shown. (South America is not a standard Reuters category. Country names and their mapping to continents were generated by the country-and region-spotter experts. A design feature of the ZWrap system is that specialized topics can be crafted when there is sufficient need.) It is not surprising that both precision and recall for the rules generated from augmented features were more than three times as accurate as for the rules generated without augmented features, since there is a nearly "perfect" feature that the system can use for classification. However, there is no reason not to add experts for a classification whenever possible.

Statistics in Support of Machine Understanding

The approach of using statistics on observations to develop rules for a knowledge base date back to at least Drescher, where an expert made observations about the results of its actions in a simulated world and developed rules that it could later use to perform tasks. This is a goal of the ZWrap system but it is too ambitious a goal to implement in its entirety. One difficulty is that the ZWrap system cannot influence the news, but rather must make its observations based on the news. This limits the ability of the system to design experiments to fill the gaps in its understanding.

Rather than abandoning this approach altogether, the ZWrap system seeks to identify potential causality and brings this to the attention of a person or expert with the broader understanding to "fill in the blanks" and decide whether the observation is indeed valid.

A data-mining experiment was performed to evaluate the impact of statistical classification on knowledge-base construction as implemented in the ZWrap system. Association-rule data mining was applied to proper-noun features and those features with high co-occurrence rates. (Both human knowledge engineers and deep machine-understanding processes are treated as expensive, limited resources, to be used sparingly.) By looking for implications among high-occurrence features, the system seeks to focus development on those areas that will have substantial impact. The experiment was performed on proper nouns occurring in a two-week period of news in February 1999. The association rules that were identified had a minimum support of 20 articles and a confidence of at least 50 percent.

CONCLUSION

This work was motivated by four observations:

(1) the general lack of an efficient, flexible way to deal with large, evolving corpora in a nontrivial manner and the general notion that large corpora require simpler techniques than small corpora;

(2) the perceived hard division between machine-understanding approaches to information retrieval and those developed from a purely statistical basis;

(3) the tendency of systems that perform any understanding of their text to quickly move to representations that are opaque to human comprehension; and

(4) the extent to which information retrieval systems fail to share any of their understanding with their human users.

The consequence is that the user has little opportunity to enhance the development of meaning, although we have found that representations that allow discretionary use of human judgment are of great value. From the ZWrap architecture, developed to address these issues, two test applications were constructed.

The architecture overcomes the traditional deficiencies of the blackboard architecture and uses this approach to build rich representations of large, dynamic corpora. In doing so, the architecture provides a framework in which a "society of agents" approach can be scaled up and applied to large text-understanding problems. Experts are allowed to interact in a controlled way through the blackboard and can be distributed over available computational resources. In addition, the architecture provides a light-weight, reusable structure.

The architecture allows computationally intensive investigation of articles to be performed ahead of time, and the resultant structures stored. This allows more in-depth examination of articles at search time without the need for the user to wait for the results.

Linking statistical and machine-understanding systems, the ZWrap system demonstrates the suitability of frame-type techniques for very large (i.e., millions of documents) collections of information. It exemplifies the use of data-mining statistical methods to assist in the creation of knowledge bases for machine-understanding systems and it exemplifies the use of machine-understanding feature identification to assist in statistical clustering. The ZWrap system also demonstrates that such a system can maintain a human-readable internal representation and yet still perform efficiently.

Finally, the task of an editor is to assess both the news and its context. The augmented-frame model used in the ZWrap system offers some help with this task by providing a structure for the sharing of information that it develops with the user. But, as the ZWrap system currently uses only a cursory model of the user, editorial questions such as "What would the reader like to know about?" are difficult to answer with any precision. Still, the ZWrap system fosters a collaboration between the system and the user, and like all collaborations, the better the communication, the better it works.

A distributed but structured approach to on-line news brings the possibility of more participants in the editorial process, each adding value to the whole. This might result in a reversal of roles-the reader becomes the editor. It will certainly result in a new relationship between readers and editors.

7

BASIC EDITING SKILLS

Professors and professionals agree that text editing, headline writing and design are fundamental and crucial skills. Professors, however, think students need a wider variety of skills. News editing has undergone several waves of substantial change in the last 25 years. The most obvious has been technological.

Computer editing, pagination and digital imaging, which were barely a dream 30 years ago, are tools of the trade today. Organizational change is a more recent development. Among its manifestations are design desks, newsroom teams and maestro approaches, as well as increased awareness of the need for better leadership and people skills.

Most Popular Articles

In Reference:

- Walking A Thin Line-...
- Pope fears Bush is...
- "The Black Dick":...
- World's Fattest Couple...

The growth of online media has spawned a third area of considerable ferment, one that has quickened in the last year or two. Aspects of this change are the integration of print and Web staffs, the introduction of multimedia coverage by newspapers and convergent newsroom experiments. Journalism educators who prepare students to enter the world of news editing have been watching these changes for decades with a mixture of fascination and trepidation. Hitting a moving target is always a challenge, but to stretch a metaphor, journalism educators feel they have to hit the old targets at the same time they're shooting at the one or more in motion.

ADVERTISEMENT

How should journalism education address these changes? The continuum is broad-from retreating to the basics of copyediting and headline-writing and letting industry handle the rest to going one better than industry and experimenting with new curricular forms to meet a multimedia world. Courses already are jammed with training in traditional skills, skills that most would agree remain crucial.

The questions are fairly simple but the answers complex: How much technology should we teach or expect students to learn by themselves? A lot, a little or none? What does the industry want, and is it appropriate to expect journalism programs to provide it? Do journalism programs have the resources-human and financial? Can they go too far too fast? If journalism programs jump wholeheartedly into multimedia education, are they running the risk of creating the 21st century equivalent of a Videotext curriculum? Another way to phrase the question is as follows: Where should journalism educators focus when they design editing curricula? Should they teach skills from the past and present, should they try to predict and prepare for the future or all of the above? There has long been a belief that the industry is closer to the cutting edge of innovation because it has access to more expertise and the latest technology. Is that belief supported by data? Which group, for example, is more inclined to say multimedia skill is important?

This study, which is based on a survey of ACEJMC-accredited programs, examines what professors say is important for students to know about editing. It also compares what professors at accredited programs say about necessary skills with what professional copy editors say is important. The issue that lies beneath the surface of many such discussions is where the academy should be. Should it lead the industry or follow? It is difficult to begin to answer that question without a clear sense of where the academy is now in the teaching of copy editing skills.

BACKGROUND

For some in the academy, the question of which skills to teach is overshadowed by another: Should journalism and communication programs continue to emphasize professional skills that prepare students for jobs in traditional media industries, or should they focus their energies elsewhere? This criticism takes different forms; one version holds that journalism and communication programs should pay much less attention to practitioner skills training because of its vocational nature. Instead of ensuring that students will have industry-specific entry-level skills, schools should concentrate on conceptual and critical issues.

The University of North Dakota's School of Communication, for example, "abandoned a subservience to career tracks in favour of a curriculum organized around significant communication issues." Blanchard, Christ and others have made similar arguments in favour of an integrated curriculum that focuses far less on practitioner skills and more on communication issues and critical-thinking abilities.

Others disagree. Medsger, for example, argues that professional coursework remains crucial and itself is liberal in focus because it emphasizes critical thinking and other hallmarks of a liberal education. A recent study by Dickson and Brandon found that professionals and professors disagreed that journalism programs should move from industry-oriented sequences to more general mass media studies. Christ and Hynes, in a study of mission statements collected in late 1995, indicated that many, if not most, journalism and communications programs attempted to strike a balance between professional preparation and liberal arts education. "It is clear," they wrote, "that many programs embrace the idea that media education involves preparing a liberally educated professional."

A second broad criticism of skills training is that it typically is too narrowly focused for a changing media world. Some media educators look to the idea of media convergence to support an argument that industry-specific training is anachronistic and that students need to develop skills they can apply in various media environments.

In 1993, for example, Rakow said that "technologies, media industries and careers are changing so rapidly and in such unpredictable directions that preparing students for today's media occupations is shortsighted and ill-advised." More recently, Pavlik argues that new digital media present "a fundamental challenge to journalism education" and that to work effectively in the new media era, journalists will need to be comfortable with text, audio, video and interactivity. Outing, who writes a popular online column about the online news industry, says that because newsrooms of the future will publish to different media, "Reporters, obviously, will have to master using new devices to communicate, collect news and do research." But, he adds,"...It's editors whose jobs will change the most... tomorrow's editors will foremost have to understand how content must be presented appropriate to each medium."

In October 2000, the first of five recommendations of the subcommittee on educational technology of the AEJMC task force on journalism and mass communication at the millennium took a similar position with respect to journalism education. It said that programs should "work toward reconceptualizing and re-organizing their curricula to emphasize cross-media JMC education, rather than media-specific education." The report also points out that "a growing number of leading JMC educators and JMC professionals are increasingly convinced that the approach proposed here makes sense and will likely produce the types of JMC professionals the industry will need in the years ahead."

It is clear that the development of online journalism has created a demand for newsworkers who have new skills, particularly in HTML and digital image processing. It is less clear whether much demand exists in online news media for convergence skills such as video. Within the last five or more years, many universities have created new-media classes or even new curricula that attempt to provide students with a more broad-based set of skills. Recent reports of convergence experiments within traditional news media industries also have raised suggestions that traditional training of journalists may not meet industry needs for long. Recently, The New York Times publisher Arthur Sulzberger Jr. added his voice to those preaching convergence: "Whether it is the printed pages of the paper or the digital realm of the Internet, in magazines or books, on television or radio, we have become single-minded in our efforts to reach this knowledge-hungry audience, regardless of the means of distribution." Several newspapers that have experimented with multimedia reporting and editing have been featured in trade journal articles.

The experiments of several major news organizations to create linkages between print and television stations within a common newsroom have been widely reported, though the level of actual integration of staffs has not been great. Such experiments also have been the focus of much discussion at professional and academic conferences, such as AEJMC, prompting calls for multimedia training of students.

On the whole, though, beyond anecdotes, speeches at conferences and position statements, there has been little evidence to suggest that journalism students are ill-served by traditional sequence-based curricula, much less to support the idea of a wholesale turning-away from industry-specific education. Indeed, there is evidence many online journalists have been drawn from the ranks of print, and online startups have done well luring talent from traditional newspapers. In the academy, this debate about sequence separation vs. integration is likely to continue against the backdrop of the continuing development of online journalism and other forms of media convergence.

NEWSPAPER INDUSTRY ISSUES

Focusing more narrowly on the newspaper industry, several studies have indicated that industry-specific skills remain in great demand, particularly for editors. A study by Auman and Alderman found general agreement between editors and educators on what skills were important for new copyediting hires to have. Both groups ranked traditional word editing skills most important. Auman reported in an earlier study that editors did not believe that new hires had adequate preparation; they felt entry-level hires were deficient in traditional editing skills, page design and general knowledge.

Technology skills appear to have grown in importance throughout the 1990s, which is no surprise, given the increasing reliance on computers for page design and photo handling in the mid-1990s. Russial found a substantial discrepancy between what skills editors said were important in an APME survey and what skills newspapers sought in job advertisements. Editors ranked technology skills relatively low and critical thinking abilities very high in the APME survey, but job descriptions for copyeditors were largely silent about critical skills and made it clear that very specific skills, such as Quark pagination, were quite important and becoming more so.

There is additional evidence that technology skills have become important in newsroom hiring. In a survey of photo editors in 1998, Russial found that specific technology skills, such as knowledge of Photoshop and negative scanning, were considered nearly as important for new hires as traditional photography skills but that convergence skills, such as video, were considered extremely unimportant. Have technology skills become as important for copyediting hires?

Besides facing technological upheaval, many newspapers have experienced other institutional changes in the last decade, and some of those changes may mean that editors will need to develop new skills. These include the movement to newsroom teams and team-like structures, cross-training of editors, the growth of design desks and a general re-emphasis on management, leadership and working together. These issues have been discussed in trade journals and in several academic studies, and they remain popular topics at national conferences, such as those of the American Copy Editing Society and Society of News Design. Taken together, these innovations suggest that new hires may need new organizational competencies and people skills. Are these newer skills as important as traditional skills?

Professors of editing know about these organizational changes in the industry, but they already are puzzling over how to cram traditional and technological skills into their classes, not to mention training in multimedia.

Editing teachers can perhaps be forgiven if they occasionally wonder just which of the many aspects of editing they need to teach and how much time they need to spend on them. Previous research has indicated that there's a need for more than one editing course-one basic and one on advanced skills, such as layout and design, visual journalism and coaching writers. Schools that have added this course or one in design have taken some of the pressure off the basic editing course, but with convergence, the pressure is on again to figure out how to incorporate editing for the Web and Web design skills.

RESEARCH QUESTIONS

(1) How much time do copy editing professors spend on traditional editing, headline-writing and design skills, which one might think of as skills from the past (though still necessary for the present and presumably for the future)?

(2) Is there much time for other types of training, such as technology and organizational skills, the need for which has been articulated in the trade press more recently?

(3) Are professors responsive to future trends relating to media convergence?

(4) Is there overall agreement between professors and professionals on necessary skills?

(5) *Advertisement:* Do the skills break into discrete bundles, and if so, do professors and professionals place the same skills in the same bundles?

(6) If not, what are the key differences? Is there a difference based on size of paper?

Method

Surveys targeted the principal editing instructors at 109 accredited journalism programs in the United States. Potential respondents were identified by telephone and e-mail contacts. The first mailing was made in early spring 2000, and a follow-up mailing was done three to four weeks later. Sixty-nine surveys were returned for a 63 percent response rate.

Questions addressed how much time is spent in the copy editing course on traditional tasks, such as grammar, spelling, punctuation and style; text editing (other than grammar); headline writing; design and other.

Survey questions included 39 Likert-type scale items addressing a variety of proficiencies editing professors might expect students who had taken copyediting courses to have developed. These questions were scaled 1 to 5 (1=very unlikely to be proficient to 5=very likely to be proficient). Broadly speaking, the proficiencies cover text editing, headline and caption writing, teamwork and organizational abilities, technology and multimedia.

Another set of questions asked how important it is for graduates to have a more limited set of 16 editing skills. These were included to provide a basis for comparison with a national survey done in 1999 that asked the same questions of copy editors and copy editing supervisors.

The national survey used a modified random-sampling procedure for papers of more than 15,000 circulation. They were divided into four circulation categories, with each group accounting for 12 million to 14 million daily circulation. Papers were asked to return either two, three or four surveys, depending on circulation size.

An initial mailing was sent in early 1999. Follow-up phone calls or e-mails were made within the next four weeks to newspapers that had returned no surveys. A second mailing was made to contacts at those papers. Additional follow-up contacts were made to non-responding papers in the smallest circulation category, which was underrepresented in returns.

The overall response rate was 174 returned surveys or 59 percent of the sample of 295. Of the 117 newspapers, 88 returned at least one survey, representing about 75 percent of the sample.

RESULTS AND DISCUSSION

Time Spent on Traditional Skills

More than 60 percent of the time in the basic class is spent on text editing-on grammar, spelling and punctuation (29.3 percent) and on other editing skills (31.3 percent). Headline writing and design account for a total of about 30 percent in the basic class.

In advanced editing classes, which are taught by fewer than half of the programs that returned surveys, more emphasis is placed on design (33.8 percent), the same on headline-writing (16.5 percent) and considerably less on text editing issues (about 37 percent total). Time spent on "other" skills is less than 15 percent in basic and advanced classes.

These percentages suggest that traditional skills remain the core of copy editing classes. They also indicate that not much time is available during editing classes for anything beyond the basics of text editing, headline-writing and design.

Proficiencies

The 39 item responses to the question "How likely are typical editing students at your school to become proficient in the following at the time they graduate?" produced a complex picture. Grouping the proficiency items into broad sets of skills yields a somewhat clearer picture. In general, text-editing skills and computer competencies (including knowledge of the widely used design program Quark) were ranked most important. Headline writing was about the middle, and new media skills were at the bottom.

Sprinkled throughout are organizational skills (meeting deadlines, thinking independently, planning coverage with others and coaching). Proficiencies that would appear to reflect media convergence (designing Web pages and knowledge of multimedia) generally rank at the very bottom, even lower than earlier production proficiencies such as character-counting headlines, which has not been done at most newspapers since the late 1970s, and cropping and scaling photos by hand, which is done rarely given the near ubiquity of digital imaging in U.S. daily newsrooms.

The message here seems to be that students are graduating with traditional editing and headline-writing skills and knowledge of the typical computer applications used in newsrooms. To a lesser degree, they are graduating with organizational skills. And to a much lower degree, Web production and multimedia skills.

Skills on the Job

Another way to look at the issue of competencies is through factor analysis of skills copy editors need on the job. Sixteen skill items were factor-analyzed using principal components analysis and Varimax rotation to see whether ostensibly related skills vary together. In the analysis of the professors' responses, four factors emerged. The first was a versatility factor, with high loadings on a range of technical competencies: Photoshop knowledge (.927), Quark pagination (.794) and graphics (.802) and on reporting ability (.927).

Factor 2 also reflects a variety of skills but centered more on critical thinking (.842), solid background knowledge: current events (.714) and general knowledge (.664) and time-management skills (.698).

Factor 3 appears to be an organizational factor, with high loadings for coaching (.805), teamwork (.800) and interpersonal skills (.594).

Factor 4 is a production factor, with high loadings on headline and caption writing (.761) and page design (.577). It also had a high negative loading for video skills.

In a similar analysis of professionals' responses to the same 16 items based on the earlier survey, four factors also emerged, though the makeup of the factors was somewhat different from those shown in the analysis of professors' responses. Factor 1 was similar to Factor 2 in the analysis of professors, loading highly on critical thinking, background knowledge and word editing skills.

But headline writing (.788) also loaded highly on Factor 1, which suggests that professionals think of headline writing as part of the same skill set as editing while professors may associate it more closely with design.

Factor 2 was a technical versatility factor, similar to the professors' Factor 1, though not as broad-based as in the professors' survey. Page design and Quark pagination did not load highly on this factor, but reporting skill did (.856), as did video skill (.715). Factor 3 was similar to that in the first analysis, and Factor 4 was a design-production factor (page design (.886) and Quark (.879).

Professors, however, rank coaching, reporting, page design, Quark pagination, Photoshop, graphics and Internet skills fairly or very important, too. Neither group reports that video/audio skills (perhaps the key skills in a media convergence environment) are very important.

The t-tests show that many of the differences are significant, though some of the differences are not very large.

Charts put the differences more in perspective. Professors' responses and those of the professionals across all circulation categories.

The lines are essentially similar in the categories that reflect traditional skills in word editing and headline writing, background knowledge and organizational skills. They diverge in page design, graphics and reporting skills as well as in a variety of technology skills, such as knowledge of Photoshop and Quark.

The differences between page design and Quark ability practically disappear, and the differences between professors and professionals on the need for copy editors to have coaching and reporting skills decrease, too. The lines converge further when the analysis is limited to papers of less than 50,000 circulation.

CONCLUSION

Professors at ACEJMC-accredited programs appear to believe that traditional skills, reflecting text editing, headline writing and design, remain fundamental, which should come as little surprise.

The need for those skills, particularly those involving word editing, is long established, and whatever form news presentation takes, those skills no doubt will remain crucial. Headline writing and design, too, are considered very important skills, though less time is spent in class on them.

The data on proficiencies students are likely to have and the skills they need for jobs also indicate that those traditional skills are important, but skills that have emerged in recent decades also have become essential.

Those include technology competencies, such as ability to use Quark and the Web, and organizational abilities, such as interpersonal and teamwork skills. Looking at the range of possible proficiencies that can be taught and the time that is now devoted to traditional skills, one might conclude that anecdotal reports are correct-there aren't enough minutes in the class to do everything that professors think should be done.

Comparing professors and professionals on skills shows that there is considerable agreement on a number of traditional and technology skills and disagreement on the need for a number of others. The data show that, unlike professionals, professors seem to feel their students need it all-editing, reporting, technology, organizational and a variety of Web skills. The professors appear to reflect the view of professionals more closely at smaller papers, where copy editors often do need to have it all. Larger papers have larger staffs and can afford greater specialization in jobs. In effect, then, professors seem to be closer to professionals at papers that are more likely to hire students out of college. Perhaps instructors also are more likely to encourage flexibility in their students to better prepare them for the job market.

One interesting finding is where headline skills fit into the picture. To the professors, headline writing falls into a design factor; to professionals, it goes with story editing. The difference might in effect be a "Quark effect."

In many classroom situations and at many small papers, copy editors do most of their work in Quark-design, headline writing and sometimes even text editing. At larger papers, copy editors tend to edit and write headlines on front-end systems, and designers spend their day designing pages on Quark or other systems.

This study suggests that professors and professionals are largely in agreement about how to prepare students for traditional print newsroom technology.

The data also suggest that neither group feels that preparation for a multimedia future is particularly crucial at this point, though professors appear to be more comfortable with one key convergence skill-video-than so their counterparts in print newsrooms.

One is tempted to conclude that the professors are actually closer to the cutting edge. The data here are merely suggestive, though. A different picture might well emerge if professors were compared with professionals in online newspaper newsrooms.

It would seem to be good news that professors and professionals are largely on the same page. Whether it is the right page is a different issue, somewhat beyond the scope of this study, but the results suggest a few observations about the future.

For example, the great importance both groups place on traditional skills of editing and presentation should serve students and the industry well no matter which direction it moves. Even converged media will need editors who have a love for language and the ability to improve writing and present stories in compelling ways.

The importance placed on technology skills needed for news production in the short term, while an understandable concern for professors and professionals, could prove to be shortsighted in the long term if it becomes a straitjacket. Copy editors who are facile with Quark, for example, are versatile in today's newspaper world. Whether such training will help them much if media change to different forms of delivery is an open question.

Perhaps it will. An openness to learning one system is often the key to learning others. A greater problem may be the relative inattention currently paid to the conceptual tools needed to shift gears to new forms of news delivery. Knowing when to use which forms to tell which stories may be as valuable a skill tomorrow as knowing how to import a photo into a Quark page is today. One might say that students are in good shape as far as the past and present go in copy editing but that the future is somewhat cloudy.

8

COPY EDITING

INTRODUCTION

Copy editors perform quality control for publications. Within the industry, they are known as "the last line of defense." Although copy editing is concerned with style, there is no universal form for the term itself. In magazine and book publishing, it is often written as one word. The newspaper industry writes the expression as two words or hyphenates it. The terms "copy editor" has a similar division between one word or two. The job is called "sub-editing" in the United Kingdom.

OVERVIEW

Copy editors correct mechanical errors, such as with grammar, spelling, punctuation, and style, and otherwise polish the writing. Copy editing is an essential task for newspapers, magazines, and other publications. It involves the review and correction of journalistic articles submitted by writers. This process includes checking for factual and content errors, as well as spelling, grammar and punctuation errors. "Copy" is a journalist's term for text. Copy editing is performed by copy editors, whose job is to read copy, look for and correct obvious errors, and question the writer concerning ambiguities and possible factual errors.

Preparation, Traits and Skills

Many copy editors have a college degree, often in journalism or communications. Copy editing is often taught as a college journalism course, although the name of the course varies. News design and pagination are often include in such classes. The Dow Jones interns receive a couple of weeks of training before going to their newspapers.

Besides an excellent command of the language, copy editors should have broad general knowledge (to be able to suspect inaccurate information), good critical thinking skills (to spot inconsistencies), and diplomacy (mainly to deal with writers). In the United States, midcareer training for newspaper copy editors and news editors (who supervise news copy desks) is offered at the American Press Institute, the Poynter Institute, the University of North Carolina at Chapel Hill, and conferences of the American Copy Editors Society.

Tests and Try-outs

Most U.S. newspapers and many other publishers give candidates for copy-editing jobs a test or a tryout. These vary widely. They may be timed or not, they may last an hour to a week, some are "take-home" tests. They may include questions, and usually include copy to edit. The length of the copy may be anywhere from single sentences to many articles. Tests and tryouts may include items on:

- acronyms
- Associated Press style (for U.S. newspapers)
- critical thinking
- current events
- fairness
- general knowledge
- geography
- grammar
- headline writing (for newspapers)
- infographics editing
- math
- news judgment

- punctuation
- skepticism
- spelling
- taste
- usage

External links:

- Test question examples, compiled by the American Copy Editors Society

The Work

Copy editors also try to prevent more serious problems, such as with accuracy, clarity, fairness, logic and taste. They also write headlines and captions, known as "cutlines" in the industry.

In the late 20th century, copy editors at many publications were given more production work because of the advent of pagination. This has expanded with the Internet. Most copy editors work nights, weekends and holidays.

Miscellaneous

The Texas Daily Newspaper Association gives the John Murphy Award for Excellence in Copy Editing. The award alternates each year between copy editors at large and small newspapers, with daily circulation of 100,000 being the dividing line. In days before computers, most newspaper copy editors worked together at large U-shaped tables or desks. References to that era survive in the jargon terms "rim" and "slot," indicating where they sat. A senior copy editor would sit in the slot and check the work of those on the rim.

Top Ten Reasons Why Editing Is COOL!

Compiled by Jane Harrigan, University of New Hampshire

(1) It's like solving a puzzle.

(2) You find a whole world of other people who go crazy over the"10 items or less" sign in the grocery store. (Or, as one new editor put it, "I can constructively satisfy

my obsessive-compulsive anal-retentive tendencies and get paid for it.")

(3) Your job changes constantly; you're never bored.

(4) You become a more interesting person. You can talk about Arafat, Albright, Agassi or Aguilera and sound like you know what you're talking about--because you do.

(5) You have responsibility and power. You decide how readers will perceive the news, how they'll perceive the world.

(6) Catching a dumb mistake before readers see it is a rush. Helping someone make a story better is the best drug there is.(Or, as one person wrote, "It's a clóse as an English major can come to being a doctor, or God.")

(7) Newspapers never ask writers to edit, but they love it if editors write.

(8) You could be the world's best quiz show contestant because you're a dictionary of useless information.

(9) You can move anywhere and find a job.

(10) You never have to wear decent clothes.

BALANCE AND FAIRNESS

Be alert for accusations, statements or characterizations that cast another person or a group of people in a bad light.

Beware of stories that use only one source. Even if it's a speech by someone, make sure you try to provide some background or context.

News Value

Ask yourself, What's the news here? Is it worth this much type? Worth the front page?

Diversity, Stereotypes

Be alert for phrases or descriptions that seem rooted in stereotype: e.g., a feisty senior.

Taste

It's a weird, wacky, sometimes ugly world out there. We shouldn't sugarcoat it. But we do need to keep our readers in mind. If it makes you go "Ewwwwww!" maybe it doesn't belong in the story.

Overwrought Prose

Not every story needs a dramatic, narrative lead. Like the courts' definition of pornography: You'll know it when you see it.

Buried Lead

Be aware of how long it takes to get to the nut graph. Anything further than five or six paragraphs down needs to be discussed.

Skepticism

Be aware of poll stories or medical breakthroughs or wonder drugs. Watch the language. Flowery adjectives and adulation, or biting criticism, is a big tip-off.

Clarity

It goes without saying: Check the math. Follow the logic. Make sure the example is correct.

Dissonance

Make sure the story's tone matches the news.

Quotes

Make sure your paper has a policy about when you clean them up (if ever) and when you leave them alone.

Sensitivity

Sometimes details can illuminate. Other times, they can risk offending readers. Sexual assaults, gruesome accidents, descriptions of living conditions-all have potential for going just over the line (and maybe sometimes way beyond).

KEEPING THE PUBLIC'S TRUST

John Carroll had 'em rolling in the aisles... well, ethics demands I admit I'm speaking metaphorically... during the session on ethics and standards he presented at the American Copy Editors Society's national conference.

Carroll took more than a dozen questions from participants and touched on the usual ethical suspects of anonymous sources, credibility, balanced coverage, gifts and oh-sooooo-much more during his 90-minute session in Houston. He also spoke about the Jayson Blair fiasco at the New York Times and defended his own paper's coverage of the groping allegations against then-gubernatorial candidate Arnold Schwarzenegger.

What it all boiled down to, Carroll said, was that such incidents as the Blair scandal are betrayals to the readers the newspaper serves. "It was an unthinkable breach," he said.

But he also tempered his criticism by finding a silver lining in the media's collective despair, pointing out that despite the glaring failure of editors the newsroom found strength in its recovery and a re-dedication to not let it happen again.

"There will be ethical breaches, but we also have staffs who see those ethical breaches like a dagger to the heart," he told nearly 100 editors during his late-morning session. "That tells you how strong those newspapers are. That feeling doesn't always exist at some news organizations."

ETHICS AND STANDARDS

Of course, he said, he was referring to Fox News, which was the first quip that drew laughter and a smattering of applause from the audience.

"There is in America a whole galaxy of organizations that have the trappings of news, but are not news organizations because their ethical core is a whole different genre," Carroll said.

"They are into marketing. They are into politics, and a truly pernicious subset of politics that we know as attack politics.

They use data when they have it. When they don't, they use falsehoods," he said.

An example of that genre, Carroll said, were the radio talk shows, attack Web sites and other "pseudo media" that picked up the "fabrications" written by a self-employed columnist regarding the series of stories the L.A. Times ran about Schwarzenegger. The Times' editors knew the stories would be controversial, they knew they would be criticized, and they knew there would be anger and angst. But Carroll said they didn't know they would face attacks that questioned the paper's integrity.

Carroll said that if he were responding to such criticism again, he wouldn't let 24 hours go by until the next news cycle; he would respond immediately by e-mail and copy it to every news Web site.

"If someone says something false that attacks your integrity, you should attack that like a lion. You have to kill these things before the attacker becomes a national celebrity," Carroll said.

The so-called dead tree media does not have to suffer in silence, in other words.

Among the other topics he covered:

--Anonymous sources: In Washington, D.C., and Hollywood, using anonymous sources are the coin of the realm, and each news organization has to decide how to handle the situation. But the L.A. Times is trying to tighten up its use.

--Balance coverage with community standards: Newspapers run controversial stories and pictures all the time. The trick is to remember that complaints are a sign of vitality.

"A newspaper without complaints is a newspaper near death," Carroll said.

--Gifts: The Times doesn't accept gifts from people its reporters cover. At the same time, Carroll said he doesn't see a need to issue a blanket statement outlawing every type of gift.

"I believe in treating our journalists as if they are adults who understand these things," he said.

--Credibility: In a wide-ranging set of issues on the topic, the Times strives to maintain its integrity. Sounds like a no-brainer, right? But what about the political reporter whose spouse or partner puts political signs on their front lawn? Well, it's a no-no.

"You can't do both," Carroll said. "At the Times we want to take a reportorial stance rather than advocacy."

--Role of the copy editor: Simply put, the copy editor must establish the same relationship with a reporter as he or she does with the reader. The copy editor should be an advocate for the reader, to insist that the reporter tell the story simply and cleanly. And sometimes that may mean be assertive--but diplomatic.

That means, of course, that the copy editor who is used to putting time in front of a computer screen rather than caring about the overall package in the paper, who cares more about the speed of copy flow than the readers, has to rethink the job.

"I urge all of you to be good advocates in your newsrooms," Caroll said. "Get back to being part of the whole process rather than sit at your tubes."

9

THE SCREENWRITING

Screenwriting refers to the art and craft of writing screenplays for film or television. Writing for film is potentially one of the most high-profile and best-paying careers available to a writer, and as such, it is perhaps the most sought after.

It is increasingly difficult to make a living as a Hollywood screenwriter, but that does not stop tens of thousands of people from trying every year, as the capricious nature of the film industry makes it possible for a complete unknown to launch a career simply by writing a commercially-appealing screenplay and getting it into the hands of the right people.

Status of Screenwriters in the Industry

Historically, screenwriters have had a low social position in the film industry. Despite the fact that a screenwriter is often the genesis of a project, directors-not writers-frequently get their names associated with the films they make (as in, "a film by..."). Screenwriters usually do not get this honour, unless the screenwriter is also directing. Before Alfred Hitchcock, the reverse was the case. The Writers Guild of America agreed to make an exception for Hitchcock, which other directors took advantage of (and insisted on using "a film by...") and gradually screenwriters were marginalized in this respect.

However, the situation has improved dramatically as the resurgence of the independent film in the late 20th century gave new rise to the idea of the screenwriter as the amateur, and creative generator of cinematic product. In the past few years, news of multi-million dollar screenplay deals is a sign of increased respect for the role of the screenwriter in film production.

Recently, the Writers Guild of America (WGA), the labour union representing writers in the American film and television industries, has made great efforts to limit the use of the "a film by" title in the credits of motion pictures, to preserve the respect for level of input made by the writers.

Theories on Writing a Screenplay

Writing a screenplay requires the creativity of a storyteller and the skills of both the dramatist and the filmmaker. Because of the particular combination of skills and standards required by the motion picture industry, many writers find screenwriting more challenging than writing novels or other narrative fiction.

Fundamentally, the screenplay is a unique literary form. It is like a musical score, in that it is intended to be the basis of other artists' performance, rather than standing on its own merits. For this reason, a screenplay is often written using pre-determined technical jargon when describing stage directions. Nonetheless, a good screenwriter will use interesting visually-descriptive language when setting up a scene or its characters so as to conjure up images. There are several main screenwriting theories which help writers approach the screenplay by systematizing the structure, goals and techniques of writing a script. There are also numerous screenwriting programs available to help a screenwriter set up scenes and keep track of structure. Scenes are usually short and dialogue clipped, i.e., the way people actually speak in real life. The First Act is typically anywhere from fifteen to twenty pages leading to a major conflict. Second Act--the story--is about seventy pages. The Third Act or resolution is the rest. [See Act structure (Film)] Screenplays are usually one-hundred-and-twenty pages in length, or two hours, a page of screenplay roughly corresponding to a minute of movie.

The most common kinds of theories are structural. Screenwriter William Goldman is widely quoted as saying "Screenplays are structure." The first, most basic theory of screenwriting is Aristotle's Poetics, which explains the Three Act Structure. The Three Acts are Beginning, Middle and End, or more functionally, Setup, Complication and Resolution. A common way to paraphrase the Three-Act structure is "get your character up a tree, throw rocks at him, then get him down out of the tree." Many screenwriters also draw inspiration from Joseph Campbell's Monomyth which also employs a variation of the Three Act Structure.

SYD FIELD

Screenwriting guru Syd Field wrote the seminal book Screenplay, and posited a new theory, which he called the Paradigm. Others refer to it as the "Three Act Structure". Field noticed that in a 120-page screenplay, Act Two was notoriously boring, and was also twice the length of Acts One and Three. He also noticed that an important dramatic event usually occurred at the middle of the picture, which implied to him that the middle act was actually two acts in one.

So the Three Act Structure is noted 1, 2a, 2b, 3, resulting in Aristotle's Three Acts divided into four pieces. Field also introduced the idea of Plot Points into screenwriting theory. Plot Points are important structural functions that happen in approximately the same place in most successful movies, like the verses and choruses in a popular song.

In subsequent books, Field has added to his original list, and students of his like Viki King and Linda Seger have added to the list of Plot Points. Here is a current list of the major Plot Points that are congruent with Field's Paradigm:

Opening Image: The first image in the screenplay should summarize the entire film, especially its tone. Often, writers go back and redo this as the last thing before submitting the script.

Inciting Incident: Also called the catalyst, this is the point in the story when the Protagonist encounters the problem that will change their life. This is when the detective is assigned the case, where Boy meets Girl, and where the Comic Hero gets fired from his cushy job, forcing him into comic circumstances.

Turning Point 1: The last scene in Act One, Turning Point One is a surprising development that radically changes the Protagonist's life, and forces him to confront the Opponent. In Star Wars, this is when Luke's family is killed by the Empire. He has no home to go back to, so he joins the Rebels in opposing Darth Vader.

Pinch 1: A reminder scene at about 3/8 the way through the script (halfway through Act 2a) that brings up the central conflict of the drama, reminding us of the overall conflict. For example, in Star Wars, Pinch 1 is the Stormtroopers attacking the Millennium Falcon in Mos Eisley, reminding us that the Empire is after the stolen plans to the Death Star that R2-D2 is carrying and that Luke and Ben Kenobi are trying to get to the Rebel Alliance (the main conflict).

Midpoint: An important scene in the middle of the script, often a reversal of fortune or revelation that changes the direction of the story. Field suggests that driving the story towards the Midpoint keeps the second act from sagging.

Pinch 2: Another reminder scene about 5/8 through the script (halfway through Act 2b) that is somehow linked to Pinch 1 in reminding the audience about the central conflict. In Star Wars, Pinch 2 is the Stormtroopers attacking them as they rescue the Princess in the Death Star. Both scenes remind us of the Empire's opposition, and using the Stormtrooper attack motif unifies both Pinches.

Turning Point 2: A dramatic reversal that ends Act 2 and begins Act 3, which is about confrontation and resolution. Sometimes Turning Point Two is the moment when the Hero has had enough and is finally going to face the Opponent. Sometimes, like in Toy Story, it's the low-point for the Hero, and he must bounce back to overcome the odds in Act 3.

Showdown: About midway through Act 3, the Protagonist will confront the Main Problem of the story and either overcome it, or come to a tragic end.

Resolution: The issues of the story are resolved.

Tag: An epilogue, tying up the loose ends of the story, giving the audience closure.

Final Thoughts

Perhaps the most daunting theory of screenwriting comes from Pulitzer Prize-winning screenwriter David Mamet, who has advised that a screenwriter should simply read Aristotle's Poetics and write a lot until they get good at it. Professional screenwriters often recognize the importance of learning about style, craft and structure by reading the screenplays of popular/ successful movies.

The time necessary to write a screenplay varies widely upon the writer and the circumstances. Professional television writers frequently are called upon to write an hour-long script in less than a week. Some major movie scripts have literally taken years of rewrites before they are ready. Most professional writers can complete two to three original screenplays in a year.

Screenplay Format and Elements of the Screenplay

A screenplay has very rigid set of standardizations in place, beginning with proper formatting. These rules are in part to serve the practical purpose of making screenplays uniformly readable "blueprints" of movies, and also to serve as a way of distinguishing a professional from an amateur---if a screenplay doesn't follow the simple rules of formatting, it is generally disregarded as a lesser product, regardless of content. Most screenplays are expected to be written in 12 point Courier or Courier New typeface, with no bolding or italicizing. Specific elements and formatting defined below.

Screenplay Format

This section describes the components used to build-up a screenplay.

Title Page

The title page of your screenplay is the first clue to a producer that you're either a professional or an amateur. The title should be about 20 lines down the page and either underlined or in quotation marks. Two lines down, in the same font, should be the words "Written By", "Adapted From (insert title here)", or just plain "By". In the bottom corners put contact information, as well as any copyright information. In shooting scripts, the title page contains in the upper right corner a list of every set of revisions distributed thus far.

Some writers are tempted to insert eye-catching fonts or images on the title page. However, such deviation from industry standards is seen as unprofessional and is not recommended.

Scene Headings

Scene headings (or slug lines) define the beginning of a new scene in a screenplay. They either begin with "EXT."---if the scene is an exterior, or takes place outdoors---or "INT."---if the scene takes place indoors. Following this descriptor, the name of the location of the scene should appear in all caps (example: "BOB'S PLACE"). This is followed by a space, a hyphen, another space, then the time of day (example: "-DAY," "-NIGHT," "-EVENING," etc.). The finished heading should read something like "INT. HOUSE-DAY". Scene headings have a margin of 1.5 inches (37 mm) from the left, 1 inch (25 mm) from the right.

Scene numbering: It is rare that you will find a "spec script" (speculation script, the one written by a screenwriter, before it is sold) with the scenes numbered. This is a tool added later in the production as the "spec script" becomes a "shooting script." The numbers are generally found immediately to the left of the scene heading.

Action

Two lines below the scene heading and with the same margins, the action begins. Action describes what can be seen on the screen, and is always in present tense. Here, screenwriting varies most from standard fiction writing, in that elaborate prose describing the feelings of a character is to be avoided. When introducing a character, the character's name should appear in all caps (example: "Bob turns and sees JOAN, whom he has never seen before."). Afterwards, capitalize according to standard grammar.

Page Breaks

Scene headers, dialogue cues, and transitions-in (such as FADE IN:) should never appear at the bottom of a page. When a paragraph of action or dialogue is split across pages, the break should come between sentences and not before the second line of the paragraph. When dialogue is split, (MORE) should appear at the bottom of the first page, aligned vertically with the dialogue cue. The cue should be replicated on the subsequent page, with (CONT'D) appearing alongside it.

Dialogue

In screenwriting, dialogue refers to anytime a character is speaking, even if it is a monologue. A dialogue "cue" is the name of the character speaking, with a margin of 4.2 inches (107 mm) from the left of the page.

The name should be in capitals letters in cues. Unless there is a parenthetical (see below), dialogue is placed one line below the cue. The standard length of a dialogue line is 35 characters starting at 3.1 inches (79 mm). Hyphenation of words in a dialogue is frowned upon.

Parentheticals

To show minor actions or revealing body language, a parenthetical, or subtext, is placed after the cue and either above or within the dialogue, within rounded brackets. e.g:

Jack

I can get a better price.

(to Megan)

Let's bounce!

The margin for parentheticals is 3.7 inches (94 mm) left, 1 inch (25 mm) right. Many script readers prefer limited use of parentheticals. They are also looked upon unfavourably by actors and directors, especially when they become too specific about emotions or actions.

Transitions

Transitions are short descriptions describing how the film will move from one scene (or image within the scene) to the next. They are justified to the right side of a properly formatted screenplay, and followed by a colon. Some of the most common transitions seen in screenplays are:

- CUT TO:-Indicates a direct transition (cut) to a new scene, or to a new shot within a scene. If a scene header follows the cut, this transition is usually omitted.
- DISSOLVE TO:-Indicates a dissolve, where one scene gradually fades into another. Dissolves are commonly used to indicate the passage of time.
- INTERCUT WITH/INTERCUT BETWEEN:-Indicates that a sequence of cuts back and forth between two scenes is about to begin. Subsequent transitions between the two scenes are indicated with the transition BACK TO:. Intercuts are commonly used when portraying telephone conversations, or to contrast action taking place in two locations at the same time.

Intercut example:

INT. ADULT BOOKSTORE--DAY--INTERCUT

Max is on the phone by the register, ringing purchases.

MAX

(into phone)

Dino Velvet... yeah, he's like the

John Luc Godard of S+M flicks,

supposed to be a real weirdo.

WELLES (O.S.)

(from phone)

A weirdo making S+M films? Who'd

have thought it?

MAX

(into phone)

His stuff comes out of New York.

WELLES (O.S.)

Speciality product.

Dialogue and Description

The following is an example from an unproduced screenplay which may give the reader an idea of how a scene without camera angles can be descriptive, and perhaps even poetic, so as to convey the proper time frame (1910) and/or feeling:

A BUNCH OF GARDENIAS

makes a sudden burst of BRIGHT RED. A hand removes each petal--one at a time. The petals fall on the ground.

Following the petals--

A part of a woman's SHOE is seen. It is strangely ornate with a shabby heel.

Giggles erupt, and the extravagantly painted face of a very young prostitute appears.

Her hand is at the arm of a man who is older by at least a couple of decades.

Imagery

Imagery can be used in many metaphoric ways. In The Talented Mr. Ripley, the title character talked of wanting to close the door on himself sometime, and then, in the end, he did.

Rain is commonly used to express a character feeling depressed, while sunny days promote a feeling of happiness and calm. Use imagery to your advantage to sway the emotions of your audience and to clue them in to what is happening.

Imagery is well defined in City of God. The opening image sequence sets the tone for the entire film. The film opens with the shimmer of a knife's blade on a sharpening stone. A drink is being prepared, The knife's blade shows again, juxtaposed is a shot of a chicken letting loose of its harness on its feet. All symbolising 'The One that got away'. The film is about life in the favelas in Rio-sprinkled with violence and games and ambition.

Character

It is very important to develop your characters, because that is who the viewers will be relating to. Characters, especially major characters, should be original and interesting. A character's true nature is revealed by his or her actions in overcoming obstacles.

Dialogue

Dialogue is very important to the film industry, because there are no written words to explain your characters or the plot; it all has to be explained through dialogue and imagery. If your script has weak dialogue, there is a good chance it will lose a reader's or viewer's interest. Make your dialogue sharp, snappy, and easy to follow.

Plot

While the story is what will be told (narrative); the plot is how the story will be told (narration). This vocabulary is not indisputable, though. Sometimes in literature story and plot are used exactly the other way round. Develop your plot before you begin work, write a treatment or a short outline for a film and follow it, but feel free to branch out in other directions if you feel that it would make your script more interesting.

ACT STRUCTURE (FILM)

Act structure explains how a plot of a film story is composed. Just like plays (Staged drama) have 'Acts', critics and screenwriters tend to divide films into acts; though films don't require to be broken down as such in reality.

Whereas plays are actual live performances that need 'breaks' in the middle for change of set, costume, or for the artists' rest; films are recorded performances shown mechanically and therefore don't need actual breaks. Still they are divided into acts for reasons that are in aesthetic and structural conformation with the original idea of Act in theatre.

Act breaks in a film are usually very obscure for lay audience and only a trained person can detect the ending of one act and the beginning of the other in the progression of a movie.

The idea of Act structure is of more value while writing a Screenplay than watching a film, though the Act breaks are never actually written in the final copies of screenplays. But television scripts called Teleplays almost always include clear denotions as such.

Act is the broadest structural unit of enacted stories. The most common paradigm in theatre, and so in films, is that of the 'Three-Act structure' proposed by Aristotle. It simply means that any story has a 'beginning', a 'middle' and an 'end'. Playwrights and screenwriters divide their stories into three major parts viz. 'Set up', 'Confrontation' (alternatively called as 'conflict' or 'complication') and 'Resolution'. These form the basic three acts of any performance-staged or screened.

Though various theories have been proposed and debated, the Three-act structure stands as the most popular one. Also, this is what Hollywood has discovered and proved as the most successful. The rest of the world cinema may have its own ways of looking at the plot.

The 'Three-Act Structure'

According to Hollywood, feature films are considered as audio-visual narrative forms which can be seen in distinct parts called 'Acts'.

It follows that the enacted story opens with the introduction of characters and situations, backdrop, locale etc. It creates interest in the audience and takes them to feel concerned as to what the real problem is and what may happen with it. Plays, and screenplays, usually revolve around main characters-the 'Protagonist' and the 'Antagonist' who engage themselves into a battle. That is "Set up".

The next part-and considered to be more important-is complication of the problem of the story. It intrigues the audience all the more, giving them more and more information and putting various points of view for imaginative comparison. This eventually leads to higher points of audience interest. Because this second Act of most screenplays adds all the possible dramatic values to the plot, this is considered to be the core of the same. The Antagonist and the Protagonist try and experiment with all their strengths (and weaknesses of the other) to win the battle. That is "Confrontation".

This takes us to the third-and the most important-act, the "Resolution". This means it tends to 'solve' the problem (-s) of the story developed so far. But this is not obvious, as it is expected to bring the 'climax' (or a series of climaxes) to give the audience the pay-off. The tool usually implemented is a 'do or die' situation where doors of escape for either or both of the two characters go on closing one by one, leaving them with only a thin chance that demands the fullest exploitation of their qualities and energies. This so called jaw-dropping, breath-taking, arm-rest-grabbing moment for the audience leads to the final outcome of the entire plot. And it is usually the triumph of the good (Protagonist) over the evil (Antagonist), with rare exceptions.

Limitations

This framework can not be rigidly applied to all the film stories, and there are a good proportion of Hollywood movies that defy this theory. Many films follow this pattern only to a subtle extent, where their genre demands a more delicate handling. Screenwiters and Script doctors have tried to provide alternative ideas, which again are open for debate. As said earlier, cinema across the world and 20th century has evolved its own ways of putting a story. Also, this theory may not be fit for non-fiction films like documentary or corporate films, which may not have a 'plot' at their base with 'characters' and all their 'actions and speeches' predecided, like the feature films have. Such non-fiction films require their own forms of arrangement.

What is important here is that ideas of Act structure help us understand films better. More importantly, these are 'tools' of the screenplay writers who can break down the story at hand

and play with various ways of presenting it to find the best possible one. Experts have gone long way ahead in dividing plot to even smaller structural units and they keep working to find the most effective formula of structuring a film story.

BECOMING A SCREENWRITER

Handling Writer's Block

Many writers get to the page and get stuck. Writer's block is what happens when you have the desire, but just can't think of what to write. The key to working through this kind of block is to push through it. Pick a time of day that works for you and write, write, write. Take time out. Relax. Let your screenplay ferment for a while. Watching movies, reading books of the same genre can spark that jolt of creative writing you've been looking for. Writer's block is quite common, both for new writers as well as tenured.

Some say writer's block is simply a lack of research. It is in the writer's best interest to know the world about which he or she is writing backwards and forwards. Meaning, if you don't know what to write, perhaps it's because you don't know what you're writing about.

Editing

Every writer knows that editing is an essential part of writing. Rewrite your piece several times until you are satisfied with the final product. Not only check spelling and grammar, but rewrite scenes to develop them more fully. But always check spelling and grammar. If there is improper spelling or grammar in a piece, an agent, producer, or other person that you are submitting it to will strongly judge it. Bad spelling prejudices people against work, and they are less likely to accept it.

Screenwriting Software

Various pieces of software are available to help screenwriters adhere to the strict formatting conventions (as described above):

- *Celtx-Free*-Open Source scriptwriting software. Linux version available.
- *Cinergy Script Editor*-Free Windows-based script editor program offered in conjunction with a full suite of non-free production management tools under the name Cinergy Motion Picture Production System.
- *Dream a Script*-All in one Screenwriting Software.
- *Final Draft*-Integrated professional scriptwriting software.
- *Montage*-Screenwriting Software for Mac OS X.
- *Movie Magic Screenwriter*-Integrated professional screenwriting software.
- *NTCore Screenwriter*-A little freeware software with autocompletion.
- *Practical Scriptwriter*-Requires no knowledge of script formats.
- *Rough Draft*-A simple script and creative writing word processor. Free (donationware).
- *Scenario*-Modern, intuitive interface with full 30-day trial.
- *Scriptbuddy*-Web-based screenwriting software.
- *Script Right Mobile Edition*-screenwriting software for Pocket PC and Palm OS
- *Scriptware*-The first scriptwriting word processor with real-time formatting/pagination
- *Sophocles*-Screenplay and production management software.
- *Script Smart*-Microsoft Word templates.
- *Totally Write Development Suite*-A four-module program created by professional writer Jeffrey Alan Schechter to streamline the story development and screenplay structure process.

The first screenwriting software was SmartKey, a macro program that sent strings of commands to existing word processing programs, such as WordStar, WordPerfect and Microsoft Word. SmartKey was popular with screen writers from 1982-1987, after which word processing programs had their own macro features.

COPYRIGHT PROTECTION FOR SCREENPLAYS

In the United States, completed works may be copyrighted, but ideas and plots may not be. Any document written after 1978 in the U.S. is automatically copyrighted even without legal registration or notice. However, The U.S. Library of Congress will formally register a screenplay, and some sources claim that if a work is not registered with the Library of Congress, then it is not possible to file for copyright infringement. For the purpose of establishing evidence that a screenwriter is the author of a particular screenplay (but not related to the legal copyrighting status of a work), The Writer's Guild of America registers screenplays. Since this service is one of record keeping and it is not regulated by law, other organizations can register screenplays as well, such as The Creators Vault. While there are benefits to registering a screenplay, it is considered amateurish and a faux-pas to include mention of copyright or guild-registered status anywhere on the screenplay itself.

Screenplay

A screenplay or script is a blueprint, written by a screenwriter, for a film or television program. Screenplays can be original works or adaptations from existing works such as novels. A screenplay differs from a script in that it is more specifically targeted at the visual, narrative arts, such as film and television, whereas a script can involve a blueprint of "what happens" in a comic, an advertisement, a theatrical play and other "blueprinted" creations.

The major components of a screenplay are action and dialogue, with the "action" being "what we see happening" and "dialogue" being "what the characters say". The characters, when first introduced in the screenplay, may also be described visually. Screenplays differ from traditional literature conventions in ways described below; however, screenplays may not involve emotion-related descriptions and other aspects of the story that are, in fact, visual within the end-product. For more details on the contents of screenplays, see Screenwriting.

In the United States, the Writers Guild of America (WGA) has final control on who may be awarded screenwriting credit for a screenplay in a union production. The WGA is one of several organizations in the U.S. and worldwide which recognize screenplays with awards.

A script for television is sometimes called a teleplay.

Screenplay Format

There is no unique "rule" for the writing of a screenplay, but throughout the world, within the relevant industries, several conventions are adhered to.

Film

Motion picture screenplays intended for submission to mainstream studios, whether in the US or elsewhere in the world, are expected to conform to a standard typographical format known widely as studio format which stipulates how elements of the screenplay such as scene headings, action, transitions, dialogue, character names, shots and parenthetical matter should be presented on the page, as well as the font size and line spacing.

One reason for this is that, when rendered in studio format, most screenplays will transfer onto the screen at the rate of approximately one page per minute. This rule of thumb is widely contested-a page of dialog usually occupies less screen time than a page of action, for example, and it depends enormously on the literary style of the writer-and yet it continues to hold sway in modern Hollywood.

There is no single standard for studio format. Some studios have definitions of the required format written into the rubric of their writer's contract. The Nicholl Fellowship, a screenwriting competition run under the auspices of the Academy of Motion Picture Arts and Sciences, has a useful and accurate guide to screenplay format. There is also a compact, quick-reference chart with format specifications and examples called the Screenplay Format Guide from ScriptBuddy. Most screenwriting software comes with a set of templates for various screenplay formats which are more or less standard. A detailed description of correct screenplay format can be found here.

Traditionally, a screenplay should be 90-110 pages long. Comedies and children's films tend to weigh in at the lower end.

Screenplays are almost always written using a monospaced font, often a variant of Courier although other fonts are sometimes seen, including those intended to resemble the output of an old battered typewriter such as a Remington Portable.

Television

For American TV shows, the format rules for hour dramas, like CSI, and single-camera sitcoms, like Scrubs, are essentially the same as for motion pictures. The main difference is that TV scripts have act breaks. Multi-camera sitcoms, like Two and a Half Men, use a different, specialized format that derives from radio and the stage play. In this format, dialogue is double-spaced, action lines are capitalized, and scene headings are capitalized and underlined.

The script format for documentaries and audio-visual presentations which consist largely of voice-over matched to still or moving pictures is different again and uses a two-column format which can be particularly difficult to achieve in standard word processors, at least when it comes to editing.

PHYSICAL FORMAT

American screenplays are printed single-sided on three-hole-punched letter sized (8.5 x 11 inch) paper, and held together with two brass brads in the top and bottom hole. The middle hole is left empty. In the UK, double-hole-punched A4 paper is often used, although some UK writers use the US letter paper format, especially when their scripts are to be read by American producers, since otherwise the pages may be cropped when printed on US paper. Despite the use of double-punched paper, it is common to see scripts in the UK held together by a single brad punched in the top left hand corner. This makes it easy to flip from page to page during script meetings and may have something to do with the taller page of A4.

Screenplays are usually bound with a light card stock cover and back page, often showing the logo of the production company or agency submitting the script.

Increasingly, reading copies of screenplays (that is, those distributed by producers and agencies in the hope of attracting finance or talent) are distributed printed on both sides of the paper (often professionally bound) to cut down on paper waste out of environmental concerns. Occasionally they are reduced to half-size to make a small book which is convenient to read or put in a pocket; this is generally for use by the director or other production crew during shooting.

Although most writing contracts continue to stipulate physical delivery of three or more copies of a finished script, it is common for scripts to be delivered electronically via email. Although most production companies can handle scripts in most formats, it is better practice to supply scripts as a PDF file where possible. This is because it gives the writer final control over the layout of the script, which may otherwise vary depending on what fonts and/or paper size the recipient uses to print the script out. The formatting software programs listed at the bottom of this article produce industry formatted standard screenplays in PDF.

WRITING ON SPEC OR ASSIGNMENT

Screenplays can be written either on "spec" (speculative) or as assignment ("Commissioned"). The Variety language dictionary defines "spec script" as "a script shopped or sold on the open market, as opposed to one commissioned by a studio or production company."

Writing on Assignment

Assignments are commissioned by production companies or studios on the basis of pitches from producers or writers, or literary properties they already own. Most established writers do most of their work on assignment and will only "spec" scripts which they think no-one will pay them to write, or if they cannot find assignment work.

There are exceptions: some very famous writers only write on spec because they know that they can get a better price for their work this way. Other writers spec scripts that they care deeply about so that they do not have to bend to the whims of executives and producers.

An assignment may be for an original screenplay, or for an adapted screenplay based on another work such as a novel, film, short story, comic book, magazine article or, increasingly, video game. It may also, however, be for a rewrite of an existing script, and in fact this is how a large proportion of writers in the modern studio system make their living. Rewriting scripts is an art in itself and an extremely lucrative one at that: it is not unknown for trusted writers in the higher echelons of the industry to receive $200,000 a week (2004 numbers) for their efforts. $50,000 per week is not uncommon.

Rewriting is difficult because executives often have very clear ideas about what is wrong with a script, however, they are usually unable to provide detailed prescriptions for ways it can be fixed. This is not surprising, because screenwriting is not the expertise of the executive, but of the screenwriter. The writer is therefore usually expected to come up with a detailed prescription for how the script can be improved, and then execute this in a timely fashion. During the process of choosing a writer to rewrite a script the executives may ask several writers for their 'take' and choose the one who appears to have the greatest likelihood of moving the script forward to the point where it may be granulite for production.

Before 'going to script' a writer may be asked to write a treatment, an outline, or a step outline describing the script in various granularities of detail. Some writers resist this process and will do anything to avoid it and get down the writing the script itself; others embrace the process and even deliver fairly elaborate treatments, the so-called scriptments. It is fair to say that producers tend to be wary of the former and pleasantly surprised by the latter.

SPEC SCRIPTS

A spec script is a "speculative" screenplay, one that the Variety language dictionary defines as being "shopped or sold on the open market, as opposed to one commissioned by a studio or production company."

Spec scripts are written for various reasons:

- by writers, who hope to have a script optioned and eventually purchased by producers or studios;
- by writer/directors, who want to direct a film themselves;
- by amateur writers hoping to convince a literary agent to represent them or a producer to hire them.

Attracting Producers

The process of 'going out' with a spec script can be an extremely tense and nerve-wracking one for a writer. The writer's agent will identify a number of prospective buyers who may range from small independent producers to executives working in the major studios, and attempt to build up 'heat' under the script.

The script is sent out simultaneously to all the prospective buyers, usually to be read over the weekend, in the hope of attracting a bidding war. Within a few days it is abundantly clear whether the script is going to sell or not. If it does, the writer may receive a payment of anything from a few tens of thousands of dollars to several million. If not, the script is often dead in the water because it is now in the databases of the studios and development executives, and has been marked as having been 'passed' on.

Sample Script

A sample script is usually not intended for production, but to showcase the screenwriting skills of the author, in hopes of attracting the attention of an agent or producer. Often a spec script which fails to sell goes on to be a sample script

Many Spec scripts (short for speculative) are written independently by screenwriters in hopes of optioning and eventually outright selling them to producers or studios. Other spec scripts are written by writer-directors who plan to direct the film themselves. Many so-called "arthouse" films fall into this latter category, whereas the former category tends to be filled with "high-concept" scripts-mostly action or comedy, to which a star or A-list director can be attached.

Script Costs

Script costs can include adaptation rights, but often story rights are listed separately in the development section of a budget. The cost of screenplays vary enormously, and there are often many different writers involved, some of which are uncredited. For example, Quentin Tarantino did uncredited rewrites for Silver Surfer and It's Pat (see Jami Berhard's Quentin Tarantino: The Man and His Movies).

Jurassic Park was adapted by the book's author, Michael Crichton, for a large undisclosed sum. His salary for Twister was 2.5 million, but there were many writers involved, not just him.

Out of a $72 million budget for the film Signs, writer-director M. Night Shyamalan was paid $5 million, most of which were however license fees for the story rights. For the film The Village (total budget: $71 million) Shyamalan received $327,500 for all writing costs including the screenplay fees for his production company Blinding Edge Pictures and costs for materials, supplies, script duplication as well as fringes. An additional $7.2 million were payed to Shyamalan for the story rights, almost three times the amount Shyamalan earned for his work as producer and director on the film.

Although the highest paid names are stars and directors and sometimes novelists who get their film adapted, a good screenwriter can command-and is worth-a large salary. Total script costs can easily be ten percent of the film's budget but, like other areas of a film, unless the writer is a star, it is unlikely for a big budget film to spend more than 5% in the script department. For a movie with a script budget of $500,000 that is not an adaptation, written on assignment, the payments might break down as follows (referred to as "300,000 against 500,000"):

- First draft: $150,000
- First draft revisions: $50,000
- Second draft: $75,000
- Second draft revisions: $25,000
- Production bonus: $200,000

The first four payments are paid half on commencement of the writing step and half on completion. The final payment, the production bonus, is paid only if the script goes into production and becomes due on the first day of principal photography. If a script is approved for production before all the steps have been completed, the production bonus could be bigger. This means there may be an incentive for the writer not to drag out the process.

The Development Process

Once a studio has purchased or commissioned a script, it goes through the process of revisions and rewriting until all stakeholders are satisfied and ready to proceed. It is not uncommon for a script to go through many, many drafts on its journey to production. Very few scripts improve steadily with each draft, and when a certain avenue has been exhausted the writer will often be replaced and another brought in to do a rewrite. Occasionally it becomes impossible to satisfy all such parties, and the project enters development hell.

If a studio decides it does not wish to proceed to production with the script, the project enters 'turnaround'. Another studio may purchase the script from its original owner, but the script is encumbered with the development costs the studio has already incurred. At a certain point, it may simply be uneconomic for anyone to purchase the script, even if it is a very good one. This goes part of the way to explaining why some of the best scripts in Hollywood remain unproduced.

The Shooting Script

Once a script has been approved for production, camera directions and notes may be inserted by the Director, and each scene is assigned a number to provide a convenient way for the various production departments to reference individual scenes. When a scene is omitted, its number is retained labelled with "OMITTED", so that it won't be assigned to any newly added scenes.

When the shooting script is distributed, its pages are locked, meaning that any subsequent revisions will apply to the first set of revision pages. When revisions are distributed, the pages are swapped into the outstanding drafts, and the script is once again locked. The process is repeated for each new round of revisions.

Each round of revisions is distributed on different coloured paper. The progression of colours varies from one production to the next. Since rewrites often continue throughout principal photography, most shooting scripts evolve into a rainbow of gold, pink, blue, green and cherry pages.

Transcripts

A screenplay is different from a transcript. A transcript is simply a copy of what dialogue finally appeared on-screen, without regard to the original script, the stage directions or action. A full post-production transcript may also include descriptions of the action on-screen, but since it is generally not written by a professional writer but either a production assistant or a fan, it may not be particularly entertaining to read. Many published screenplays available at booksellers or downloaded from the internet are in fact glorified post-production transcripts rather than shooting scripts.

Transcripts and screenplays often differ radically because scenes are frequently re-ordered or dropped entirely during the editing process. Moreover, actors may change lines or simply improvise dialog, and many directors will make their own changes to the script on the fly during rehearsal or shooting.

It can be extremely revealing to compare a shooting script with the film as finally distributed.

Screenwriting Software

Detailed computer programs are designed specifically for screenplays, and many have templates for teleplays and stageplays. These programs have been designed to create industry standard screenplays and are used by professional screenwriters. What should be remembered is that all such software is an aid in 'formatting' of a screenplay and not the actual 'creation' of it. A number of these programs offer access to on-line screenwriter communities where you can publish your work for feedback from fellow screenwriters. Furthermore, screenwriting software is available for handheld devices (Palm OS, and Windows Mobile / Pocket PC).

SCREENWRITER'S SALARY

A typical writer's deal usually comprises:

- *Option:* Monies paid in exchange for the right (the "option") to produce--and therefore to purchase outright--a screenplay, treatment or other work within a certain period.
- *Guarantee:* Literally, the monies the writer is guaranteed to receive, whether the script is produced or not. This amount is usually divided into payments for multiple drafts (commonly, a draft and a "set," a set being a rewrite and a polish). The guaranteed monies are sometimes referred to as the "front-end."
- *Bonus/Bonuses:* Also known as the "back-end." Typically, a production bonus is paid once the script goes into production, or, if there has been more than one writer, after the final credit has been determined. A typical contract will specify a smaller production bonus for shared credit. There may also be bonuses contingent upon budget (e.g. "if the movie's budget is greater than x...") or grosses. The cousin of the bonus is the "penalty," which might be paid by the writer if, for example, the

script has not been put into production by a set date. Penalties are rarely included in writer's deals, however.

Definitions

- Five figures: under $100,000
- Low-six figures: under $300,000
- Mid-six figures: between $300,000 and $600,000
- High-six figures: over $600,000
- Seven figures: Over $1 million
- *Spec Script:* Short for "speculative." The writer writes the script without being paid, and, subsequently, tries to sell it.
- *Pitch:* The writer works up a five-to-twenty minute presentation of a prospective movie and presents it to buyers in a short meeting.
- *Assignment:* A rewrite-for-pay of someone else's script. The writer pitches his "take" much like he would an original pitch.

History of Screenwriters' Pay

- 1900: One of America's first screenwriters, New York journalist Roy McCardell, is hired to write ten scenarios (each about 90 seconds long) for $15 each (has the buying power of about $332 today).
- 1947: The original screenplay Woman of the Year is bought by MGM for $100,000 (about $950,000 today).
- 1949: Ben Hecht is paid $10,000 a week (about $77,000 today). Claims David O. Selznick paid him $3,500 a day (about $27,000 today).
- 1967: William Goldman's original screenplay Butch Cassidy and the Sundance Kid is bought for $400,000 (about $2.25 million today).
- 1972: Leonard and Paul Schrader's spec script The Yakuza is sold for $350,000 (about $1.6 million today). Paul Schrader and his agent receive 40% each; novelist

Leonard Schrader, who conceived the idea for the story, is persuaded to take just 20% and a story credit.

- 1984: Shane Black sells the screenplay to Lethal Weapon for $250,000, ushering in the modern spec market.
- 1985: Ex-fireman Gregory Widen sells his university thesis screenplay Highlander for $500,000.
- 1990: Kathy McWorter-promoted by her agent as a 21 year-old wunderkind, though she was in fact 28-sells her sex comedy The Cheese Stands Alone for $1 million. This was followed by nuclear-terrorist technothriller The Ultimatum by Laurence Dworet and Robert Roy Pool and WWII action comedy Hell Bent... and Back! by Doug Richardson, both of which sold for a million dollars.
- 1990: Brian Helgeland and Manny Coto sell their nuclear-armed robot spec The Ticking Man for $1.2 million. The script was sent out with a ticking alarm clock attached.
- 1990: Shane Black is paid $1.75 million for The Last Boy Scout.
- 1990: Joe Eszterhas sells Basic Instinct to Carolco for $3 million, but is replaced by Total Recall scribe Gary Goldman when he argues with director Paul Verhoeven over explicit content. There will not be another million dollar spec script for over two years.
- 1991: Front page of Variety mourns the end of the modern spec market, announcing "the candy store is closed."
- 1992: Sherry Lansing is hired to run Paramount and spends $3.6 million in less than a week, $2.5 million for a two-page outline of Jade by Joe Eszterhas, and $1.1 million for the for the script Milk Money by John Mattson. At the time, both deals are records, respectively, for outlines and romantic comedy specs.
- 1994: After a bidding war, Shane Black is paid $4.5 million by New Line for The Long Kiss Goodnight.

- 1999: M. Night Shyamalan-who received $2.5 million for breakout script The Sixth Sense-is paid $5 million for Unbreakable, plus another $5 million to produce and direct. Later receives same sum for Signs.
- 2003: M. Night Shyamalan is paid $7.5 million for The Woods, later renamed The Village, but with a reduced fee of $3.21 million for producing and directing.
- 2004: Peter Jackson is paid the higher of $20 million aggregate or 20% of the gross to write, produce and direct King Kong. Jackson wrote the screenplay with his wife, Fran Walsh, and Phillipa Boyens.
- 2004: Bobby Florsheim and Josh Stolberg are paid $1.5 million against $2.5 million + 2% for "The Passion Of The Ark", later becoming Evan Almighty. Daily Variety reports this as the highest price paid for a spec script by unproduced writers.

Current Records

Some of the highest amounts paid to writers for spec screenplays:

$4 million:

- The Long Kiss Goodnight by Shane Black

$3 million:

- Basic Instinct by Joe Eszterhas
- Medicine Man by Tom Schulman
- The Ugly Americans (Eurotrip) by Alec Berg, David Mandel and Jeff Schaffer
- Bad Dog (unproduced) by Dale Launer
- Married in the Morning (unproduced) by Harry Elfont and Deborah Kaplan
- Panic Room by David Koepp. $2 million against $3 million.

$2.75 million:

- Mozart and the Whale (The Newports) by Ronald Bass. $2 million against $2,750,000.

$2.5 million:

- The Sixth Sense by M. Night Shyamalan
- Twister by Michael Crichton and Anne-Marie Crichton
- Jade by Joe Eszterhas
- A Knight's Tale by Brian Helgeland
- Untitled Will Davies Romantic Comedy (unproduced) by Will Davies
- Jackson (unproduced) by Brandon Camp and Mike Thompson
- The Superconducting Supercollider of Sparkle Creek, Wisconsin (unproduced) by David Koepp and John Kamps. '$2.5 million against $3.25 million with an additional deferred bonus of $1.5 million for Koepp.
- Deja Vu by Terry Rossio and Bill Marsilii. $2 million against $5 million.

$2.25 million:

- Untitled Disney Family Comedy (unproduced) by Kevin Bisch
- They Came From Upstairs (unproduced) by Mark Burton
- You, Me and Dupree by Mike LeSieur
- The Break-Up by Vince Vaughn, Jeremy Garelick and Jay Lavender

$2 million:

- The Arrangement (unproduced) by Kevin Bisch
- Stalker: A Love Story (unproduced) by Michael Carnes and Josh Gilbert
- The Worst Man (unproduced) by Michael Carnes and Josh Gilbert
- Manhattan Ghost Story (unproduced) by Ronald Bass, based on the novel by T.M. Wright.
- Radio Flyer by David M. Evans
- Forever Young by Jeffrey Abrams

- Showgirls by Joe Eszterhas
- Sacred Cows (unproduced) by Joe Eszterhas
- Reliable Sources (unproduced) by Joe Eszterhas
- Courage Under Fire by Patrick Sheane Duncan
- Tennessee (Pearl Harbor) by Randall Wallace
- River Road (unproduced) by Andrew Niccol
- The Mark (unproduced) by Rob Liefield
- Untitled Tim Herlihy Comedy (unproduced) by Tim Herlihy
- The Game by John D. Brancato and Michael Ferris
- Untitled Firestein-Pesce Action Project (unproduced) by Les Firestein and PJ Pesce
- Executive Search (unproduced) by Gerald Di Pego
- Going West (Switchback) by Jeb Stuart
- Untitled Michael McCullers Buddy Comedy (unproduced) by Michael McCullers
- Alpha (unproduced) by David Benioff
- Ghost Town by David Koepp and John Kamps
- Male Pattern Baldness (unproduced) by Joe Eszterhas. $2 million against 4.5 million.

$1.8 million:

- RPM (unproduced) by J.H. Wyman
- Stay by David Benioff

$1.5 million:

- The Passion of the Ark by Bobby Florsheim and Josh Stolberg. $1.5 million against 2.5 million.

$1.25 million:

- 99 Problems (unproduced) by Deborah Kaplan and Harry Elfont. $1.25 against $2 million.

$1.1 million:

- Milk Money by John Mattson, bought outright by Paramount in 1992.

$1 million:

- Foreplay (unproduced) by Joe Eszterhas. $1 million against $3.5 million.
- The Cheese Stands Alone (unproduced) by Kathy McWorter.

$750,000:

- Steinbeck's Point of View (unproduced) by Brandon Camp and Mike Thompson. $750,000 against $3,750,000 with an additional potential $2 million bonus cast contingent.
- Man-Witch by Bobby Florsheim and Josh Stolberg. $750,000 against $1.5 million.

ACT STRUCTURE (FILM)

Act structure explains how a plot of a film story is composed. Just like plays (Staged drama) have 'Acts', critics and screenwriters tend to divide films into acts; though films don't require to be broken down as such in reality.

Whereas plays are actual live performances that need 'breaks' in the middle for change of set, costume, or for the artists' rest; films are recorded performances shown mechanically and therefore don't need actual breaks. Still they are divided into acts for reasons that are in aesthetic and structural conformation with the original idea of Act in theatre. Act breaks in a film are usually very obscure for lay audience and only a trained person can detect the ending of one act and the beginning of the other in the progression of a movie. The idea of Act structure is of more value while writing a Screenplay than watching a film, though the Act breaks are never actually written in the final copies of screenplays. But television scripts called Teleplays almost always include clear denotions as such. Act is the broadest structural unit of enacted stories. The most common paradigm in theatre, and so in films, is that of the 'Three-Act structure' proposed by Aristotle. It simply means that any story has a 'beginning', a 'middle' and an 'end'. Playwrights and screenwriters divide their stories into three major parts viz. 'Set up', 'Confrontation' (alternatively called as 'conflict' or 'complication') and 'Resolution'. These form the basic three acts of any performance-staged or screened.

Though various theories have been proposed and debated, the Three-act structure stands as the most popular one. Also, this is what Hollywood has discovered and proved as the most successful. The rest of the world cinema may have its own ways of looking at the plot.

THE 'THREE-ACT STRUCTURE'

According to Hollywood, feature films are considered as audio-visual narrative forms which can be seen in distinct parts called 'Acts'.

It follows that the enacted story opens with the introduction of characters and situations, backdrop, locale etc. It creates interest in the audience and takes them to feel concerned as to what the real problem is and what may happen with it. Plays, and screenplays, usually revolve around main characters-the 'Protagonist' and the 'Antagonist' who engage themselevs into a battle. That is "Set up".

The next part-and considered to be more important-is complication of the problem of the story. It intrigues the audience all the more, giving them more and more information and putting various points of view for imaginative comparison. This eventually leads to higher points of audience interest. Because this second Act of most screenplays adds all the possible dramatic values to the plot, this is considered to be the core of the same. The Antagonist and the Protagonist try and experiment with all their strengths (and weaknesses of the other) to win the battle. That is "Confrontation".

This takes us to the third-and the most important-act, the "Resolution". This means it tends to 'solve' the problem (-s) of the story developed so far. But this is not obvious, as it is expected to bring the 'climax' (or a series of climaxes) to give the audience the pay-off. The tool usually implemented is a 'do or die' situation where doors of escape for either or both of the two characters go on closing one by one, leaving them with only a thin chance that demands the fullest exploitation of their qualities and energies. This so called jaw-dropping, breath-taking, arm-rest-grabbing moment for the audience leads to the final outcome of the entire plot. And it is usually the triumph of the good (Protagonist) over the evil (Antagonist), with rare exceptions.

Limitations

This framework can not be rigidly applied to all the film stories, and there are a good proportion of Hollywood movies that defy this theory. Many films follow this pattern only to a subtle extent, where their genre demands a more delicate handling. Screenwiters and Script doctors have tried to provide alternative ideas, which again are open for debate.

As said earlier, cinema across the world and 20th century has evolved its own ways of putting a story. Also, this theory may not be fit for non-fiction films like documentary or corporate films, which may not have a 'plot' at their base with 'characters' and all their 'actions and speeches' predecided, like the feature films have. Such non-fiction films require their own forms of arrangement.

What is important here is that ideas of Act structure help us understand films better. More importantly, these are 'tools' of the screenplay writers who can break down the story at hand and play with various ways of presenting it to find the best possible one. Experts have gone long way ahead in dividing plot to even smaller structural units and they keep working to find the most effective formula of structuring a film story.

PLOT POINT

In television and film, a plot point is a significant event within a plot that digs into the action and spins it around in another direction. Noted screenwriting teacher Syd Field teaches that the 'ideal' movie plot has the first plot point occurring around the 30th minute of the film, then the second one around the 90th minute. See screenwriting theories for an overview list of plot points.

Monomyth

The monomyth (often referred to as "the hero's journey") is a description of a basic pattern found in many narratives from around the world. This universal pattern was described by Joseph Campbell in his book The Hero with a Thousand Faces (1949). A noted scholar of novelist James Joyce, Campbell borrowed the term monomyth from Joyce's Finnegans Wake. Campbell's work has been consciously applied by a wide variety of modern writers and artists, for example, in creating screenplays for movies. The best known is perhaps George Lucas, who has acknowledged a debt to Campbell regarding both the original Star Wars trilogy and its prequels.

In addition, leaders in the men's movement, notably Robert Bly and Michael J. Meade, have used Campbell's insight as a guide for personal spiritual growth. Campbell's insight was that important myths from around the world which have survived for thousands of years, all share a fundamental structure. This fundamental structure contains a number of stages, which includes

1. A call to adventure, which the hero has to accept or decline
2. A road of trials, regarding which the hero succeeds or fails
3. Achieving the goal or "boon," which often results in important self-knowledge
4. A return to the ordinary world, again as to which the hero can succeed or fail
5. Application of the boon, in which what the hero has gained can be used to improve the world

In a well-known quote from the introduction to The Hero with a Thousand Faces, Campbell wrote:

"A hero ventures forth from the world of common day into a region of supernatural wonder: fabulous forces are there encountered and a decisive victory is won: the hero comes back from this mysterious adventure with the power to bestow boons on his fellow man."

The classic examples of the monomyth relied upon by Campbell and other scholars include the Buddha, Moses, and Christ stories, although Campbell cites many other classic myths from many cultures which rely upon this basic structure.

Summary of the Monomyth

In the monomyth, the hero starts in the ordinary world, and receives a call to enter an unusual world of strange powers and events. If the hero accepts the call to enter this strange world, the hero must face tasks and trials, and may have to face these trials alone, or may have assistance. At its most intense, the hero must survive a severe challenge, often with help earned along the journey.

If the hero survives, the hero may achieve a great gift or "boon." The hero must then decide whether to return to the ordinary world with this boon. If the hero does decide to return, the hero often faces challenges on the return journey. If the hero is successful in returning, the boon or gift may be used to improve the world. The stories of Osiris, Prometheus, Moses, Buddha, and Christ, for example, follow this structure very closely.

Campbell describes some seventeen stages or steps along this journey. Very few myths contain all seventeen stages-some myths contain many of the stages, while others contain only a few; some myths may have as a focus only one of the stages, while other myths may deal with the stages in a somewhat different order. These seventeen stages may be organized in a number of ways, including division into three sections: Departure (sometimes called Separation), Initiation and Return. "Departure" deals with the hero venturing forth on the quest; "Initiation" deals with the hero's various adventures along the way; and "Return" deals with the hero's return home with knowledge and powers acquired on the journey.

Other Formulations

Campbell's proposed structure has been expanded and modified since its conception. Many modern characterizations of it add in new steps (such as the hero having a miraculous birth) or combine or prune others. For instance, Phil Cousineau, in his book, The Hero's Journey, divides it up into the following eight steps:

1. The Call to Adventure
2. The Road of Trials
3. The Vision Quest
4. The Meeting with the Goddess
5. The Boon
6. The Magic Flight
7. The Return Threshold
8. The Master of Two Worlds

Another eight-step formulation was given by David Adams Leeming in his book, Mythology: The Voyage of the Hero:

1. Miraculous conception and birth
2. Initiation of the hero-child
3. Withdrawal from family or community for meditation and preparation
4. Trial and Quest
5. Death
6. Descent into the underworld
7. Resurrection and rebirth
8. Ascension, apotheosis, and atonement

Use of the Monomyth by Modern Artists

The monomyth has influenced a number of artists, musicians, poets, and filmmakers, including Bob Dylan and George Lucas. Mickey Hart, Bob Weir and Jerry Garcia of the Grateful Dead had long noted Campbell's influence and agreed to participate in a seminar with him in 1986 entitled From Ritual to Rapture.

George Lucas and Star Wars

George Lucas's deliberate use of Campbell's theory of the monomyth in the making of the Star Wars movies is well-documented. In addition to the extensive discussion between Campbell and Bill Moyers broadcast in 1988 on PBS as The Power of Myth (Filmed at "Skywalker Ranch"), on Campbell's influence on the Star Wars films, Lucas, himself, gave an extensive interview for the biography Joseph Campbell: A Fire in the Mind (Larsen and Larsen, 2002, pages 541-543) on this topic.

In this interview, Lucas states that in the early 1970's after completing his early film, American Graffiti, "it came to me that there really was no modern use of mythology...so that's when I started doing more strenuous research on fairy tales, folklore and mythology, and I started reading Joe's books. Before that I hadn't read any of Joe's books.... It was very eerie because in reading The Hero with A Thousand Faces I began to realize that my first draft of Star Wars was following classical motifs"(p.541).

Twelve years after the making of The Power of Myth, Moyers and Lucas met again for the 1999 interview, the Mythology of Star Wars with George Lucas & Bill Moyers, to further discuss the impact of Campbell's work on Lucas' films.

In addition, the National Air and Space Museum of the Smithsonian Institution sponsored an exhibit during the late 1990s called Star Wars: The Magic of Myth which discussed the ways in which Campbell's work shaped the Star Wars films. A companion guide of the same name was published in 1997.

Chris Vogler, The Writer's Journey, and Hollywood Films

Christopher Vogler, a Hollywood film producer and writer, created a now-legendary 7-page company memo, A Practical Guide to The Hero With a Thousand Faces, based on Campbell's work which inspired films such as Disney's 1994 film, The Lion King.

Vogler's memo was later developed into the late 1990s book, The Writer's Journey: Mythic Structure For Writers, This story structure is evident in a vast number of successful Hollywood films including the Matrix series.

Orson Scott Card and Ender's Game

In his book, Ender's Game, Orson Scott Card gives a very complete example of the monomyth structure, with the main character, Ender Wiggin, fulfilling all eight primary stages of it:

- *Miraculous Birth*-In a world where only two children are normally allowed, Ender is born as the third child by special government decree
- *Initiation*-Ender shows remarkable intelligence at a young age
- *Withdrawal*-Ender is removed from his family and sent to Battle School
- *Trial and Quest*-Ender learns of the threat to humanity from the Buggers
- *Death*-Ender grows despondent after his unit is broken up, and he is sent back to Earth
- *Descent into the underworld*-Ender's sister helps him feel like part of humanity once again
- *Resurrection and rebirth*-Ender refuses to play the "simulations" anymore, and ends the "game" by destroying the Buggers' homeworld
- *Ascension, apotheosis, and atonement*-Ender realizes that the simulations were in fact real and has to cope with this

The narrative structure within Ender's Game doesn't follow this structure perfectly linearly. Many elements of it are actually repeated throughout the book. For instance, the latter four steps can also describe the psychological states Ender went through after his realization of what he'd done to the Buggers.

Modern Applications of the Monomyth

Each of the seventeen stages of the monomyth (below) can be found in popular works, including movie series such as the Star Wars movies, The Matrix movies and even the anime Fortune Dogs.

DEPARTURE (OR SEPARATION)

The Call to Adventure

The adventure begins with the hero receiving a call to action, such as a threat to the peace of the community, or the hero simply falls into or blunders into it.

The call is often announced to the hero by another character who acts as a "herald". The herald, often represented as dark or terrifying and judged evil by the world, may call the character to adventure simply by the crisis of his appearance.

Campbell: The Call To Adventure-"A blunder-apparently the merest chance-reveals an unsuspected world, and the individual is drawn into a relationship with forces that are not rightly understood" (Joseph Campbell, The Hero With A Thousand Faces, 51).

Modern Applications: In Star Wars, Luke Skywalker, the hero, begins the story in frustration over being unable to leave home. The heralds are the two droids who carry a message from Princess Leia. In The Matrix, the call comes in the form of Morpheus and his followers who encourage the hero, Neo, to question reality. Morpheus literally calls Neo using a cell phone.

Classic Examples: Sometimes the call to adventure happens of the character's own volition.

In the story of the Minotaur, Theseus learns the tale of the beast and the terrible sacrifice to appease it, which sets him on a quest to destroy it.

In Herman Hesse's book Siddhartha the main character, Siddhartha, becomes weary of his way of life and decides he must venture away from his accustomed life in order to attain spiritual enlightenment. Most Buddhist myths describe the Buddha as becoming bored with his royal life and venturing into the world.

Other times, the hero is plunged into adventure by unforeseen events. In Homer's Odyssey, Odysseus is caught in the terrible winds of the angered god Poseidon and sent off to distant lands.

REFUSAL OF THE CALL

In some stories, the hero initially refuses the call to adventure. When this happens, the hero may suffer somehow, and may eventually choose to answer, or may continue to decline the call.

Campbell: Refusal of the Call-"Refusal of the summons converts the adventure into its negative. Walled in boredom, hard work, or 'culture,' the subject loses the power of significant affirmative action and becomes a victim to be saved" (Joseph Campbell, The Hero With A Thousand Faces, 59).

Modern Applications: In Star Wars, Luke is refused adventure by his uncle, a man who seeks to protect Luke from the inevitable dangers of fate. Subsequently, Luke's family is killed by stormtroopers. In The Matrix, Neo refuses to take the window washing scaffold to escape and is captured by the Agents.

Classic Examples: Myth and history are rife with examples of what happens to those who refuse the call too long or do not take it seriously. A Persian city was turned to stone, inhabitants and all, for refusing the call of Allah. Daphne was pursued by the Greek god Apollo (a herald), but refused his advances at all costs.

She prayed to her father, Peneus, to take away her beauty to be rid of Apollo; Peneus turned the nymph into a tree, the only semblance left of her past self being her beauty. In Judeo-Christian mythology, Lot's wife is turned into a pillar of salt for looking back with longing to her old life when she had been summoned forth from her city by Yahweh. One of the clearest references to the refusal and its consequences comes in the voice of Yahweh in Proverbs 1:24-27 and 32:

Because I have called, and ye refused... I also will laugh at your calamity; I will mock when your fear cometh; when your fear cometh as desolation, and your destruction cometh as a whirlwind; when distress and anguish cometh upon you.... For the turning away of the simple shall slay them, and the prosperity of fools shall destroy them.

SUPERNATURAL AID

After the hero has accepted the call, he encounters a protective figure (often elderly) who provides special tools and advice for the adventure ahead, such as an amulet or a weapon.

Modern applications: In Star Wars, Luke encounters the Jedi Master Obi-Wan Kenobi who presents Luke with a lightsaber and teaches him the ways of the Force. In The Matrix Neo meets with The Oracle who gives him advice which proves invaluable in his journey.

In The Hitchhikers Guide to the Galaxy, Ford Prefect gives Arthur Dent the copy of the guide.

Classic example: In Greek mythology, Ariadne gives Theseus a ball of string and a sword before he enters the labyrinth to confront the minotaur.

THE CROSSING OF THE FIRST THRESHOLD

The hero must cross the threshold between the world he is familiar with and that which he is not. Often this involves facing a "threshold guardian", an entity that works to keep all within the protective confines of the world but must be encountered in order to enter the new zone of experience.

Modern applications: In Star Wars, the threshold is Mos Eisley, a spaceport that acts as a doorway between Luke's home planet and the wider universe; Luke must avoid capture by the threshold guardians, the Imperial stormtroopers. In The Matrix, Neo must choose the red pill to leave the Matrix and enter the real world.

Rebirth

The hero, rather than passing a threshold, passes into the new zone by means of rebirth. Appearing to have died by being swallowed or having their flesh scattered, the hero is transformed and becomes ready for the adventure ahead.

Biblical applications: In the gospels, John the Baptist baptizes Jesus before Jesus begins his public ministry.

Modern applications: In Star Wars, it is the Death Star, in which Luke is engulfed and in which he learns how to be a hero. In The Matrix, Neo finds himself waking up in a bio-electric cell where he is one of the humans being harvested by the machines.

INITIATION

The Road of Trials

Once past the threshold, the hero encounters a dream landscape of ambiguous and fluid forms. The hero is challenged to survive a succession of obstacles and, in so doing, amplifies his consciousness. The hero is helped covertly by the supernatural helper or may discover a benign power supporting him in his passage.

Marriage

The ultimate trial is often represented as a marriage between the hero and a queenlike, or mother-like figure. This represents the hero's mastery of life (represented by the feminine) as well as the totality of what can be known. When the hero is female, this becomes a male figure.

Modern Applications: In The Matrix, Neo confronts the Oracle. In The Matrix Reloaded, Neo takes Trinity as a lover.

Woman as Temptress

His awareness expanded, the hero may fixate on the disunity between truth and his subjective outlook, inherently tainted by the flesh. This is often represented with revulsion or rejection of a female figure.

Modern Applications: In The Matrix Reloaded, Persephone attempts to seduce Neo. In Star Wars, there is tension between Luke and Han Solo over their love for Princess Leia--this is resolved in Episode VI, Return of the Jedi when Luke finds out that Leia is actually his sister. Luke is also tempted by the dark side itself, as demonstrated by his vision in the cave on Dagobah.

Atonement with the Father

The hero reconciles the tyrant and merciful aspects of the father-like authority figure to understand himself as well as this figure.

Biblical Applications: In the gospels, Jesus wrestles with his impending death in the Garden of Gethsemane, before submitting to his Father's will.

Modern Applications: In The Empire Strikes Back, Luke confronts Darth Vader and learns that he is his father and a former Jedi; in Return of the Jedi, he is reconciled with the reformed Vader. In The Matrix Revolutions, the Oracle explains to Neo that she and the Architect are two programs that work together to keep the Matrix working, the latter to "balance the equation" and the former to "unbalance" it.

APOTHEOSIS

The hero's ego is disintegrated in a breakthrough expansion of consciousness. Quite frequently the hero's idea of reality is changed; the hero may find an ability to do new things or to see a larger point of view, allowing the hero to sacrifice himself.

Modern Applications: In The Empire Strikes Back, Luke sacrifices a part of himself (losing his hand) rather than turn to the dark side. In The Matrix, Neo faces off against Agent Smith resulting in his death and resurrection as the One.

THE ULTIMATE BOON

The hero is now ready to obtain that which he has set out, an item or new awareness that, once he returns, will benefit the society that he has left. Modern applications: In the climactic scene of Star Wars, Luke uses the Force to successfully destroy the Death Star by firing torpedoes down a narrow ventilation shaft of the Death Star.

RETURN

Refusal of the Return

Having found bliss and enlightenment in the other world,

the hero may not want to return to the ordinary world to bestow the boon onto his fellow man.

Classic Examples: After obtaining Nirvana, Buddha doubted whether he could communicate the path to enlightenment. (Actually, some Buddhist traditions hold that this was only cunning politics by Buddha: by saying this he gave people the impression that he didn't want to teach them, which made them curious and eager to hear all about it).

The Magic Flight

When the boon's acquisition (or the hero's return to the world) comes against opposition, a chase or pursuit may ensue before the hero returns.

Classic Examples: In many fairy tales and folktales, it is literally a magic flight, with the hero or heroine transforming objects to stop the pursuit (The Master Maid, The Water Nixie) or transforming himself and any companions to hide themselves (Farmer Weathersky or Foundling-Bird).

Modern Examples: In the Metroid video game series, Samus Aran frequently has to outrun the destruction of a collapsing structure after defeating the final boss.

Rescue from Without

The hero may need to be rescued by forces from the ordinary world. This may be because the hero has refused to return or because he is successfully blocked from returning with the boon. The hero loses his ego.

Modern Application: In The Empire Strikes Back, Luke is rescued by the Millennium Falcon as he hangs on an antenna beneath Cloud City after a battle with Darth Vader. In The Matrix: Revolutions, Neo is physically trapped in the limbo-like Mobil Avenue subway station construct, and Morpheus and Trinity have to help him escape.

The Crossing of the Return Threshold

The hero returns to the world of common day and must accept it as real.

Master of Two Worlds

Because of the boon or due to his experience, the hero may now perceive both the divine and human worlds.

Modern Application: In Return of the Jedi, Luke becomes a Jedi. He has mastered the force and defeated the one true temptation, the Dark Side. In The Matrix Neo returns from death now able to see and control the world of The Matrix, stopping bullets and defeating the Agents. In The Matrix Reloaded, Neo destroys several Sentinels in the real world using only his mind.

Classic Example: In the Christ story, Jesus is able to return to the ordinary world after resurrection.

Freedom to Live

The hero bestows the boon to his fellow man.

Modern Application: In "The Return of the Jedi" Luke has overcome the Empire and his rebellion is free to live and thrive, the ending scene establishes the peace restored by Luke's victory. In The Matrix Revolutions, Neo realizes that machine life is as valid as human life and gives his own life in order to reconcile the worlds of man and machine.

According to the Gospels, Christ returns to the ordinary world after his resurrection, but not as an ordinary man. He can seem to be as others are and interact with them, but his body is a "glorified" body, capable of assuming visible and palpable form, but freed from the bonds of space and time; he is able to appear and disappear at will, for example.

Other traditional examples of something similar, are Elijah, Enoch, and Khidr, the "immortal prophet" of the Sufis.

Use of the Monomyth by the Men's Movement

Poet Robert Bly, Michael J. Meade, and others involved in the men's movement have applied and expanded the concept of the hero's journey and the monomyth as a metaphor for personal spiritual and psychological growth, particularly in the mythopoetic men's movement.

Characteristic of the mythopoetic men's movement is a tendency to retell fairy tales and engage in their exegesis as a tool for personal insight.

Using frequent references to archetypes as drawn from Jungian analytical psychology, the movement focuses on issues of gender role, gender identity and wellness for modern men. Advocates would often engage in storytelling with music, these acts being seen as a modern extension to a form of "new age shamanism" popularized by Michael Harner at approximately the same time.

Among its most famous advocates were the poet Robert Bly, whose book Iron John: A Book About Men was a best-seller, being an exegesis of the fairy tale "Iron John" by the Brothers Grimm.

The mythopoetic men's movement spawned a variety of groups and workshops, led by authors such as Bly and Robert L. Moore. Some serious academic work came out of this movement, including the creation of various magazines and non-profit organizations, such as the Mankind Project.

"The Hero's Journey"

The phrase, "the hero's journey," to describe Campbell's theories first entered into popular discourse through two documentaries. The first, released in 1987, The Hero's Journey: The World of Joseph Campbell was accompanied by a 1990 companion book, The Hero's Journey: Joseph Campbell on His Life and Work (with Phil Cousineau and Stuart Brown, eds.). The second was Bill Moyer's series of seminal interviews with Campbell, released in 1988 as the documentary (and companion book) The Power of Myth.

The phrase was then referenced in the title of a popular guidebook for screenwriters released in the 1990's, The Writer's Journey: Mythic Structure For Writers, by Christopher Vogler. Though they used the phrase in their works, Cousineau, Moyers, and Vogler, all attribute the phrase and the model of The Hero's Journey to Joseph Campbell.

Criticism

Thoughtless use of monomyth structure is often blamed for lack of originality and clichés in popular culture, especially big-budget Hollywood films. In addition to the popularity of Campbell-influenced guides such as The Writer's Journey, the influential book Screenplay by Syd Field also proposed an ideal three-act structure, which is easily compatible with modern screenwriters' attempts to craft a monomyth.

However, since the peak popularity of cinematic monomyth narratives in the 1990s, some would-be blockbuster movies that have been seen as conscious attempts to follow the structure have met with indifference from critics and often disappointing performance at the box office, as in the case of Cinderella Man and George Lucas' three Star Wars prequels.

THE HERO WITH A THOUSAND FACES

The Hero with a Thousand Faces (1949) is the seminal work of comparative mythologist Joseph Campbell. In this text Campbell discusses his theory of the journey of the archetypal hero found in world mythologies and religions.

Since publication of The Hero with a Thousand Faces, Campbell's theory has been consciously applied by a wide variety of modern writers and artists. The best known is perhaps George Lucas, who has acknowledged a debt to Campbell regarding the stories of the Star Wars films.

Summary

Campbell's insight was that important myths from around the world which have survived for thousands of years, all share a fundamental structure, which Campbell called the monomyth.

This fundamental structure contains a number of stages, which include: (1) a call to adventure, which the hero has to accept or decline, (2) a road of trials, regarding which the hero succeeds or fails, (3) achieving the goal or "boon," which often results in important self-knowledge, (4) a return to the ordinary world, again as to which the hero can succeed or fail, and finally, (5) application of the boon in which what the hero has gained can be used to improve the world. In a well-known quote from the introduction to The Hero with a Thousand Faces, Campbell wrote:

> *"A hero ventures forth from the world of common day into a region of supernatural wonder: fabulous forces are there encountered and a decisive victory is won: the hero comes back from this mysterious adventure with the power to bestow boons on his fellow man."*

The classic examples of the monomyth relied upon by Campbell and other scholars include the Buddha, Moses, and Christ stories, although Campbell cites many other classic myths from many cultures which rely upon this basic structure.

While Campbell offers a discussion of the hero's journey by using the Freudian concepts popular in the 1940s and 1950s, the monomythic structure is not tied to these concepts. Similarly, Campbell uses a mixture of Jungian archetypes, unconscious forces, and Arnold van Gennep's structuring of rites of passage rituals to provide some illumination.

However, this pattern of the hero's journey influences artists and intellectuals worldwide, suggesting a basic usefulness for Campbell's insights not tied to academic categories and mid-20th century forms of analysis.

TELEVISION WRITING

Chad currently works as a Creative Executive at the Littlefield Company/Paramount Studios. He has previously worked in television development and production at 20th Century Fox, CBS Productions, NBC Studios, and Regency Television.

If you think writing for film and television is essentially the same, here's a helpful hint: Think differently.

Although teachers often lump feature and television writing into one category, they're actually separate, rarely overlapping worlds. This article focuses on the industry and craft of television. We'll explore the industry's structure, how shows work and how writers break in. The television industry consists of three main entities: networks, studios and production companies. They may look similar on the surface, but each works in a unique way.

Networks program and broadcast material. The non-cable networks are NBC, CBS, ABC, FBC (Fox), the WB, and UPN. Although they suggest shows to studios and production companies, networks don't always produce their own programming.

Studios hire writers to develop material for networks. While most studios are owned by networks, they may sell product anywhere. Twentieth Century Fox is owned by FBC, but ABC airs Twentieth's The Practice.

Production companies, like studios, produce material for networks. Production companies are independent entities that make deals with studios wishing to partner with valuable producers. Imagines' Ron Howard is an acclaimed director/ producer with a Twentieth deal. Warren Littlefield ran NBC for nine years before partnering the Littlefield Co. with Paramount. By joining forces, studios and production companies can access each other's stables of talent (writers, directors, producers).

Studios and production companies make two kinds of deals with writers:

A development deal employs a writer to develop a single idea (paying from $30,000 to $500,000, depending on the writer). Because development deals focus on one project, writers can have simultaneous deals at different companies.

Overall deals pay more than development deals (usually in the low millions) and bind the artist to a particular entity. Overalls are the holy grails of TV development. Jason Katims (Roswell) has an overall at Twentieth. Although Katims develops only for that studio, Twentieth may sell his shows to any network (Roswell aired on WB and UPN).

Thus is the basic structure of Hollywood's TV machine. But how does this machine work? Let's follow a show from conception to airdate. A show begins in... Development season. From July through November, writers pitch shows to studios and production companies. Executives rarely meet first-time writers. Most developing writers have sold features or worked on staff. Had Kevin Williamson never written Scream, he wouldn't have sold Dawson's Creek to Columbia-TriStar (which sold the series to WB).

Studios also hire writers to write ideas conceived in-house. Warner Brothers Television owned the rights to Superman before hiring Miles Millar and Alfred Gough to write Smallville.

Studios then work with writers to perfect network pitches. Networks rarely buy scripts; they buy concepts. This allows input in shows' development and spares writers from finishing scripts that don't sell.

After hearing approximately 1000 pitches, networks buy 50 to 75 ideas, or script commitments. Writers then develop scripts and networks receive about 75 pilot scripts. Thus we enter... Pilot season (January-April). From these scripts, networks shoot 15-20 pilots. Scripts that don't get picked up may be sold to other networks. Ed was developed and axed at CBS before being picked up at NBC.

Networks view finished pilots in April and May. Mid-May brings the upfronts, enormous affairs where networks announce season lineups to advertisers. Each network debuts two to six new shows each fall and a handful more at midseason (January-March). When a show goes, we enter...

Staffing Season. Between April and June series hire writers for the upcoming season. Agents submit clients' materials, and creators and executives meet with writers they like. Of the hundreds of submissions received, most shows staff 4-10 writers. Staffs begin writing immediately. Because most new shows premiere in fall, they commence shooting in early August.

HOW THE STAFF WORK

A staff is the hierarchy of writers that writes a TV Show. At the top of this hierarchy is the showrunner, often the program's creator. Running a show isn't simply visualizing a series; it's hiring, inspiring, and organizing an entire writing team and production staff. Most showrunners have spent years writing television and receive an Executive Producer credit on the series. Before running 8 Simple Rules To Dating My Teenage Daughter, Tracy Gamble paid dues on Home Improvement, My Two Dads and others.

While staffs arrange their hierarchy differently, here's the basic ladder (from top to bottom): executive producer, co-executive producer, supervising producer, producer, co-producer, executive story editor, story editor, staff writer.

Most writers begin as staff writers, or "baby writers."

Each level comes with its own perks and payscale. TV writers are salaried (except for those with overalls), and baby writers make between $60,000 and $80,000 a year. Showrunners-depending on their cache and the show's success-make closer to a million. As writers ascend the ladder, they eventually get offered development deals and-hopefully-overalls. All shows use staffs, although different staffs work differently. On half-hours (sitcoms), writers write as a group. They sit in "The Room" and discuss jokes, stories, characters, etc. While individuals may write first drafts, scripts are always revised by committee. On hours (dramas) the staff structures the season together before assigning individual episodes. Writers then write alone, often under the showrunner's supervision.

How to break in:

Unless you sell a movie that earns a development deal, there are two basic ways to get staffed:

Have a great agent. As any agent will say, "breaking a baby" (getting a job for a first-time writer) is nearly impossible. Many shows don't hire low-level writers. Those that do want specific voices, and-in an ever-diversifying world-shows strive to find ethnically diverse babies. Even with a great agent, it may take three years to break a baby.

Get promoted from being a writers assistant. Writers assistants do everything from taking notes in the Room to making copies and offering story feedback. Naturally, showrunners like hiring people who know office dynamics and the voice of the show.

Writers assistants begin at the bottom. Jobs as production assistants (grunt work) abound. After a year. P.A.'s graduate to "writers P.A.," slaving away for writers themselves. That leads to a writers assistant gig, which-hopefully-becomes the coveted staff job.

Aspiring writers need two weapons: strong original material, and strong specs.

Original material consists of plays, screenplays or sketch material. Showrunners want writers who have unique voices and can fashion characters and stories. But they also need writers who can mimic others' tones and characters, so it's important to have....

Specs, or sample episodes of shows currently airing. Showrunners use specs to evaluate one's grasp of character voices, the ability to tell stories within a particular structure, and knowledge of a series present state of affairs. To write a spec, watch and outline several episodes of the show. How are the stories structured? Are there B Stories and runners (subplots and continuing gags or themes)? Write down lines for each character.

Does one character always have the sassy comeback? Does another speak in one-syllable words? Scrutinize the show till you know it in your sleep; if you can't think the characters' thoughts, you're not ready to write.

Outline your spec based on original ideas. Continue watching and revising as you write. With each episode, update the script. The more current your spec, the stronger a showrunner's response.

Also pick a series that's frequented by showrunners and executives (The West Wing, Sopranos, etc.) You may love Yes, Dear, but few people watch it. If readers don't know the show, your spec won't get rave reviews.

Get your material to as many people as possible. In an industry based on networking, you can't shy from peddling your work. If everyone's six degrees away from an agent or executive, you must find those paths.

Don't send specs to their own shows. Showrunners feel they know their show better than anyone, and-regardless of what they actually produce, and regardless of what you may have written-your two visions probably won't connect.

Rather, send your specs to similar shows. CSI specs go to Law & Order, Malcolm in the Middle to Bernie Mac.

Of course, most shows won't accept cold submissions. They take scripts only from agents and mangers and, even then, mostly from agents or managers they know well. Your job, then, is to make friends. Once you know a story editor, an agent's assistant, or even a camera operator, ask them to read your stuff. Or pass it to their boss.

I recommend finding a job in the industry. Even P.A. jobs or studio receptionist gigs provide industry knowledge and access to contacts. This not only helps you move forward, it impresses agents who want clients in positions of upward mobility. Now that you understand the fundamentals of the industry, there's only one thing left to do. Keep writing. Television, first and foremost, is a medium of storytelling. If you have the chops, you'll get there. It just helps to know the ropes.

SEVEN STEPS TO A SUCCESSFUL SPEC SCRIPT

It's easy to learn the format of writing for television from a book or writing class. It's a much harder thing to capture the voice and the tone of a particular series,Use this exercise to learn what makes your favourite TV series work, then craft a spec script that showcases your writing talent.

And to make your script fit flawlessly into the run of the show. Television is the one medium where you don't want your own unique voice to shine through. The characters' voices and thoughts and ideas need to stay true to the ones already established by the series' creators. Here's an exercise to help you capture the established voice of the show you wish to write.

Videotape a new episode of a show you love and that you watch often. Watch the first half, then shut off the television You are going to write the ending yourself.

Start by brainstorming all the possible ways the episode could end. For example, on the show I work on Sex and the City, in the first half of the episode "Ghost Town," Carrie and Miranda learn that Steve and Aidan are opening a bar together. At the halfway point, Carrie has just run out of the bar after hearing Aidan's voice because she is afraid to face him again. Think up as many ideas as you can for ways to resolve this story. Carrie could see Aidan and discover that he's married to someone else.

She could realize she never loved him. Or maybe she realizes that she loves him still. Maybe she never sees him at all-she goes back to the bar only to discover he's left New York for good. There are dozens of possible resolutions-let your imagination run wild.

Pick the ending you think best suits the characters and the show, then write it out, keeping in mind the way the characters act and talk and behave. You know these characters; how do you think they would solve their problems? You have about 12 pages to resolve the main story line, plus tie up any subplots or "B" stories.

When you finish, put your pages down and turn the television back on. Watch the broadcast ending straight through. Compare the ending you wrote to the one your just watched. As you go through your script, ask yourself these questions.

1. Why did the writers pick the ending they did?

   This particular episode of Sex and the City ends with Carrie discovering she has been in love with Aidan all along and decided to try to get him back. Think about why this particular ending works best for the show. If you ended your script with Aidan having left town, there are fewer possibilities for future stories between the two characters. Carrie scheming to get Aidan back, however, gives the writer plenty of material for many more episodes to come. Does the ending you wrote help move the series forward?

2. Is your ending believable? However you chose to resolve the episode, make sure that your story episode, makes sense in the world set up by the series' creators. You should never have a major character die, move to a different city, or do anything which would have permanent repercussions on the character and the show. A spec script needs to show that you understand the constraints of the series and are able to work within them.

   You might write a hilarious scene where Charlotte and Mr. Big get drunk and get married. Funny though it may be, it would never happen in the world of Sex and the City, and writing a story line like that would hinder your script form being taken seriously by anyone familiar with the show.

3. Did you leave any loose threads in your ending? Contemporary sitcoms are often intricately plotted, with four or five story lines all intertwining and building upon one another, leading to a resolution which affects all the characters. A show like Seinfeld will throw half a dozen plot elements into the mix, and all need to be resolved by the show's end. Make sure the ending you wrote satisfies all the questions raised in the beginning of the script.

   If you have trouble resolving each story line thoroughly and appropriately, try doing this exercise on an older series like Mary Tyler Moore or The Odd Couple. These shows tend to have simpler, more linear story lines and fewer subplots. They are great practice for building up to writing a more complicated script for a contemporary show.

4. Does the language you write fit the character? A joke that would be hilarious on Malcolm in the Middle would

fall flat on Fraiser. The character in your script should talk the way you expect them to. If you have Malcom's brother Reese using 25-cent words or Fraiser's brother Niles using poor grammar, viewers will instantly recognize the inconsistency in the characters, and you will lose your audience.

5. Have you taken care of business? All shows have recurring elements they always feature. Each episode of Sex and the City shows Carrie typing a question for her column on her laptop computer. Just Shoot Me begins scenes by showing words from the cover of Blush Magazine. Frasier always included a scene at the radio station, with Fraiser giving humorous advice to the caller.

   Including these elements in your script can ground your story in the world of the series, and establish that you thoroughly understand the parameters of the series for which you want to write.

   Many shows also often have recurring "bits'-themes or character which appear frequently but are not mandatory parts of each episode. "Itchy and Scratchy" cartoons are certainly an important part of The Simpsons, but they do not occur every episode. The same goes for Jacks' cabaret act on Will & Grace, and Ross' line "We were on a break!" on Friends. Using some of these elements in your writing can add specificity to your episodes and are a good way to show your understanding of the series' history.

   Similar to business that always appears is business that never appears in a show. No one would believe a Sex and the City script which referred to Mr. Big by his real name or a Fraiser episode where we actually see Niles' wife Maris. Make sure you don't break any of the rules of the show by revealing something the staff writers intentionally keep secret.

6. Have you covered the basics? Shows vary in terms of length and number of scenes. The second half of a

Fraiser episode might take place in three long scene, one each at the radio station, Fraiser's apartment and café.

A show like Sex and the City, however, will use 10 or 12 shorter scenes, cutting quickly from the girls' apartments to bars to stores and back again. Only a few lines are said at each location before moving on to the next scene.

The ending you write should have roughly the same number of scenes as the ending that was broadcast. Also be aware of the number of exterior scene in your show. While there are numerous scenes in Sex and the City of the women walking down the street or sitting in the park, we rarely see the Friends characters outdoors. Make sure the number of exterior shots in your ending is comparable to the broadcast ending.

7. What's the tone of your ending? "Sitcom" is short for situation comedy, and comedies need to be funny. Even sad or moving story lines are invariably lightened with a joke. When Miranda's mother died on Sex and the City, the writers contrasted her sorrow with Charlotte's outrage at the giant, glitter-covered flower arrangement the florist mistakenly sent. And Monica and Chandler's wedding on Friends was all the more touching for Joey not being able to remember all the parts of the ceremony he was officiating.

BIBLIOGRAPHY

Bliss, Edward: Now the News: The Story of Broadcast Journalism, New York, Columbia University Press, 1991.

Callahan, Christopher: A Journalist's Guide to the Internet, Boston, Allyn and Bacon, 2002.

Carey, James W.: Public Opinion and the Communication of Consent, New York: Guilford Publications, 1995.

Crowley, David. J. and Paul Heyer: Communication in History, Boston, Allyn and Bacon, 2003.

Earl, R.: Writing for Mass Communication, White Plains, NY: Longman, 1996.

Eiseman, Leatrice: Pantone Guide to Communicating with Color, Cincinnati, North Light, 2000.

Frank, Reuven: Out of Thin Air: The Brief Wonderful Life of Network News, New York, Simon & Schuster, 1991.

Graber, Doris A.: Processing the News, N.Y., Longman, 1984.

Hudson, Robert V.: Mass Media, New York, Garland Publishing, 1987.

Langman, Larry: The Media in the Movies, Jefferson, NC: McFarland & Company, 1997.

Nora Paul: Behind the Message: Information Strategies for Communicators, Boston, Allyn & Bacon, 2004.

Ross, Lillian: Reporting Back: Notes on Journalism, Washington, DC: Counterpoint, 2002.

Sims, Norman: Literary Journalism in the Twentieth Century, New York, Oxford University Press, 1990.

Startt, James D. and W. David Sloan: Historical Methods in Mass Communication, Hillsdale, NJ: Lawrence Erlbaum, 1989.

Suggs, Henry Lewis: The Black Press in the Middle West, 1865-1985, Westport, CT: Greenwood Press, 1996.

INDEX

♦♦♦